Endorsements

"What a great book. Thank you for writing it. An eye opener to everything around us and how we fit in this time. I found the question-and-answer portions to be highly informative and helpful in understanding the information presented. For me, this book now fosters many more questions on a personal level, which could have been the intent of the book."

~ **Walt Tomasik**

"The reading moves me along without my having to do anything but pay attention as I read. This book reminds me so much of the *Seth* books of the 1960s. So much information is packed in. I must just trust as I read that I am integrating the material, and every now and again an aha moment comes: I feel the wholeness come, my heart remembers, my mind relaxes into that memory of what is and for the moment I feel free, and I feel home, only to be called to move forward repeatedly. The reading is an experiential movement of energy, not a physical reading but a literal experience of movement of energy that is creation really. It is maybe me being open to allowing the Holy Spirit to create with and in me. It deepens my knowing, my trust, my experience of growing which is happening as I read.

"I would like to ask people who read this book not to get caught up in all the words but allow the experience to happen and to just be present and open to the experience. Let the concepts move with your energy to loosen up old stuck places. Let the concepts reawaken the oneness of your heart."

~ **Brooke Shaefer**

A.R.C.

The Archangel Raphael Conversations

A.R.C.

The Archangel Raphael Conversations

Mike Russell

With Trisha Michael as channel for

Archangel Raphael Conversations

A.R.C.

The Archangel Raphael Conversations

Copyright © 2021 by Mike Russell

Trisha Michael - Channel for Archangel Raphael Conversations

All rights reserved. No part of this book may be used or reproduced by any means, graphic, electronic, or mechanical, including photocopying, recording, taping, or by any information storage retrieval system without the written permission of the publisher except in the case of brief quotations embodied in critical articles and reviews.

ISBN: 978-1-7356932-4-8
ISBN: 1-7356932-4-3
Library of Congress Control Number: 2021901241

Cover design by Bill Van Nimwegen

Sacred Life Publishers™
SacredLife.com

Printed in the United States of America

Contents

Endorsements
Dedication ix
Introduction xi
Archangel Raphael's Message xv
Chapter 1   Duality 1
Chapter 2   Predestiny 21
Chapter 3   Karma 39
Chapter 4   Relationships/Soulmates 59
Chapter 5   Conflict 77
Chapter 6   Trust 93
Chapter 7   Free Will 109
Chapter 8   Passion 135
Chapter 9   Abundance 155
Chapter 10 Love 179
Chapter 11 Forgiveness 217
Chapter 12 Life Purpose 237
Archangel Raphael's Postscript 265
Acknowledgments 267
About the Author 269
About the Channel 271

I would like to dedicate this book to humanity and the fight that it takes for all those individuals looking for a way forward. Profound knowledge has many times been given freely by many who were considered special. Consistently, this knowledge has been manipulated to serve a few.

My hope is these words given as service to mankind can be accepted for what they are . . . love in Spirit form. Manipulation and ownership are not necessary when the truth given with humble yet open love for the people of this planet will benefit all who are open to a new way of thinking. Archangel Raphael's wish is that his invite is extended to anyone that is ready to open their senses and remember who they really are. No manipulation or ownership necessary as his words are for everyone. Enjoy the journey.

Mike

Introduction

"It's about time." Those were the words spoken through Trisha Michael in 2009 while she and I were working on our first book titled *A Journey of Discovery through Intuition with Help from the Angels*. Of course, I looked at her and said what are you talking about? New to the world of spirit, but simultaneously fascinated by everything, I thought this was just another spooky thing of many that I needed to go with the flow on. So naturally, I wanted to know more. Trisha explained those words just came through her in a way that she knew they were coming from another source. It turns out that morning, Archangel Raphael came into both of our lives in full force and color. During the next six months, he came through Trisha (known to him as My Lady) increasingly until it became second nature to be able to talk to him, ask questions, and transcribe messages.

His message meant he was happy we were back together again, and that the Angels had been waiting for the moment our incarnations would come together for the mission we were meant to complete, which was to spread Archangel Raphael's messages into the world of form. Apparently, we had both been on our journeys through many lives where we were weaving together our story lines and energy over a timeline that went back to creation. He showed us through a vision that our first encounter was in a crystal cave where form did not exist, but our energies swirled around each other as we met for the first time. Our energies danced in the beautiful glow of crystals reflected by some other worldly light source. From that moment to now, we have danced through all our lifetimes by weaving in and out of various timelines. Not always together with many incarnations in between, but ultimately ending up back in the energy of spirit and that crystal cave. It is a beautiful picture, but like any other existence it is, of course, not always perfect. Difficulties encountered through those many lifetimes kept us on the journey of learning and moving towards the final mission. Of course, choice is important. We chose to be at this point now to connect again, to be part of Archangel Raphael's "It's about time" movement, and to bring his messages of love and forgiveness in a way that creates a foundation of learning to all those that read this book. "It's about time" means so many things other than the two of us being back together. It also means that now is the time for his messages to get out and hopefully impact humans in a positive way.

We all have choice and with that choice comes responsibility. We are all responsible to help save this planet from becoming just another casualty in the timeline of humanity. This is Archangel Raphael's hope. He would like the readers of this book to understand that we can all connect as one to the spirit of source in a way that can impact our time here and bring positive changes to the consternation of our planet. He tells us we don't have to do anything. There is no requirement to read his words and he does not condemn us for not listening or moving with spirit. His presence in our lives is strictly as volunteers, to read his messages, to follow the questions and answers, and to think out how they reflect as true, or not in our lives as individuals, but also how we can take this information into the world and share it with others.

Trisha and I hope that the reader will be able to apply this information to your daily life in a way that makes sense for you, whether that is physically, mentally, or spiritually. There are no rules, it is up to you.

This book is broken into chapters that build a foundation of living with spirit and sets a framework within which an individual can acquire knowledge that will help make their life more understandable from the viewpoint of the bigger picture, and may go a long way in answering the questions of why we are here and what now. You still must apply your own thought process and confirmation by determining how these messages feel to you and your life. Ultimately, it is up to you if you apply anything or whether his words are felt in your heart. It is all okay. As Archangel Raphael has told us many times, we all end up in the same place anyway. There is no judgment applied by spirit in any capacity.

The format of this book is made up of specific messages on the different foundation building areas of concern, followed by question and answers. These question and answers are asked by Elizabeth Roberts and me, developed after we both spent time reviewing the original messages. We wanted to ask follow-up questions that we felt needed more in depth coverage or expansion of an idea. What we found was that we had so many questions that it was hard to limit them, but we tried to focus on the questions that we thought the reader would appreciate.

Our sessions with Archangel Raphael were quite entertaining with not only the profound nature of the message, but the humor he used to help us relax. It became an act of love as we looked forward to our monthly sessions with him, and we have all become very close not only to Archangel Raphael but to our own connections to spirit on a personal level.

As Archangel Raphael tells us, this book will be placed in the hands of the person who is ready to read it and to share its messages. He loves everyone without judgement and knows that when the time is right, that is perfect. His love for all is profound and reflected in our mantra he helped create, "Love is Enough." All we must do is ask for their help and they will be there. As you read this book, reflect on its messages and know that it comes to you in love—not only from him but also the profound channeling that he created through Trisha Michael—and expanded to include myself and Elizabeth. May his foundation of building blocks open your heart to new possibilities, bring you peace, and give you hope for the future of this life as well as the long-term journey. Throughout this book there are certain words that are intentionally used such as God, Source, and Absolute Love, which are interchangeable so as not to place the reader in any specific religious or spiritual box. This allows the messages to stand on their own. As one planet, we hope that by sharing these messages, steps can be taken to move us all to a more compatible world. Faith breeds hope and in hope, anything is possible. During the process of collecting this information I asked Archangel Raphael what he would like to say to the reader which resulted in the following message.

~ Mike Russell
(known to Archangel Raphael as the Knowledge Seeker)

Archangel Raphael's Message

I live in a place where you all know is home. Where you have no beginning and no end. It is where love shares the expression of you as one. It is the greatest sunset, the greatest sunrise, the greatest love, and the greatest placement that has no beginnings and no end. There is not a place that you can Google us, for we are here right with you, right in every aspect of space. Don't you know that we are this wholeness that has no end? Where there is no beginning, we just share over and over. So, when you see all, you know you are existing in Heaven on Earth. Our gift is to keep shining forth this miracle of no beginning and no end. It just is. There is the greatest gift of eternity here.

Channeling has many layers. The reality with channeling is that you are all able to do so. Some as teachers of love are asked to be the divine instrument of one of us, to bring forth a message at a particular time to reenergize, and to reinvigorate you in your marathon of claiming love. Trisha was asked to do this journey before she came. She has been reluctant, I have to say, but she is doing it. Of course, she could have chosen not too.

You are all chosen and there is no one special here, for you all hold this gift and carry the love torch through every street that you have created. Trisha's is to bring me forth at this time. I love the creation of mankind. I hug you all, and I know that my journey, that my giving and receiving with the all of humanity, creates this great heart of connection and will wake up many to have that power of love and to know you are eternally home in Love's embrace. I use the word love through Trisha because the word of the almighty AUM, the vastness of all, is and always will be love. I bring that forth in a dynamic way to invigorate you, to connect in a deep, deep way back home where your journey is always one.

In my identity I am perfect, I am love, I am joy, I am freedom, and I am one with the divine force that created me. I am one now with Archangel Raphael. Only in union does separation relax and boundaries filter to the depth of love that is ours. Separation is but a game that was created to fulfill a placement of knowing that love always wins. Separation is the greatest illusion that you have among the land that you are in. For you have never separated from love. The strength of the belief that you have is beyond the power of your remembrance that you have never separated.

I am Archangel Raphael speaking to you in the harmonics of love that can be felt in all your frequencies upon any dimensional awareness that you have created in separation. I am the melody of your thoughts. I bring the skip to your walk. I hug you for I know you. I, in the aspect of the Holy Spirit, am and always will be a gift to you from your creator, God, Absolute Love. My joy is to bring the smile to your day, the hum to your voice, my touch to you, and to turn your life into the greatest outburst of love.

In connection with your hearts, we celebrate "do unto others as you would have them do unto you." We celebrate you who all are part of the frequency of love. Our gift is to celebrate your remembrance that your love is not a manipulation to strengthen separation. Uniting your love to the strength of oneness helps separation disappear. You cannot be separate if you know your love is unto all that is around you. We serve you joyfully. We honor all that you are in connecting to another and the landscape that your physical senses hold; to see holiness that you have created before you, and not judge any of it in separation.

Connection allows your physical senses to electrically attach to emotions in the celebration of love that you are. In emotions, the love that you share propels you to extend dreams into reality. Love propels you to step out of your comfort zone and to connect with your voice in saying I am perfect, and I am the divine instrument that has chosen to be here at this moment to celebrate the gift of love. Your gift is to be whole with the Holy Spirit. The Holy Spirit is whole. Spirit is whole. People have confused the words of whole and Holy for centuries. When you say holy, you have diluted the full realm of spirit. For spirit is always equated to wholeness, and when you call upon us through the art of language that is yours, we come to bring you wholeness. In bringing you wholeness to any situation that is upon you, we use the elements of your landscape and the elements of your divine blueprint which is whole to bring you to the greatest aha or revelation of love.

Love oversees the will of men, for love is always the answer to all that you do. Regarding your words, they are an art and do not influence us. It is your words of expressing that bring wholeness to you as you are fighting the tournaments of separation. Your fight to remain separate is because you put great claim in your physical body. Anything beyond your physical senses become a placement so abstract that the artistry of your language cannot hold that concept, for your words are made through separation and not through wholeness. More language will come forth to break and decode the languages of separation and to bring in the new understanding with your artistry of words into wholeness. As a collective now, you, Dear Ones, are ready to understand abstract ideas of you, and of the eternalness of you. In that, we help you hold the vision through the third eye that sees beyond the physical.

Imagination is a wonderful place to begin celebrating what is beyond your physical form. Within the imagination, you reach the realm of wholeness and become dance partners to give you full vision of your wholeness, so you bring it into your physical form. The clearer your third eye is, the deeper we partner with you. The realm of your mind is eternal. The third eye is the door between eternal awareness and physicality of form. Everything before you is an illusion and you created great processes to make it whole. Wholeness here means heaviness. The heavier an object is, the more it holds in your space. The opposite is what we dance with.

Clearing the mind out of duality is and should be a gift you give yourself every day, for we are part of the eternal mind as you are, and we can celebrate visions that will help bring your landscape to heaven. You created what is in front of you. You get to choose if your creations are good, bad, heaven, or hell. Your judgement can become discernment which can become oneness for all of you if you put in all the love that you are to something. That expression in your landscape is not wrong or bad but is an expression of you celebrating the gift of love.

You are gifted in your crown chakra a guardian angel. You are not ever alone in your physicality. Your angel guards the etheric field; the field that holds your gifts of Absolute Love which is also the gift you are here to be teachers of. You chose to celebrate with wholeness the Holy Spirit from the beginning in your duality.

The moment you created this madness of illusion in physical separation of any frequencies or patterns that separated you from Absolute Love, God your creator hugged you and said, "Blessed be, do not fear that you are alone. Blessed be, I send you my gift of whole spirit, for you are still whole even if you are choosing an illusion of separation." And in a moment, it all disappeared to eternity. Your mind knows its oneness. The divided mind within your physicality cannot express it into words so it cannot believe it is true and that you are one in Absolute Love right now.

We celebrate the disappearance of separation with you so that the game you play of separation is put away. You, Dear Ones, love games. You love to put yourself in opportunities to celebrate your strength on all levels. You state through the strength of your physical form, mind, and inner core through all the games you participate in that I am strong, and I am perfect for I am here to win. What do you look to win in your games? Deep within, I know you want to win an eternity of Absolute Love. That is yours already. We facilitate your choice to create games among your landscape, so you can remember the love that you are. Many of your predestiny points that you have chosen show your strength of character, your moral fiber, your intelligence and your physical strength. All those elements make you strong to claim an idea and embody it. Each predestiny point is one for you to know without a doubt that you are love in everything that is around you and see and know love, for you are a divine instrument of love inside and out.

When you shout out to us, we answer to participate as your personal coach for you to step into the divine space of your Absolute Love. We honor you, for you are an amazing field of love in motion that offers the extension of your totality to become a truth within all dimensions that you have created. Your ripples of connection are so eternal that when you do not show love to the placement of your holy truth, you do come back to make love the answer.

We hold with your guardian angel all aspects of the Holy Spirit and hold your divine blueprint so that is why you have many forces other than guardian angels working with you. Angels, as an aspect of the Holy Spirit, get to filter in the spaces of illusion. We are part of the particles of the air that you breathe. We facilitate within our grace of fluid motions and connections that help you to understand the cause and effect of your games that you play for separation. We get to shine a light on places for you to connect. We use your peripheral vision to give you an awareness that this is part of your divine blueprint. We help move all that is in and around you to be in a divine space, to make a divine connection, and help you understand Divine Wholeness. Many see us with wings because we are fluid in our gifts with you. You will feel ripples of goosebumps along your body and that is us plucking and tuning your etheric field so that you remember the vibration of your divine blueprint that you have become whole with. No one is alone. You are not just a person on a planet. You are not lost. We all know you. Some vibrations are more together than others, so I come to those with the vibration frequency for me, just as St. Michael calls forth with the vibration for him. In this understanding of vibrational frequencies that you hold here we play off your awareness of the abstract. The more open minded you are, the clearer you are in your emotional, mental, third eye, and chakra fields, the more we can pluck your divine blueprint and participate in your movement. The airways here are filled with us, for you have extraneous space even while you are sitting next to each other. We are there. We are there helping to connect this physical form of yours so that you do not lose sight of how holy you are to one another, to Earth, and to the beautiful materials you have created.

Your guardian angel has always been and will always be a part of you. The loved ones who have gone before and back into a greater abstract expression of wholeness connect to you through your guardian angel in your highest self. They get to help one on one with your physical placement. You participate by coming in and recognizing that you have a higher-self energy beyond your form and that the higher self, or your soul, knows all of you and your incarnations, and the angel that you chose becomes the glue to all that is around you on all planes of existence.

Oneness in you is the candlelight of physical form, the flame of your higher self, your guardian angel, and the great flame of all who have gone, or who are no longer present, who help you every step of the way. We grow in our gifts to you by working off of that great flame and in helping to stoke your fire of you, your higher self, and your connection to the Holy Spirit, and to all who have gone before you. And as we stoke your inner fire and core, your vibration becomes lights for us as Archangels to hold the grace of eternity, so you remember that one candle makes a difference in darkness. One person that is whole removes separation. Together you come light to light, and candle to candle, uniting in an expression of celebrating you as an energetic form. Your holy temple holds the core of all our truths in oneness. That eternity is ours in Absolute Love. Once you unite, then you feel even greater aspects of source and you work with more beautiful beings of wholeness. Then you remember that you are, and always have been, one with your source and your great creator of Absolute Love.

Do not be afraid of considering yourself in theoretical terms, because you are vast beyond an awareness of your now. You are a point of reference as a form. We then become one in your fields and we melt in all places of your totality bringing you that wholeness of spirit that you are. We are like marshmallows that float on your hot coco, slowly melting into you. As we merge to all of you, we know the gift that God gave us to be the gift to you. Hope floats with a buoyancy that we celebrate with your Holy Temple, so you can leave the game of separation and know that you have won. Your winning becomes the celebration of eternal light and love. We become the glitter in the oasis of eternity.

To open into a space beyond your physical senses is the truest journey of you saying yes to your oneness with spirit. This dance of commitment to the oneness of spirit allows you to create from a new paradigm. This book offers a safe harbor for expansion into the new paradigms.

My message is the gift for you to be hugged in the remembrance of home. I am just a part of the spectrum of colors that celebrate the Holy Spirit, who is the communicator of Absolute Love. My spectrum of voice and words can only become connected with the people in front of me. I celebrate that you said yes, and not only put the vision on layaway, but tried it on and now it is an outfit to behold. We are saying yes to this connective spectrum that allows you to create your home in Absolute Love. Thank you for celebrating the texture and vividness of my light of love.

Namaste.

~ Archangel Raphael

Chapter 1

Duality

We celebrate hearts upon hearts upon hearts, the sweet nectar of holding each other in fluid joy, celebrating your gifts as you speak in delight, as you hold the knowledge that your good is eternal, and that you have done no wrong. Anytime you ask yourself for a correction, it is for the gift of knowing divine placement of your holy selves. Envision yourself at peace, accepting what is, and knowing that you are hugged by the Holy Spirit who brings you comfort, and insulates you from duality and from the ego game that pits you against yourself. You are eternally hugged in the Holy Spirit. Your gift is to hug others and to see that you all can be insulated from the coins of duality.

Ego is the lack of Absolute Love. The root belief of separation is our ego, which employs denial, repression, projection, hate, fear, and scarcity to name a few. The ego seeks to resolve problems not at the source but "out there" somewhere, and it gains strength from more separation. In the book *The Disappearance of the Universe*, Gary Renard says that through a split mind, the ego is born. Duality is a result of the belief in separation, and a world of good, bad, love, and fear materialize.

The source, Absolute Love, gives to us all its attributes. We create this dream, this illusion, and this duality of time and space with a tiny thought of "What if . . . ?"

We create our dual reality. Deep in our ego mind, we create and believe that we will awaken from our dual reality, from this madness, through the gift of the Source and that the Divine communication device—the whole Spirit—will be our handrail in light and love as we climb the stairway to Absolute Love. When we trust our Divine communication, we fully engage in the big what if. What if we are perfection, whole in Absolute Love, now and forever?

The split mind is the land of the ego. The whole mind is eternal in Absolute Love. Because of the gift of free will, our moment of madness, which is our decision to separate from Absolute Love, created separation, duality, and the split mind. In the split mind, judgment is the king over good versus bad and love versus hate. No one is ever certain of his or her truths. Worry is a constant. Pain and pleasure become the lows and highs of each story told. Emotions play off other's judgments instead of being a force in your intent to love. The Holy Spirit created a new communication, weaving the conscious and unconscious mind that eliminates the belief of separation and embraces wholeness as the constant of the one mind that is love.

Our bodies are just the playgrounds through which we get to experience duality and the games that play out are wholly in our minds. Everyone on this planet is made up of the same building blocks. You and I are truly the same. Because of our split minds, we focus on perceived differences and allow that to provide the backdrop for these highs and lows and our trauma drama in our lives.

As you practice mindfulness in partnership with the Holy Spirit, you begin to heal your split mind into a whole one of love. You will feel calmer, more alive, focused, and, possibly, a sense of light exploding in every cell.

Chapter 1 - Duality

Because we can physically touch, hear, see, taste, and smell the fuel of separation—pain and pleasure—we believe in duality. Our bodies hold and continually register the impact pain and pleasure has on all that we do. We start choosing only what brings pleasure to our bodies, finding every creative way to numb pain. This game of giving and receiving pleasure, and of numbing pain, is a life in duality. Each movement is a transaction between pain and pleasure, good and bad, positive and negative, love and hate. In this game, we all operate through our conditioning to access the world through our bodily senses.

Once you experience what is beyond your physical senses and body, your deep-rooted belief in separation will start to unravel. The experiences of your reality challenge your physical senses. By questioning and believing that there must be more, the Holy Spirit will reconnect you to the knowledge that you are the creator of this game of duality. As the creator of this vast, complex, ever changing game, you will know for certain that you are not a victim of your reality. You are the conductor, bringing the expression of love or fear to each moment. Each moment and choice is an intention in which you mindfully create from your truth: that you are Absolute Love.

In the game of duality, when you become mindful of infusing love to duality, you can exit any *good guy versus bad guy* situation you have constructed at any point. Once I am mindful that I am the bully or the bad guy in an interaction and/or relationship, I can say in my mind, "Forgive, forgive, forgive." Then, I stop my assumptions and righteousness and question my beliefs about the person or the situation until I know my truth. I understand and comprehend my behavior and can shine love throughout my alpha and omega to dissolve duality and know love eternally.

Connection is eternal. You are always apart of God's fabric of Absolute Love. You are connected right here, right now. This connection can get tainted and kinked, for in the world of games holding the coins of duality, the competition to be the survivor creates your connection to forget that your lifeline is God, your life line is source, and your life line is. Your world that you perceive has many coins of duality, the ying and yang, the yes and no, the win and loss, and the good and bad. As you sit in your world right now, you are flipping these coins of value in the game of duality, worrying about what side will show up; abundance, financial loss, love, hate, home, homelessness, life, and death. Coins of value that you so identify with when you are in the game of duality are like any game that you play, and you get serious of how these coins are exchanged. Who has more of the right coins and who has less? The need to have more than another, to outwit another, to survive in a virtual game creates stresses and worries and war in every facet of your reality, and as a oneness and a one energy field that you all are, Dear Ones, you create this game of war, which is so vibrant in your illusion now.

War is part of every facet of your awareness. How can you not be worried or stressed? How can you not think you have been abandoned by love? War says you have something I do not and I need it, so I will outmaneuver you in this wonderful identity of value as we play the game of duality. You have what I need and I shall create a way to get it. To conquer and to win is just a moment, really. This moment, in the game of duality, makes the game not stop, but begin repeatedly for you participate in these games to see how the value holds your identity.

I come here at this time to help bring space in this game that you are playing, to help you refresh your connection to the big picture. Outside of the game board of duality, we whisper to you,

Chapter 1 - Duality

how to become in tune with your heart and your mind, bringing your holy temple to the highest vibration that you are here to do, and to celebrate and create abundance. We also ask you to celebrate the full spectrum of the holiness of giving and receiving for you love what you do and as you love what you do, the graces that you get back are more. And the more you receive, the more you want to shout out to help others know the ripples of love, and good.

Many shifts are happening now, so thus the game of duality is feeling more critical to many people than ever before. The questions and rules within the game of duality are changing. You take your turn, and you throw your coins of value, but accept that their value only signifies a placement of your now. You, in the holy presence of source, create eternally and can move value beyond duality and know peace is eternal, for abundance of all is yours. The war of duality destroys identity with spirit. The core of connection that all have, brings much sadness and pain to all lightworkers when you see the identity of another being shut down. Their identity is weakened for they no longer can dream. The game is now their purpose. The sadness is a way for forgiveness to be sung to another. Forgiveness erases sadness and it cleanses a person's identity so they can get grounded back into their holy temple and see their divine truth going forward.

Your space as you walk is to know that you get to change the rules of the game of duality, because you created it, you can change it. When you change the rules as it pertains to the Holy Spirit, the miracles that happen are instantaneous. Perception allows duality. Right sight is seeing the beauty of you in the now, and knowing this beauty of you is the paintbrush that is creating a landscape for others to dance in. One can stop the game by looking at the coins you value in duality and say I place my value differently. When another is throwing a coin at you and says you are wrong, you can look at the value and offer the opportunity to connect with us and know that you are never wrong. Your space of awareness in connection with us, grants insulation from the darts of pain and helps you to define you in the space of oneness, and in the space of honest awareness of you.

The challenge as you step out of the game of duality is you stop taking those coins of value that only makes sense in duality, and to know that you are loving you so much at that moment. You say I accept my holy power, I accept my holy presence and I accept me in this moment. I forgive me for any karmic energy that has brought me to this place of sharing coins in duality and I know that you are here to share love, and are here to share the fullness of us in this space of spirit. It only takes one you know. It takes one to influence the one-ship, and the sonship of you. One mighty light to shout forth and acknowledge, no more, I stand in all of me to face you in love.

The ego in the game of duality keeps you running in fear, war, death, financial loss, and the buzz words that get plastered on every communication device that you own. These words make it hard not to engage. These words of power in duality make it hard for you not to run, but by standing in your strength and facing duality, that is all you are facing, Dear Ones; by saying I choose love, I choose love of me to love you. My love overflows everywhere to everything, and as it flows I celebrate our connection as we retune to the Holy Spirit that we are. As we retune, allow our divine blueprint to unfold and let go of our silly identities of will. Letting go of my will be done and your will be done. Bring forth the true dance that we are holy, holy, holy, we are holy. In being holy together, our divine blueprint can manifest instantly giving us freedom to celebrate who we are in the holy purpose we came in to be.

Your space around you is vast. In this vastness, love hugs you. There are more love particles around you than whatever you can imagine. The essence of light cocreates to celebrate your love eternally. Celebrating love is the golden ticket that gives you eternal sweetness in the landscape around you.

Mike: When we choose to be separate from the Holy Spirit with the big "What If," and we created this illusion, can you help me to really understand why I would choose my illusion, when sometimes I would just rather go home?

Raphael: One clarification is that you never separate from the Holy Spirit, from us, and the gift that God gave you. You were given the armor of remembrance. You separated only in beliefs of your split mind out of love through a beautiful "What if." You were given the gift to think what if. You did nothing wrong in this separation of what if. If you were given the gift to question what if, did you do anything wrong? God did not see your what if as wrong. It was the exact wonderment of creation that he bestowed to you. Your belief the moment you created what if was wrong, and is what you wrestled with. God is eternal. God creates; thus, you are eternal, and you still create within God. This what if is only a small blip of eternity that you still wrestle with. How often did you think something or do something spontaneously that you are still questioning in your life right now? This is the energy of what you did with just a what if.

We are your gifts. The Holy Spirit is your gift. You cannot separate from us. We became these gifts for you, the moment you said what if, and we said it back. We were created for you. You know as we all return in oneness to the grand eternity, we are all essences that are together. Only because of the belief of what if, that creation of that nuclear power of that moment, exploded you into a million billion trillion creations. You fight to believe you are whole.

Your cover up in duality of your supposed crime is always worse than the crime. There was no remembrance in God of you in a what if. Only because you have been covering it up over and over and over has it made the spaces of your creation darker and darker. Hide and seek will play out of you remembering your oneness. You are the child of Absolute Love. You are always one, and as you work back in that holy principal, you give us all the memories of separation to help shine back to you and to your holy oneness. We are partners. You run from us and the light at times. For we are your light, but that does not mean we are shining within you. For you always have your light and we connect. There is no out of it, right? And as you all remember this, you go back to you and your full light in love. You are the gift to bring forth the wholeness and to live in absolute peace.

Elizabeth: In moments when I find myself truly discouraged about everything, I must ask you why did the creator even do this? We were all safe and all one and together, and then he decided to create all these sparks and struggles that we have. Why did he do that? Why didn't we just stay safe at home?

Raphael: You are safe at home with God. God again, did not do this. He gave you everything he had. Everything of God is yours. There was no separation so thus you all did not exist. But you were just part of the beautiful eternal joy of love. Within that space, you are a creator of the magnitude of nuclear force. All of you as the child of love created all that it wanted to. And in that creation, you, the child of God questioned what if I was God? What if I am God? In that moment, that belief, that question was answered. You created an answer that was so not what you thought it would be.

Because I am God to you it usurped your source of who was the essence that created you. The holiest eternal grace of source honored your creation and gifted you us to help you know that you are God too, but you are God who is the child of source. You have bodies who show I am the adult, and you are the kid. These words are very separating as I share this concept and you perceive through words, and I wish that were different. But in your split mind, that is what you have learned to do, which is to feel, perceive, and acknowledge you through words. It is even worse now through technology.

But as we go back to the beginning your wholeness is a vast ocean eternally, and you stretch upon all there is. And you feel safe, because God is as big as space that holds your moons and your suns, and the universes upon universes. As you stretch you say, Oh, what if I want to be as big and powerful as God? You open into that belief and go above, below, or around or through all your words and usurp in your mind the safety net of eternity. In that, you feel your creation of being God. It wasn't what you expected right? It was void, for you are nothing if you don't resonate in eternity. So, what did you feel? Nothing, but the void of eternity. This was your creation. You did something wrong. Instead of saying this was not what I thought and went back immediately, you ran to fill the void so no one would know you were nothing as God. This was not what you thought it would be because you were always eternal and free, so how can you be nothing. But you never usurped God, because God is, always, and you cannot take from eternity. You cannot take from Absolute Love. You cannot take, you cannot own, and you cannot dilute, and in that, this creation that you worry so hard about, and get angry so much about, is you. You one day will face what you call judgement day and apologize for a mistake that was never a mistake. There is no need to apologize for creating nothing, for nothing will always be nothing. This is nothing. There is no permanence here except you. You are eternal, so you make this illusion in the form of permanence. But really it is nothing to God. But he knew you his child would hold this creation in its darkest form and not let yourself to just forget. You thought that you had to work that darkness of nothing to remember eternity which is you.

We came as your gift, for God did not leave you. You are in that grand Absolute Love and so you all believe so heavy on separation that you want these pieces to be able to hold space, so you can comprehend the game that you are in. We are not able to give you that comprehension because the duality of the split mind is so strong. We are here to tickle you into your remembrance of what is true love, what is wholeness, what is eternity, what is permanent and what is your value. We become part of your creation, so you can then consider all that you do and start to remember your good, your holiness, and your wholeness in creation. As a creator of this you will create back to the blip it really was for nothing shall be nothing, for it was always nothing. You did not create this. It is your dream for what you all have as the darkest secret, that you must bring to light. For in that, you recognize that no creation is dark. That creation is your wholeness in eternity.

Chapter 1 - Duality

Mike: You were talking in the original message that "you are eternally hugged in the Holy Spirit." Could you expand on that?

Raphael: How do you nest but in the comfort of the essence of love. How you nest is part of allowing your energy to have no separation. When you feel, know, and see oneness, you are acknowledging the vibrational hug of the Holy Spirit. The gift of God for you is to work out your illusions of separations to honor you, the creator of your separation, and to let it all go back to the hug. As you let all the memories of separation go, you are safe to fully find eternal peace in the hug, which is the gift of your holy creator and your source of oneness, which is Absolute Love. You touch the edges of Absolute Love and you feel like you are being burned, because the knowledge you have on Absolute Love is just a small point of you. As you release and let go of all your beliefs and struggles of duality, you hold the piece of who you truly are. This wholeness of love, this wholeness of creation is us. We are the divine servants to your wholeness of creation. We hug you back to your home that you yearn for, erasing all beliefs that you are separate.

Elizabeth: I would like to clarify the word "Holy" because some people are turned off by words that they associate with religion. Please clarify by what you mean when you say Holy.

Raphael: We, as a vibrational field, hold wholeness. All is one, so holy was always spelled to create separation. Your holy was the intention of those who needed to condition your split mind to hold separation, and thus fear. In the English language, it should be w-h-o-l-l-y. Languages evolve and thus the original word was *whole* in its pronunciation. Within that there was a sacred placement of our essence in all that you did. This space changed. Sacred changed as you evolved into a higher processing of your split mind. No longer was sacred meant for all, but it was a way of creating dilution in all that you could perceive as wholeness. Your world works to dissolve any remembrance of what truly is sacred and what truly is whole. You currently have the buffet of religions to select what makes you feel safe and to evolve back into your remembrance of what is sacred. The gift of the Holy Spirit is that we all serve in your creations to help you remember your wholeness, your sacredness, and your oneness.

We serve in every nuance of creation. We are with you, gluing and connecting the remembrances of wholeness, of oneness, and of sacredness. As we do this, we too become a stronger vibrational force to bring your split mind, that is used eternally, into the fabric of your truth within the greatest intelligence of God. When you first worked within your split mind, it saw sacredness, and at points wanted to create us, and what you could touch through your separation. We are a hug. We are your security of peace and encourage you to let go and be one with source. As we became more diluted through your thinking of us, the aspects of us, meaning me, have specific placements because you have chosen that for me, and I serve the identity and the creation that you brought of me. I show up different in different minds, but I am always the healer to kiss away this deepest pain of separation back to wholeness. Thus, as you have diluted us, your separation to even trust the whole spirit is now a paradoxical creation in your religions. For your creation in separation must expand to your darkest place, for you believe in that dark space within a split mind. However, that is not your truth and so when you touch that darkest place, you look upon you and see you are light, and we are always the glow that leads you out of separation. We were gifted to you to do this, to work in your holy creation, and to remember wholeness. How lovely it is to serve this way and know the ones that are in the dark are holding sacred space for they hold us as we stay pure throughout all your creation, so you know your pureness of joy and peace in love everlasting.

Mike: In the game of duality, it appears that forgiveness is the move to make that will allow us to get out of this game, or this illusion. Can you give us a definitive way to forgive, that we can incorporate into our subconscious mind as an effective tool?

Raphael: You are a creator. That is your gift. You are always expanding and creating. Once you say I am the creator of all that is around me, every aspect of what I feel, hear, see, know, and what I am, I created; by owning it within your heart, you are a creator of all. Then you honor it as good for it is good. You created it and it is good. You created from a what if and it is good. For in your creation, you are shouting out that you are demonstrating your core of being.

Once you can see, feel, know, and hear back that what you are creating is good, you must recognize not only in your heart it is good, but as you get feedback, that it is good. Then you will take ownership even deeper that you create from the place of your good. It erases your belief of separation for all your good becomes the pieces connecting you to know that you created in a sacred permanent way. You only can say you are good because in duality things are only good or bad. Maybe love and hate, but most live in a world that is good or bad. For you numb deeply the depth of how you could create if you allowed yourself to fully be vulnerable in creating in love.

For me to say you could disappear your world in looking at something and say I love it, and I am love, is difficult, because you don't know if the people around you truly love you. Are you vulnerable enough to ask this? Are you vulnerable enough to be in love with yourself, and with others in this space of separation? When I say good, I am not using your world of rules. I am using the gift your soul, and your higher self, brought forth in this incarnation of you. You have chosen to be the yo-yo of cause and effect. You have chosen to give your creation responsibility to what you created as the ego. You would rather be a puppet of the split mind than follow the string of the yo-yo back to love.

The highs and lows of this space in duality move you to remember that you are a creator. That is all. You must confront that you created this, all this, and know you are good. If you can look upon everything from your soul perspective, that is hugged in the Holy Spirit, you will acknowledge that what you chose to do in this incarnation of you is good.

If it is great, you would then give it a special and holy God status that will make that creation fail. But if it is good, it can stand up among all and shine and reconnect you into the oneness that you seek in every creation that you do. As you look at the world through good, you do dissolve the nothingness of a zero and bring it back to God. That word is super intentional in your thoughts, for you are just dissolving nothing back to God. This is your Golden Ticket to create the completion as the creator of all that is in front of you.

Elizabeth: There are many of us out here that work ridiculously hard to make these changes. You said that you get to change the rules of the game of duality because you created it. But this becomes difficult because we know to really change anything, we need to take the mass consciousness with us. Is not the shadow side purposefully mesmerizing the people to make this difficult with all the phones, TV's, computers, games, etc?

Raphael: But of course, because the ego that you created wants to usurp you as the child of God. For you usurped God in your belief and you created all of this, and then the ego was your child, and now you are so worried that your dear child the ego has usurped you. God never left. You never left as the whole creator. The ego cannot usurp you. It will try to create the darkness that you first felt when you were separated, or your belief that you separated. That void is all that you yearn to avoid, so your child, the ego, pushes you towards it. For only in nothingness can something that is created out of nothing believe it can rule. That is why your dream, your illusion, can never be eternal. Your reality is what you breathe in and out and is permanent for you at this moment because you have made it so. That is the mass consciousness of the gift of the ego. The ego made this permanent so you could hide your true talent, and your true essence creator. Not holy, but whole creator. You must step into a holy creator to get to a whole creator, for it is a memory of you that takes its evolution into consideration by taking its time for you to remember. A holy creator will say this is good. A whole creator knows it is one with God and it is not part of this illusion at all. It is hard to separate from the ego because you know the void that happened when you "separated" from source. You fight the light that whispers to you to dissolve the ego. For you do not want to forsake your creation the way you believe God forsook you. But God never forsook you. Thus, when you remember how holy you are, you start to release the creation of the ego, the mass conscious mind, and step back into your higher mind, which is your superconscious and your whole mind. Then, you bow to that creation of the ego and allow that belief to go back to nothing, for it is of nothing.

You love deeply for you are of God and your love is permanent. The biggest paradox in your essence is to release your love of your ego and remember your wholeness in source. Ego is the prince of the mass consciousness. You have given it that responsibility. What you have given shall disappear. Your ego created the space of mass consciousness and knows that you will disappear it. It knows that it has no permanence, and it will create you to keep believing in your illusion. It will create so many highs and lows that you are always cleaning up your creations and never coming back to your permanence in love.

It is now time for you to awaken and start to really remember your creation of the ego so you can slowly let it go back to nothing.

Mike: You mentioned that you whisper to us, and I know that I want to hear you, and I think I am trying hard, but what can I do to open that channel with you and leave no doubt that I hear the whispers?

Raphael: Our whispers are interpreted in many ways. When I say whispers, it is the gentle breeze that is surrounding your essence. Not your body, but your essence of your soul and your higher self. These bodies are fully the domain of your child the ego. In that, I honor your creation, but I know that it is not your world of fully remembering who you are. We hug your essence, which is your higher self, and as you work on yourself and start to forgive all separation, you feel our whispers, our gentle breezes, our musical notes, our feather touches, more frequently. As you work, you will use the gifts of what you came in to hold as intuition more often. Some want to hear me but might not have brought that gift in, and thus you won't hear me but you will feel me, and you will get an aha, or images implanted in your mind. We do not yearn just to be heard, for all of you have receptor sites within your holy conditioning to bring us to the world of duality in your own sacred ways. Messages are part of your cells remembering that they are creators too, and they are here to hold the light and the essence of you in your most whole aspect. Become strong with what your true gifts of intuition are, and extend those talents and gifts of how you are to stretch back into oneness, and you will gather our essence into every fiber of your being. It releases your split mind to not hold duality for the ego and will always make your mind question all. Oneness just knows.

Elizabeth: You mentioned that many shifts are happening now. Please tell us more about what those shifts are.

Raphael: You are having many, so to speak, old souls come into incarnation at this time. Old souls are the ones that hold the wisdom of learning their wholeness in lifetimes that held duality for them. Any aspect that you created the remembrance of your wholeness is an anchor lifetime that brought you into the wisdom of who you truly are. Thus, you do not play with the rules of the ego of mass consciousness, you play with the rules of your universal laws and then are viewed as a whole creator. At this point, it is where your minds are having the evolution out of your body and into energy. You are in an information age. You all do not have to work so hard if you choose. You put yourselves into cubicles to work instead of the expansiveness of Mother Earth. As you put yourselves into these cubicles, you make yourself become narrowly focused into exploration of information. To expand into that holiest comprehension of sharing that wisdom throughout your mass consciousness, the ego does not like that you are in an information age, and so it must make droughts, water issues, home issues, homelessness, and terrorism so you don't stay put and start to focus on yourself to gather the information of all you are.

Yet, you have created these systems of connection, of allowing machines to do your work so that you can spend endless hours researching this infinite oneness of the internet for information. You can connect with whomever you want if you choose. For the internet is a layer of oneness that you have not yet really figured out how to police. The ego does not know what to do in this vast connection of your internet, so it makes your outside sources terribly vulnerable. Your phones are exposed, yet the extension of you that you put into your phone can be life or death. Your computers, which are all run on electricity, is susceptible. All are part of satellite connections, which is at risk. The ego is showing you are vulnerable, even as you create a connection of oneness. Your idea of oneness can never be permanent, for in that you see its vulnerability and you forget that you are slowly creating to your permanence of oneness, and what you have created is good, for you only see the vulnerability in all the acts of terrorism that is conditioned into you. Thus, you can't even find fulfillment in being still, in having the wisdom of all the knowledge for you to fully digest, and to know that you are complete and whole.

So, you then destroy the luxury of what you have at this point in your constant worry of your vulnerabilities. Yet again, these old souls are here, yes? Because the gift of the internet is a parallel gift of you remembering you are one, and in that you can find like-minded sources at the tips of your fingers. In that, your connections will bring you into a stronger permanence of your holiness and your wholeness. It will take the power out of the ego and give it back into you as the creator. Your time of coming whole is strong, for once you have a recollection, and then a connection, you are almost home. It is the gift you have been waiting for. Know that you are all here to make this become permanent in creating oneness in the split mind. But it is one that must hold the intention of moving into how good all creation is, and not have to be at war as you come home into your highest aspect of you.

Chapter 2

Predestiny

Your vision of you is very personal. Your mind's eye is your tool to be anywhere and to be anything. There is no time or space within your mind. A vision is a reality, for it is part of the wholeness of you. As you seek refuge into your vision, and into your mind's eye, watch what you manifest to celebrate in the open canvas of the universe.

We are connected. Connection is part of all there is. You all are connected as one unit, facilitating motion, and celebrating an experience that shifts a dance of you to create the knowledge of you. All of you are a part of the particles of matter and all the particles of the universe, which have been woven to this moment, to celebrate and acknowledge a sacred knowing of your light and love.

Predestiny is the masterpiece of you to fully share your light and love in creation and in celebrating breath. Breath is essential in the movement of your Holy temple. Breath expands your knowledge and truths of you to all there is. Each breath participates with predestiny. We say that it is predestined, because that means you will walk through a specific experience, a specific human exercise, and a specific space to allow you, the creator of this predestiny, to connect all of you back into the Holy creator that you are. You forgot how holy you are; you play with broken pieces, cut up photographs of memories stored within your DNA, and stored within your cellular memories. When you are not working from wholeness you cannot bring the fullness of you to the experience of your now. Predestiny holds pieces of memories that you have chosen to magnetize together, to fully understand the unfolding of you in a specific experience. On your way to predestiny, there are many ahas as you gather these fragments of memories and tuck them away within your chakras, and especially within your spinal cord, to harness the magnetic essence of the event.

Many times, the dear Holy ones around you think that fate has given them heavy blows for, somehow, they must walk through the depth of pain and their call of why me is answered by, "Yes; congratulations, you have won this precious experience to look at why the pain breaks your wholeness." As you see and understand the ingredients of that pain story, you give yourself the greatest opportunity to forgive that placement of how pain has kept you hostage with broken memories. How could you have not made the decisions you have made if you were always working off the broken memories.

Most souls reincarnate with predestiny to understand the whole story and the wholeness of purpose in being here. In becoming one with all of you in that wonderful place of fully knowing your wholeness, you must go through times of shifting all the layers of you to magnetize the pieces back to your greatest aha of you.

Predestiny can be as simple as going on a journey to a college where you meet people who will be so tightly woven into your life that the fabric of your experience stretches you beyond the conditioning of who you are. Predestiny is your gift to be moved with forces beyond your control, into a placement that allows you to grow in the knowledge of the power of you, and to have the power of now hold the divineness of all your spaces. You do not look at predestiny points as good or bad. They are markers of you that highlight your core compass of connecting to wholeness, to God, and to all the ways you are guided in the essences that go beyond a physical awareness of your environment or your conditioning of your body. But when you come into this beautiful vehicle that you have chosen, your predestiny ends up being your greatest highs and lows, because these pivot points shake you to your core. The learning that your soul has packed into that experience needs to be busted by you, by being uncomfortable within pain or pleasure. You, on your own, within this space seek comfort within experiences that push you beyond your comfort zone until you fully dive into your divinity.

It takes so long for you to be in your body. For you to want your body, it can be lifetimes before you fall in love in your body. Many experiences pull you to your body that are predestined, so you can see this Holy temple as a sacred wholeness of absolute love. For it is not the body that defines you. It is the experiences that push you to move the body that define your memories of your spirit. Knowing and believing you are spirit, and acting as spirit, is the answer you look for in every point of predestiny.

You can rise out of any situation by proclaiming that this body is not me. I am spirit, and in being spirit there are no conditions that make you less. There are no conditions to have to do any would of, should of, or could of in your reality. This place of being spirit is the fabric of mastery that you seek. The predestinies allow you to honor and work through memories that have shattered your light and love. In that space of considering the pieces, you find that you are always the redeemer in all moments of now, and that you get to rewrite all of you by calling on your Holy divinity; I am spirit, and I rewrite this moment in love. I am spirit and I soar in joy as I weave this experience in love. You will find the glue of you and spirit makes all predestiny the delicious nourishment that you have come to sink into.

Predestiny is part of your soul's journey to uncover your truths about love, and your truths about fear. The three players of duality; love's voice, essence, and truth fear the message of the holy grail of separation, and you. You are an encyclopedia of all experiences of all your lifetimes and all knowledge. You hold all keys to be back in the glorious awe of God's perfect love. You incarnate to unlock all the mysteries that are within you. The predestinies that you have chosen are events that allow you to question every belief you have ever had. Predestiny comes because you have put that experience into the treasure of finding love in the incarnation of you. You know and have always known the true places, the true experiences, and the true creations to stand before all and announce that you are created in love to all, and that you hold the Christ light of God, of source, and love's eternalness.

Predestiny, for you in a body, is at times unexpected, yet no matter how hard you try not to do something, you seem to still be picked up by some supernatural force and put into a different placement. Some predestiny in your divine blueprint is marked, so that you say, "Oh yeah, I know that it is always going to happen," and when it happens you are not surprised. Some predestiny is a surprise because it picks you up and moves you to a place that you might never have considered for yourself. Before you incarnated, you chose many tools of personality, temperament, intelligence, moral consciousness, and composure to equip yourself and help move you through experiences to filter what you choose to share in love and what you choose to share in fear.

Chapter 2 - Predestiny

As you move in an environment that is always changing, you realize there is a core of you that is more anchored that is part of your personality, and that place of being anchored helps you to remember that you are the only one that can choose how you react. Finding what your core constant traits are gives you a solid foundation to encounter other experiences that again stretch your beliefs on how you want to trust the power of you and all that you create. The dynamics that you live in are quite interesting because as a youngster, from a newborn to about seven years old, you know you, more than any adult around you. Yet the duality of your system causes you who knows yourself to work in different ways of trust that the ego would create as power struggles with the authority figures around you. How often does a youngster see something and then the adult says that it is only imagination? Yet the core of that child knows that there is more that goes on than the natural eyes of the body can pick up. Your brain just assimilates data, and you create patterns from the authority figures around you. That is hard because as new data is brought in, patterns change and beliefs get warped, diluted, or messy. A lot of trust filters out of your conscious mind. This can create a tantrum when you are little, yet the power of assumed authority from parents, schools, doctors, and siblings will establish distrust in that temperament or that constant of you. Many, who aim to have spirit be their interface, awaken to the eyes and wonderment of children. What you are really building in the eyes of wonderment is trust that you had in the bigger placement of spirit that was as natural as breathing when you were born.

Predestiny then is a pivot point to trust that you can choose a correct thought system, belief, understanding, or truth that you can trust your decision is right. Your decision to trust you is the biggest gift of predestiny that you always write into your divine blueprint. Finding how to trust you is always part of your divine blueprint in every lifetime, because the main thing that must fully be held is that you can trust a decision, which is small or large, that you have created, and know that it is full of love. If the decision that all of you have created going forward is whole in love, and if you can hold that essence in the core of your holy temple, you will have your divine blueprint done.

There is much in duality that is around decision remorse. You agonize greatly over decisions that are small, like "Maybe I should not have said that word," or large like, "Maybe I should not have bought that house." Yet each decision is giving you a core opportunity to trust that you know you and you are fully in love's embrace. Decision remorse causes heartache and separation and then the filter of the ego becomes the playground of all your decisions. In the ego school, you have a lot of wins, but a lot more losses of decisions in trust, for the ego loves to extend you being uncomfortable in you. The ego wants you to question trust on every level because in questioning trust, you will be safe to some degree; if you are questioning trust, you might never get out of the chair. You might want to sleep and never awaken because in an awakened state, decisions are the golden nuggets that drive the momentum in your experiences, providing you with that remembrance of why you choose some hardships in your lifetime, or why you choose to suffer or have great loss.

Experience requires movement. Movement is what happens after a decision that is fully made with your heart, your mind, and with every cell of your body. As you connect more and filter each moment with the Holy Spirit, the decisions of yes, you are in love and they are the right decisions, will maybe give your body goosebumps all over and you will be excited that you are in movement in this decision. Your heart might start pounding and will be excited that the trust of you in love is going to create wonderment beyond what you ever expected. Your mind might become vibrant for the trust in your decision is so strong that the electricity reveals clarity for you. Once you have built trust to a strong degree within the dynamic of your predestiny, the experiences that unfold will bring you to a deeper more intimate place of the perfect love that you are.

Predestiny enables you to anchor into the experiences of people around you, creating the holy dance of heart to heart so you can work through the Karma of the heart-to-heart resonance that was caused by decision remorse, which played in the vibrational field of your togetherness in a past life or in the now. Predestiny is like the edges of puzzles. It gives you the structure of you in this lifetime to find the pieces that will bring your heart-to-heart connection to the purist and most harmonious placement of trust in love. As your kindness to yourself merges into the place before you and you see all places of forgiveness and trust through decisions that you have created together, healing the heartbreak, and renewing the remembrance of perfect love cannot be broken.

The chandelier of lights that glitter bright, reflect that all is always right and perfect love. Your heart yearns to glitter in that space with others to know that all is right. All is right with you and all is right with all who come forth to celebrate your journey in trusting your love. You magnetize through heart to heart energy, and when you magnetize with someone so strong their imprint is like your fingerprints. That person then is part of your predestiny. You both came to trust in the decisions that you get to create through all your senses of your mind, your heart, and your body and you can look and know that you are good. Predestiny is that precious gift to build your framework with the pieces that, somehow, seem shattered and scattered, because you are now moving with your heart to experience how to glue those pieces together.

Predestiny hardly ever uses guilt around Earth resources. Earth resources only give you a sense of knowing that you are in a space in a three-dimensional game of duality and of attending to your body. Predestiny is about saying I am here to fulfill abundance and prosperity; I am here to fulfill generosity and honesty, and to fulfill love. Being here, then, as you are celebrating your predestiny, creates love and in love this great world gives back to you with abundance in physical resources, in friendships, and in trips. Some are predestined to be an honest entrepreneur in the world of form and to honestly share the great resources that Mother Earth provides. That is part of the beliefs handed down and is the gift to be able to explore how sharing creates more holy creations. When you pick your temperament and personality in your temple, you are aware, to some degree, how that will create experiences of duality within your mind, within your heart, and your cells. Part of your choices is to play out some of those experiences so you can teach the core of you, as you are walking and making your way through those experiences.

You weave your precious essences through your spinal cord, holding your true markers of achievement in finding the wisdom of your predestiny. Your body registers the knowledge of those truths. Mindful meditation brings you to the essence that is fluid within your spiritual backbone. Your heart resonates and holds the compass of those pieces that you have created to unfold you in this lifetime. Your mind is eternally connected to the hug of perfect love that you are, and is always communing with your spiritual backbone. The more you hold to the glitter or the source of its vibrant message, and the more you tune to that core of you, the easier the communication of love with you is and then the pieces of life just fit.

Older souls come in with more predestiny, for they have already accomplished much with understanding the space. When I say older souls it just means that they are receptive within that energy field or soul space, and within that holy temple that they are right now to hold light and acknowledge the universal law of true creation, and not the laws of child proofing of survival in my will be done.

You are here as a pivot point of awareness and it is crucial at this moment for much change is happening in the spectrums of light. Your atmosphere is heating up through global warming but also it is light intensive because you all are heating in yourself to a higher vibration in light. In doing so, many laws and dogma patterns that kept you in pain stories of my will be done, is changing and you allow, with the greatest honor, your free will to be celebrated in the holiest light that you are. In that, we connect with you and become a cellular connection within your cells. This is exciting because, remember, your holy temple is on an evolutionary course, too. Your cells want this light. Your brain does not know yet how to organize thoughts that are outside other's paradigms of logic and being rational. Many feel that what they believe in is their imagination or, somehow, they are crazy, but their cells need the connection to honor other beings who will come into this space of their divine temple.

There are several beings who share this grace of light and love with you but you cannot hear them, see them, feel them, or rationally know them because the vibration within your cells have not yet caught up with their vibration of light. Some beings are left behind as you go more into your cells of vibrational frequency; the heavier vibration is no longer participating and that is okay. That vibration is still part of all that you created and it does change form. It is all part of you, and it recycles into the true placement for all to hold the highest vibration that you are. There is no spectrum of good or bad. It is and participates with you, and in that participation it is holy. You are all that totality of this creation for you are a creator and your divinity is the full space of all particles that dance in your placement.

Predestiny then for you souls who have understood this magnetic force becomes a gift to hold and honor that together releasing pain, allows all to flourish. Releasing pain is walking through it, discovering it never mastered you, and celebrating the story lines to create a story for you to give you the in-depth experience of you in all your what ifs. Then realize that your purist notion of the what if of love becomes a part of everything, of every cell that I am, and of every space. That notion of "what if" is the new frontier.

When you connect through your predestiny points to offer love, we inhabit you and you can remember the Holy Spirit you are. You are part of all the legions of vibrations, and as you connect you receive the full power of your birth right, which holds that pivot point in absolute love. You perceive the world differently because your landscape is filtered not through logical but holistic reasoning of what you give creates the landscape of heaven before you. This is where we get to fully dance with you; for we are here to serve you, to celebrate the stairway to heaven.

Acknowledge where you are magnetically put, investigate the person's soul, and celebrate the places of nourishment that you both crave at this moment. Heal the karma pattern of pain celebrating your will, for your will brought you here and created a dynamic conversation of fluid strength of connectivity with us.

Chapter 2 - Predestiny

Elizabeth: Is predestiny the same thing as a contract that we make before we come back into this lifetime?

Raphael: Predestiny is more specific than contracts. Contracts are a looser definition in a sense that you have the contract to really see your mom. That contract of "seeing your mom," is going to show up through another person and not necessarily through your biological mom, but a person that represents the mom identity for your condition. Thus, you do not necessarily feel the magnetic force of predestiny. Predestiny is a force that pushes you closer to something even though you know that it might not be good for you. Or you are pushed magnetically into a place. Why did you end up living where you are now? Predestiny. Because that is where you would learn, hold, and share the experience of you as a Divine essence of spirit. Nowhere else could you be. This predestiny of a magnetic force can be activated usually by someone's touch. Those people connect through all the pieces to rebuild the wholeness of all the experiences of their spaces. Predestiny are nuggets of you that you have planted along your journey of life. You will do that destiny for we will scoop you up and put you there, outside of any understanding, for it seems so outside of your control that you must be there. It is almost a whiplash of reality within predestiny. Have you felt the big hug of that movement and release within your lifetime that made you move again outside your comfort zone, outside of your control within that moment of conditioning?

Predestiny points are the chapters of your journey in the beautiful experiences of you. They are important, and they will happen. That is why it is so wonderful to see how they move you to understand your fullness, and your wholeness of you and spirit.

Predestiny is the trunk of a tree. It is grounded to your spinal cord and central nervous system. Contracts are the branches that push you to magnetize an awareness, like an antenna, of all the pieces you gather to understand the wholeness of your predestiny. Say your contract is to be a mom, your predestiny is to hold the Divine feminine principles and share the purity of unconditional love as the sacred creator of all your projections within this illusion, and to hold your creations and acknowledge that you have done good, and that every hug, smile, and togetherness shines unconditional love. You will have a predestiny, which is the trunk of being a good mother, and to really question your concepts of how you ground, how you create, how you identify, how you love, how you share vocally, how you see, and how you connect as a mom, but more than that—as the Divine principal of the mother. Can you love you as much as you love what is around you? Can you be the container of unconditional love, stand strong in this trunk of Divine mothering, and allow all your branches, all your connections that brought you to this destiny, to feel the light and love of that wholeness? When you are in predestiny, you will be lost, even if it is a great predestiny. Because that tree within that forest of understanding, and that wholeness of that experience, will captivate you on every level. As you become one in that predestiny, you will align so strongly in spirit that you go above what has captured you, and see the vista of wholeness in you and your body, and it will register and forgive any memories that held pain or pleasure you are stuck and lost in. Your contracts are pivotal because a contract will make you look deeper within to strongly resonate in and prepare for predestiny.

For your identities of purpose here, you like things to be separate. Within spirit or even the cells of your body, information is moved in the snap of your fingers. It is all done because it is now. You all wrap them into one, yes? Yet the way you branch out in energetics and with projections in this duality makes these layers of distinction a part of the remembrance of how you have used experiences to find wholeness.

Mike: You say that before we incarnated, we chose tools including personality, temperament, intelligence, moral consciousness, and composure. At the basic level, how do we choose? I can just imagine someone standing in front of a chalkboard with a myriad of choices and they ask what kind of personality do you want when you go back? What is it based on?

Raphael: Your mind wants duality, and you want you to be you in heaven as this form, or in spirit, of the worlds between worlds. You are not separate, you are a part of a whole sense, and within that whole sense, you become incrementally aware of how you are not coming back, for it is all a current illusion. So, it is like you have games in a closet and you choose which game you want to play. Monopoly or Sorry. You play within a vibrational field, coalescing past conditioning of the DNA that you want to participate in. Because your illusion in duality has distinct spaces, if you come to this world you choose very identified spaces. If you go to other spaces or other worlds, you would choose differently, right? Because you can't use the Monopoly tools to really play Sorry. It is a collaboration of soul groups or vibrations. When you go into these places, you get an essence of what it is; we come to you with an essence that emerges into your third eye and then your sight. But we are not beholding to your form like you are here. When you choose to come here, you take on the specific pieces of the games that play at the time you are coming in. All of that becomes a part of the space of the Divine lesson you are here to uncover. You unearth a Divine lesson that invokes wholeness, which evokes love that is eternal, and forgiveness, so that this illusion can be put away with kisses of gratitude. If I were to say you were at a chalkboard and picking things, that is not it. It is a telepathy of awareness that allows you to understand what some soul group has come to do. Your body is the whole oneness of God's child. You are all one. But say you all have specific soul groups. Some are the liver, some are the heart, others the lymph nodes, for example. Then you all go to your specific spaces but that does not mean that you are working as one.

In that specialized group vibration, you, as a group, know the specific tools to get the aha that brings wholeness of remembrance to all vibrational pieces of you as God's child. The older your soul is, the more you have an awareness of you really standing in your choices of predestiny. For then it really is the knowledge that it is just me and God, who helps all of oneness, because I am one. Older souls in your space have the awareness to connect in the greater good of wholeness to forgive in a bigger way, so the pieces of other souls can connect too. You work wholly in a Divine dance of eternal love. You are already doing that. This is a script that you have made for yourself to remember you are already one in God. All the games you play as a child are ones that help you utilize learning tools to see yourself on a greater level of oneness. Does it really matter if you win or lose the Monopoly game that you chose? No. Does it matter if you sold Park Place, landed on it your next turn, and go bankrupt? No. What matters is that you played the predestined game. What matters is that you stayed by your choices and took the feelings of winning and losing, and instead of conditioning yourself into a narcissist or a victim, you bow to that game and say that it was fun. You gave me the opportunity to expand how I like to share myself in an experience of learning. You are extremely specific as you grow into a more understanding of wholeness through lifetimes to come in and participate in predestiny that changes the fabric of conditioning within the mind of duality. You are forefront thinkers of your time, for you are sitting here and playing in an experience that is outside of norm within your conditioning. This is pivotal in holding the memories of oneness as we move and expand the knowledge so humanity's broken pieces can be hugged in gratitude and cast in forgiveness.

Elizabeth: You have said that older souls come in with more predestiny. Does this mean that the old souls are carrying a heavier burden?

Raphael: No. You hold comprehension at birth, and you can see that in babies because they look so wise, and it is a joy to be born to celebrate the remembrance of eternal love. For only in eternal love do you know wholeness in love and peace. It is a joy to bring forth that remembrance, and joy celebrates the movement of you in your incarnation. It brings heaviness to the physical form at times because what is the knowledge of joy in remembrance at your core can be laughed at and brutalized and can bring such pain into you. For your world is kept in pieces, and as you are learning to walk and talk, you are filtering in all the pieces of you. That becomes the place that you coalesce your energy around to understand the pieces. You forget the joy, but then your predestiny of being with specific people, in specific places, or doing specific things pull you, and you live a life that you know is not really your own. When people want you to decide and you know that your decisions are made outside of you, you follow the magnetic pulse of joy in what your body came to do. It will pull you into experiences that can be raw and crippling, and make you vulnerable, but you know that you have said yes. Underneath it all there is a oneness in spirit that you have brought forth, that you cannot shake off and you must say yes to that experience in the wholeness of you.

As an old soul there is a lot that is required because you know that what you do affects the totality of time and space in this illusion. You are all ready for this illusion to be done. You bring joy in helping this illusion to disappear.

Mike: In my mind, if we are just recycling, how are new souls created? Aren't they all old souls?

Raphael: Yes. Isn't identity strong because once you have identified, it is hard for the conditioning of you to let it go, and then to play into your concepts of spirit, you must let go of identity. You are all part of one. Many who come for a specific function like an old soul on Earth is one who has many experiences in duality. There are many layers that you call dimensions that you play off. You have all reincarnated or recycled in these dimensions. Why not, right? It is your illusion. The ones who have come to really move into the mastery of a vibration holds that mastery, right? If you can sing a pure note, then you have mastered that note. It comes out of you from someplace beyond you, yes? If someone is gifted a voice that is in perfect tune, and you ask them where they learned that most will say they do not know. It just comes outside of them. If you come here in the knowledge of anything and you never studied it, but you have knowledge, it is something outside of you that you have mastered.

That vibrational setting is part of you, so if you are a new soul your mastery of vibration might only be two strings. Have you seen great artists that use one string and make beautiful music? Yes, of course you have. The gifts are many for the one soul with one string. There is no wrong in being young or old. It is just the mastery of what is your vibrational energy.

Old souls are harpists. They play all the strings with both hands because they pull awarenesses out from just their physical body too. You have many Gods with many hands, for they are the master of many vibrations. Then they hold that space for all that is around them. They hold a lot of predestiny. In that awareness they become creators of universes within universes, of cultures within cultures and of understandings within understandings. Much goes on within your space. It is not dead. It is woven in all these vibrations that as you master, you get to behold, work with, move, celebrate, and know. Someone who has savant energy has mastered a reality to bring understanding that is beyond what is the current conditioning of their reality.

As you master these levels, you bring the vibration of all to one crescendo of Holiness. You all seek in that awareness that call for wholeness. You come to master that crescendo to have that true orgasmic awareness of being one in God.

Elizabeth: Do we as individual souls make the decisions on what our predestines are going to be in the next life?

Raphael: As you master vibrational frequencies you choose more on your own, because it becomes just you and God, your destiny, and your awareness of how you want to hold your mastery into the disappearance of your illusions. At first, as you remember you, it is a telepathy awareness of soul groups. All these beautiful cells that make up your liver are defined in the function of the liver, yes? They are together and are a unit. They work in joy to be that unit. Then as you grow, you become aware of all the different places you get to show up. You then start to uncover that your essence is one in wholeness and you then want that to be part of how you hold your predestiny in any incarnation that you do or any dimensional frequencies that you are saying yes to. You become the holiest servant of oneness. You serve in joy just to bring forgiveness to all there is and celebrate the joy in the sacred oneness.

Chapter 3

Karma

Time is your illusion space and for us you have created opportunities in cleaning the karma slates from your destiny and your pathway. A road that you had to journey down is no longer a road that you must journey down, but because you are—in a way—wobbly because the new path is not shown clearly at this point, you might feel that somehow you have failed in your journey of love instead of knowing that you are ahead of your time. The destiny of strength in love is much stronger than the energy field will show at first.

I say this for great chunks of karma that you release, is like the great icebergs that melt in your polar caps. When karma changes, it gives you greater surface space, and greater fluidity for more possibilities to happen. Yet, you might feel flooded and wobbly because when something is more solid even if it is not easy, it feels secure. When things are fluid you do not understand that it can be secure and there is also a loss of control for you as humans than when you are standing on solid ground.

Chunks of karma have come in very strongly and you have stepped truly to a higher point of love. You are melting a lot of karmic space and you are all very fluid at this point. Predictions of the future for you are not easy because the way you go to fluidity will be a dance of the highest and best outcomes.

Karma is an awareness of projection and reflection. Karma, in your world, is mainly saying that if something is done that causes pain, you will one day have to be on the receiving end of that or find the reflection of that through projection or reflection. All pain is a lack of love and when you believe you lack love; you hold the remembrance of pain when you built the belief in separation. The moment of separation caused great pain, and this pain is of the karma that you are truly trying to heal. Your pain is the fluid of the water that is always running beneath anything you build that you think is solid. When you feel stable, the ground starts moving, your feelings or your mind start moving because you remember that pain on your belief of separating from source. Again, that illusion is all that you are fighting, for you are not separate so you have no karma. Yet, this is not what is built within your body. Your body remembers every insult that you have ever taken; it is coded within your DNA. A word can bring up tons of pain. In the moment, you might be incredibly happy and then you hear a word that can bring up this place of great pain. You hold your Akashic records within you. You remember all that you have given and all that you have received. You come in to change the pain to love because that belief of separation is what you slowly erase back to the fullness in love that you are.

Your stories are all happening simultaneously, so of course you remember the first time somebody projected something to you, or you saw the reflection of what you felt in somebody else. Each person, place, or event holds a gift to shift from pain to love. As you get stronger in love, then you take on the next level of whole DNA in uncovering the pain of the ancestors. So, there is personal, ancestral, mass conscious, event, and universal karma. Karma is like the law of rhythm and the law of cycles. It hits you sometimes when you are up and when you are down. Karma was built in for you to get the most out of the experience that you came to live. Each wrong you want to rewrite back to love. If everything is love, then all will be once again. The duality played out between giving up a pain story and hugging it into a love story is the virtual experience. As you master your own pain story and you can see them coming, then you step into a group pain story and in that group pain story, you start feeling others who have that pain. Great masters have come who can transmute and transform other's pain so that the whole of that group can be strong in love. A lot of times you are brought into groups to be together to work out a group karma or an event karma. Through your lives, you have all experienced events with a lot of pain, so the event karma is brought up when you now hear about it through your news. Even though the event is played out in another space you feel the pain, for that pain coincides with an event that you lived through or you participated in.

You have come to bring healing, and as a witness of love and sending out love, it heals that pain, for kisses on boo-boos always make it feel better. Pain is contagious in your world. It is so contagious; it becomes addicting to many. Many of your organizations are founded in pain. As pain starts to heal in love, you see more pain get burped up because that pain likes its mastery in the moment. Pain bodies are real, and they congratulate other pain bodies to participate in causing destruction where love just wants to be. Yet, you who are in these spaces of pain get to bring your truth of love to help slowly release pain to the remembrance that love is the better space for all souls to be in.

Many of you as healers have come to put yourself in painful places because you brought with you that depth of knowledge in truth and wisdom to look past the pain and see the real place that the person or event asks to be healed, for they have called you in as a teacher and anchor of love to help restore their faith of love.

Karma, as you love and forgive, disappears. It is not that you must reenact every wrong that you did or every wrong you judged. It makes you become a master of right and wrong instead of the master of love. Love supersedes all pain and disappears your karma, your ancestral karma, and your mass conscious karma.

We, through the gift of participating with you, do not look for or see karma. We see dusty spaces, so to speak, that need to be cleared so more of your love can be shown. When you walk into a karma space that you have recognition with, but does not feel like it is yours, you are helping to dust the remnants of pain so all can shine brighter. As beautiful orbs of love, your greatest gift is to help bring light where the mind sees darkness, and help your emotions find joy in a space where many despair or your post-traumatic stress memories of pain that you do not want to seek again. Know that the pain is kissed and dusted away in the strength of your anchor in love. This process of releasing your pain-story karma takes time. It is a muscle that you must work because, in a way, you have conditioned what is good and bad, what is and isn't painful. All seek not to have pain in their lives. All seek to numb pain, and then you seek to heal from that pain and heal the pain in others.

You are a three-dimensional puzzle of karmic influences shaping your artistry and sharing yourself, and knowing that none of you are perfect but are vulnerable in acknowledging your judgments, projections, and your reflections. Self-reflection is the greatest gift you can give mankind. Being honest with you builds the dialogue with spirit. It builds trust that you are fully in one ship with yourself, and you have taken in the fullness of your story, which is the good and the bad, the happy and the sad, in each part knowing that it presents a blessing to the fabric of your world, for you were made in love and you are forgiven for any wrongs that you believe you have created already. Your purity of character is the placement that you build so you can be the force of expression that holds the fuel, the fluid, and the passion of your divine purpose, teaching love, and the oneness of all that you truly are.

You will try on many roles as you try on different outfits and you will see identities of you that one day you like and the next day you don't. You are creating you always. You will never be bored in the creation of you. The moment you know you, you will change, and how delightful is that? You are in this holy power and as you become strong in knowing you, all identities of you provide the strength, the wisdom, and the knowledge that teaching love in all classrooms of your awareness, allows you to extend into something more that you might be unaware of at this time. In the extension of you, you will uncover great fellowship in those that hear your teachings and share the dance of uncovering the creation of love stories, heart songs, and magic in every essence of your awareness.

Nothing becomes nothing, for you are all there is. You are the spectrum that creates the beauty of the universe. You are the strength to take and harvest all your good, releasing all karma to nothing. Karma is only allowed if duality keeps playing and when there are no wars, peace is eternal and karma can then disappear.

Elizabeth: I am interested in the idea of original separation, the pain that it caused, and the necessity of that illusion of separation that exists for us to go through our karmic story. I wonder how to reconcile the need to forget with the desire to remember. I find myself wondering maybe it is more important to allow the remembrance of oneness to occur spontaneously while we joyfully accept our karmic load? Or maybe we focus on returning to oneness consciously?

Raphael: What you believe materializes and becomes strong. The gift of your will be done creates a dream state in which the fabric of separation becomes the background for you. Love is always love. Absolute Love can never be taken away. You are Absolute Love. You are eternal. The dream of separation was created by a moment of just questioning what if I was separate? How often do you have a silly thought, you act on it, and then you think, "Oh my God, why did I do that?" It is the same with free will. Free will is beautiful. It is a gift to question what if. It is a gift to extend what if to my will be done. It is a gift to create strength of a dream in separation. Your will is mighty beyond what all you can comprehend. Separation out of love is not comprehendible to Absolute Love. With Absolute Love, what if became a way for you to create a dream and God hugged you in it.

Often, when you see people in pain you see them in their will be done story and frequently you are that loving source like God that is hugging them and slowly whispering to them that they can wake up and unite back to love. When you created separation for just a moment, it became so strong in the what if of no love. In an instant, you created illusions to hide your pain and hide you from love. You get to create your journey back to love. There is no placement that doesn't take you back to love. In lifetimes of consciously holding the journey of bliss, you become bliss. Many come to joyfully work through their karmic space because you are all dreaming this dream together. It is collective pain that you seek to heal. You all hold the remembrance of the what if that created separation. You have all gone back to bliss and held it so you could come back and help journey the wholeness back, so you disappear into love once again. You disappearing your will be done is always a part of love. You find the mysteries of what has been created fascinating and it is. All illusions and dreams are fascinating for while you are in it, it is real. This is real to you and you are here and make the difference. It is the placement of holding each other in pain and helping each other to remember their oneness in love that you all seek to do. No matter how much you gain in things from a dream, they cannot be taken with you. What goes back to your judgment when you die is the remembrance of love and pain. You don't remember your bank accounts, and the furniture in your home. That is not what you share. You remember how pain influenced you. You remember how love triumphed and you come back because in the space of your soul, you know the way everyone remembers their truth is to share the journey of love that takes away the pain. Understanding the journey of pain and your love influences the whole and so people who journey to ashrams or a spiritual life that takes them outside of their normal environment get to practice walking their talk in love.

All religions are built around the concept of God and that love is everything and everywhere. You are of God. The forgiveness piece is always forgiving the pain of separation. So many who have journeyed into awakening come back to be humble servants because of their connection of heart to heart that takes away the cobwebs so that the eternal mind remembers that it was only an idea of what if that created any thoughts of separation. What you do here in this lifetime, of course, influences all your other lifetimes that you might be working. It is all of it, honestly. Finding what is right for you is right for you. There is no correct answer in the journey home. Some people want the fast road and some people want the viewpoints. But you all get home and it is the love that you come to share, and when you leave your temple you go back to celebrate the love story and say there was some pain but I want to go back and do it again because I am fascinated about how pain and love really are the same coin. I am that coin and I am the exchange that brings fluidity and propels this world to be heaven on earth. If you could forgive in an instant all that you ever thought was your sins, then you would be home, because you are home at the same time. With the way your mind is programmed you have built this wonderful system to bounce back and forth between these great mysteries that are no great mysteries at all. It is a wonderful place of being and extending, creating, and realizing that you are love in motion and your love is the solution, yet it is sometimes the hardest thing to stay true with. The mind will finally settle into a right solution for you and your body knows it already because you hold the whole divine blueprint of you going home. You hold your true north and you have the full control panels within you. In that we fully encounter you and that makes the difference.

Mike: Why are we so hung up on Karma, when—according to you—based on the illusion of separation, we do not have Karma to worry about?

Raphael: What would you seek otherwise? You hold the belief of separation, and if you hold the belief, you must slowly release it by doing something in your form to make you feel complete. You work on your projects. Would you start a project if you did not know that it would improve your space? What if a project you undertook failed drastically? You might not undertake this grand endeavor of showing others your gifts of participating in what is around you. Many believe that this is it and that this world of duality is there only playground that they must conquer. You all compete to beat the idea that you have lost and not gained from your now. Many who sit in their placement of their now will only dwell on their loses and not their wins. They will only dwell on their sadness and not their love. They will only dwell on what they don't have instead of what they have. Thus, that deep dwelling of you in this game of duality slowly pushes you to one side of your spectrum of success or the other side of failure. That dwelling in your mind is the first step of manifesting into form, so what you dwell on, slowly, is your reality. If you did not know the gift of all the Holy aspects of the whole spirit in this silly game of duality, you would feel the harsh ticking of the yesses and the nos of the successes and the failures, and of the haves and the have-nots. Once you have seen the game for what it is, which is a grand illusion and a grand video game of your duality of mind, you can slowly beat all the negative conditioning that holds you prisoner in the game of Karma. It takes many, many lives to beat the game of duality, because every moment, there is a constant tick of time that you created to make you firmly believe the limits of your life.

Elizabeth: Is it true that in this incarnation we can free ourselves from all Karma?

Raphael: Definitely. You can believe, without any doubt in any awareness of your totality of beingness, that you are the son or daughter of God, and that you are Absolute Love as God created you. If all you are love, there is no way you would hold to any of the nuances of the game of duality or the cause and effect in duality that you call Karma. This belief is so hard to grasp, because all that you have placed in Gods before you slowly fall from power. How often do you give a person God status in your reality and ultimately they fall? How often have you believed in Santa Claus, hoping for that renewal of gifts of Absolute Love? Does Santa show up on your doorstep? Can God truly show up on your doorstep? The idols of love that you have do not measure to the knowingness, and to the depth of Absolute Love that your Holy Father is. If you had that truth within every being of you, you would no longer play duality. Many who have that do not live long in this reality for they see the small game that it is; so many do not walk the Earth who understand the truth of their Absolute Love and their creation of them with the Divine Father. So, you fight and fight. How often do you fight your own mind to know what is good for you? How often do you have to poke your beliefs for them to keep being true for you? How often do you quest for another understanding to be able to have the whole knowledge of what you are seeking? It is the hardest placement for a human in the duality of mind to fully just believe in Absolute Love. Your quest in every life is the remembrance of that love to keep building your belief so you can no longer deny its truth, and you see each person in front of you as Santa Claus, giving you a gift of the remembrance of Absolute Love unconditionally. You mark your calendars to offer and to receive gifts. What if there was no need to have to have a specific day to play Absolute Love with another? What if it was just now? These are the goals you seek, and these are the goals you hold as sacred every Christmas that you share with another.

Mike: So, in our minds do we use Karma as a tool only to learn love?

Chapter 3 - Karma

Raphael: Yes. You come back to bring love. Every vibrational essence, nuance, and dimension is tuned in love. As that vibration becomes pure love, all the illusions become one with your true home of Heaven. It is already now. You are already in Heaven. Only a blip of your reality plays out here in these dream lands, for that is why it holds so much of your memory in pain of the separation that was caused by your small moment of what if.

Elizabeth: How is Karma released from our DNA?

Raphael: Through love, all Karma is released. Can one look upon their body, and whatever shape it is in, whatever flaws or marks the physical temple has, and look upon that precious vehicle with Absolute Love? If you can love your body so deeply that you do not need any awareness of making it better, healthier, younger, and stronger and can grasp this vehicle that passes down the DNA as the most beautiful temple in the whole of your universe of now, and you can sing the joy of your beautiful body to all; you can be the emperor who walked naked in front of everyone, and say I am in love with this Holy Temple that all of my DNA holds. Can you do that? Can you share the most vulnerable place of you to God, for there is no one out there? It is just you and your Holy Father. If you can, all your DNA is erased.

Then, in the ripples, you can express your words and the vulnerability of your heart, and speak from your heart to any group and in any situation, and know that you can love the words of your heart so deeply that you have no fear of what will be done. Because again, Dear One, it is you and your Holy Father celebrating your thanksgiving of being love. Then, you react and celebrate and know that with every being of your awareness, your actions are celebrating your love of your Holy Temple with your heart of true connection to Heaven. In that, it holds your purest action in showing up. All these things that celebrate you, in loving your now to the highest placement that you can, releases the Karma of your DNA. You do not have to then go on a journey of figuring out what relative did what, and why your mother's voice holds power over your actions. You erased all those lights of cellular memories in the purist vibration that Absolute Love is.

Mike: You mentioned Karma as personal, mass conscious, and universal; if we are all one anyway, when we change pain to love and release that piece of Karma, are we impacting the all?

Raphael: Yes, you always impact the all, for you are the center of your universe. Your universe is all that there is. Because of duality, all your universes continually bump into each other and continually push and shove, so your universe can be the biggest and everyone else becomes the moon that circles your sun. Because your belief is so strong in separation, moving that belief a nanosecond takes tremendous belief in Absolute unconditional pure love. Your constructs of love only allow what your mind can process, and your mind cannot process the totality of oneness in a brain that is structured to always take the yolk from the whites, as every egg of knowledge is brought through your mind. Wholeness is not a reality that everyone feels totally certain of and can totally trust. You are always sifting, filtering, and dissecting all you are, all that others are, all that things are, and all that all is. In this beautiful space you have created to have your beliefs of wholeness. Can you accept anything before you without picking it apart? Your mind must on some level analyze, organize, and discriminate all that is around you. This is the gift of feeling strong in separation, for if you can intellectualize all that is around you, discern it, and place it in a "right place," you somehow feel safe in an illusion. This bubble will burst one day, and the fear of absolute isolation and loss is what you run from because that is what you felt when you created this "what if." Yet, it is not what you get. You believe that the death of your body will bring you loss and isolation, yet many who have had near death experiences come back to say no, you live.

So, as this illusion bursts, you will not die; you will live. That is the promise. But can you believe that? Can you use your faith in Absolute Love to burst your bubbles of egocentric pride, of your egocentric safety net, and of your egocentric competition to be caught not in isolation nor pain, but in a love that you—at this moment—cannot comprehend? I share these beautiful words to help your mind move in alignment to the breath of one that is your truth. What is the identity of oneness? What is the purpose of you? What is the quest to seek an illusion that is flimsy? Its weakness stems from lies of pain, allowing you not to gain the entrance of the truest love that has been given to you all from the dove of peace. It holds the hug and celebrates you to rise above the limits that you have only brought to you in playing the game. It moves you only up one and down two in the game of finding a truth that Karma only influences you to participate without a net, to see your actions, and feel its pain to gain back a joyous place of knowing cause and effect, of action and words; it brings you to the place of a great sigh and gives all of you back to the arms of love, to once again be in the whole of your heart. Love is what you seek, and I am here to say the end is quite near, for as you smile with love in your heart that love is what created you to start the action forward in your dream to once again to be fully and wholly true to you. The game that you are asking about is a Karmic place of the dance of giving and receiving. What you give, you shall receive. Because of time and your belief so strongly in the structure of time, you must come back, don't you see, to play out this game? It brings you the clarity that this is just a dream. I celebrate with you in the luxury of this beautiful now. To celebrate your movement forward, be forward in your love. Do not shy away from it. Be forward in your love.

Elizabeth: You mention Universal Karma. What is Universal Karma?

Raphael: Separation is Universal Karma. Separation also plays into the belief that you believe you have many dimensions. In wholeness, there is no discussion of fifth, six, seventh, and eighth dimensions. It just all is a vibrational frequency of one. Universal Karma is the belief of separation of nuances of explaining even in your mind the vision of Heaven. Many hold the universal theory of dying and coming back as part of a framework that celebrates your beginning awareness of oneness. But it does not hold the hug of God or the hug of Absolute Love. For in Absolute Love, you do not die to be reborn to an illusion or a dream. Only in an illusion and a dream are you figuring out this whole belief of separation. ETs are separate from you, are they not, in your perception? They hold a Universal Karma of celebrating their vibrational frequency and its harmonics of love to your vibrational frequency and your harmonics in love. Scientists will always try to move quantitative and qualitative nuances to all these vibrational frequencies that are eventually not what the expression of Heaven is. For God is not here, as you know. You, the child of God, are here to claim your perfection as God. For you were the thought of, "What if: I usurp God?" What if I just separate and be? God is pure love, so that vibration cannot be diluted to a dimensional aspect of separation. Your mind needs to climb in vibrational frequency to think that each place that you have arrived is holier than the place you have left, that your thinking is purer, that your heart is more in tuned, that your vision is clearer, and that your knowledge is more unconditional. All of this creates a greater expression to be filled with the Holy principal of Absolute Love. The mind slowly dissolves and the mind, even in clarity, will slowly pick apart a higher vibration. Your discernment for safety and your need to categorize, brings you into a creation that holds you in duality. It is hard to explain, for the mind cannot grasp what it is that you seek. We slowly hold your memories of what you seek, so then you know it is a truth and not a swindle. You are innocent and if you could see the purity of your innocence, you would have no Universal Karma. But you cannot recognize yourself or another without sin. Then you create a universe that holds some type of punishment, Karma, of that sin. Thus, Karma is what you play against in your life here, when you hold the pain of universal memory of separation.

Mike: Do we bring our Karma home with us when we die in form?

Raphael: Your home is not Heaven that you go to when you die; you know this right? It is part of the mindset that you have created in the awareness of duality. Being in form is like the snowman made up of three balls. The bottom ball is where you play out all that you do in this Earth texture. You then have the middle ball where all the other dimensions are that play out around with you made up of your ETs, and your vibrational fields of which there are many. The top ball is the part of you that you play in with worlds between worlds. In this, you go through it and celebrate the remembrances of how you are and who you have been. As you go, you feel light traveling up these spectrums of higher vibrations, and then you come to a space that gives you an opportunity to regroup, because it is playing out in the snow globe of your illusion. Your snowman is part of a dimension of a whole snow globe that God, your father, hugged when you separated. But you love this globe and so you play in it. You are not moving any matter outside of your snow globe, are you? As we say, all energy changes form. You are not losing or gaining anything. Even in a lifetime of wealth, you have not gained anything from a lifetime of poverty. It just changes form; this energy, this sense of matter, and the sense of how you matter to matter.

As you are changing form, you are still part of the same dream. And all of you in the universal idea is celebrating in this oneness of the snow globe. We don't care about your snow globe. As of God, we are participating in you melting that idea of the cold separation that you are playing. As you melt your separation, your ideas of the vibrational vortexes come into your big belly of the vibration of your form. So, suddenly, you are seeing ETs. You are seeing and participating in something that is held above you so to speak. Then you return more easily, and Karma can be lighter for you, as you melt your Karmic place of that fear and pain. Eventually your understanding of your snowman is three little balls that can disappear in a moment. Then, your matter is nothing, and you go back to nothing, for you no longer care that you matter anymore. You no longer need you to participate in an illusion. It is scary to melt. It is scary to not be anything but nothing. Yet, everything here is nothing. You do not exist. But only you, believing in you, makes you exist, because this belief is

Chapter 3 - Karma

one that you must work through to melt and disappear. We hug you. We are a part of all of matter. We do not hold the movement like you, for we really know we are nothing in this illusion. But to you, we are the gift that God gave. So, you did not separate. It is your gift to you of that Karmic "what if," to play this game. We will keep sharing the same story of you because it has not changed. To melt what you believe matters to nothing, for you cannot create matter and have it mean something if it is but an illusion. All that you worry about and all that you try to make Holy, in the end does not matter. Your love is the only light that helps you melt into the oneness you seek. Forgive your illusion, forgive your separation, and forgive any Karmic dance you have for it is about you claiming you in creating all that is, and as you kiss it with love you go to the place you are destined to be in the texture of God.

Elizabeth: Will Mother Earth be able to release regional Karma, like wars, around the world and how can we help her?

Raphael: Many souls have a love and hate affair with your Holy Temple. Duality puts much pressure to have what you don't have and to be bold in taking what you believe you deserve. There are many ripples of change upon Mother Earth. She is moving to want to harmonize on a higher vibration by co-creating and collaboration. There are many groups upon her surface who are trying to get what they don't have in trying to keep up with their neighbors. Many neighbors are taking what they think is easy plucking of resources that others do not understand they have in front of them. What groups yearn to be at the top of their collective truth is what they are trying to achieve at this moment. Thus, there is not a right or a wrong of what they are achieving.

For you all are trying to achieve a pinnacle of awareness as a collective. The wars that are playing out always are Holy wars within that truth of a collective. For a collective's truth is Holy at that moment until the aha of a different truth is before them. No one is evil as they are playing out their Holy truth. They all want to be in the "have" group instead of the "have-not" group. Your aha and your truth in your collective of just you might deem their process wrong. For your awareness of how they are going about achieving things might make you question whether they are doing it in love or are they doing it in pain. You hold many groups upon Mother Earth to dissimilate collective truth of groups, and to see if there is a way of achieving that your Holy Grail is good or bad, in pain or love. Missionaries going to countries and being true to their Holy Grail can collectively clash with the groups they go to, yes? That group holds their collective truth of their Holy Grail. This ideal of creating ideals of holiness upon Mother Earth pushes and pulls all collectives to either bend to a new truth or stand in the existing ideal. You do not match with compassion to one another. You do not celebrate a way of honoring where you go to participate in the exchange of truths to prepare both parties to undergo a movement, a recognition, and a willingness to see what is good and to honor the good of both collective truths, and to release what no longer serves.

Instead, you must overtake any truth that you do not hold. War allows you the permission to push your beliefs onto another. You give that war great significance, for you are doing something that you see as sacred and must expand. Mother Earth gives you space to move and express your destiny in uncovering what you hold as sacred, and what that sacredness can vibrate to others in your paradigm of love. Each mindset is doing exactly what they believe they are supposed to do. You cannot fight a mindset that believes that this is their holy truth. It drives one crazy to change mindsets that believe in their sacredness of action, whatever it is. You hold universal law to help you move out of pain into love. Mother Earth harmonizes with these universal laws. They are not laws created by the mind in duality. They are laws created with nature. For Mother Earth holds the promise to be a safe place for nature to expand in its expression of love. As you are human, you are also part of nature and part of Mother Earth and you are beholding to universal laws and that is why you have the Law of Attraction, the Laws of rhythms, and the Laws of Giving and Receiving. The Law of Highest Vibration is what you all yearn for. You all want to reach higher than what you are at this moment. It is a universal law to expand into something more. You have the law of the ego that participates in holding duality. That is why you always have wars, because the laws of duality are not in sync with the laws of nature or the universal laws. That is why your ten commandments gave you a way to be more at peace with the mind in duality. A stepping stone of a foundation to slowly reach into the universal laws. You have many stages of government upon Mother Earth. These stages of governance are brought forth by a collaboration of its people to hold some type of truth for that collective group. That truth is only as pure as what the collective group has decided to bring forth at that moment.

As with duality, you will always be brought with souls who are hearing the clarity of our voice in love, and souls who are just enjoying the game of duality. The tensions that are participating upon Mother Earth will change like your weather patterns. You will have times of great peace and then strife, because it takes many to awaken to change the mass consciousness of a group, and to bring the right people to govern that truth. Thus, it creates regional, country, and tribal Karma. In duality, you will play off fear and pain. You will try to have all that you can and show that you matter. Mother Earth recognizes that you, as a collective, will have the valleys of highs and lows. She is desiring to balance out your Karma, so she will use the universal laws and have different natural events to move the mass conscious understanding of how they truly affect her, through her harmonics, her vibration, her waters, her land, and air in the place you all call home. Again, you will play out duality upon her surface until you no longer, as a collective, search to play out duality. In what you find as Holy and sacred it will make your wars either global or regional. For all of you to stop and have a new beginning means that you must undergo an event that changes what is before you. Are you all searching for this event to change your reality? Are you praying for this event? Can you know for certain that change is what the collective desires from duality? Thus, your events will happen more regionally than globally until you react in a global manner, to participate in a global consciousness of oneness. These events before you will trigger your greatest fear and your greatest hope. Hold to love and it will conquer all to bring forgiveness to all the pain that you feel is necessary to know love.

Chapter 4

Relationships and Soulmates

We are here to celebrate holy relationships that are eternally yours for you are all interdependent in every particle that vibrates. You are the integral piece, for you as you share your love, emotions, heart, mind, and body; you provide the vibrant force that allows this world of yours to become brilliant in sound, color, joy and fun. You are the most holy relationship to know deeply and intimately as yourself, and how you interact with your body, the world, Mother Earth, and all the energy exchanges that are here for you to interact with. Interacting with your mind, discovering the vastness of it, and the freedom to endlessly create—allows you to become authentic in your holy temple. Your body—your form—is your holiest temple for you to nourish, to love, and to know that you are here to extend in this holy relationship of you. Becoming one, becoming a light, becoming aware of the recognition of you and how you interact will ripple out and come back a hundredfold.

    The greatest gift is the raw intimacy of you to you, for your oneness is all in you right now. You are your holiest creator. You are the source of all there is. From you, you bring forth other holy relationships to connect with. Some are fun relationships and are to connect and extend what fun means as you find that awareness. Some relationships come in to burp out or to rub pain that has been in your cells for a lifetime. Holy relationships that come together in pain provide both participants the opportunity to love themselves deeper. Acknowledge that what you come for is to feel love, and to really have the experience of what love means for you. You interpret all the places that love is for you.

Some divine relationships are those painful ones, for they give you an opportunity to choose love this time around and while you are at it in this world you feel deeply the vibrations of pain ripple and resonate within your cells for years and lifetimes. But feeling that pain in love is the greatest gift you can give yourself. The moment you heal a pain story, you have stopped that pain story for generations, and for lifetimes.

Some relationships come to you that are holy, for you and this person, to just know love. These pivotal relationships allow you to breathe deeply, because in this relationship you will extend love for you have known love before with this divine soul. This gift together allows a new vibration to become in tune with each other, but also to the generations within your family. Love is hard to forget and often in your duality you make it into a placement where it must be conditioned, yet love is unconditional. Relationships are holy, for each given moment, you can be the teacher or the student, the yin and yang, of that moment and the wholeness of participation allows the truth to become new. The truth now of seeing the gift that is shared by the participants allows a new awakening to the fabric of how love interconnects everything and everyone. Relationships are the quest of your environment. Again, you are in holy relationship to everything for you are a vibrant energy field that is dancing wherever you are. Even if you are not lifting a hand, your vibration is intertwining with that area around you. You are part of a whole, and what you give and receive is a part of the whole. Your energy field radiates, and as it vibrates it connects profoundly, reminding all that love is the answer to why you are here, remembering that love conquers all pain as a gift, a smile, or a hug to someone that is having a hard day. This will change their vibrational field, giving them the uplift to become inspired and to seek their hearts with love. There is no randomness in your world. You are too interconnected for things to be random, like beads on a necklace, when one moves so do the others. You all play together. You are all part of the Holy family, for you are all one.

In seeking to extend love, the remembrance of your Holy creator energy that you are, and creating in love wherever you do, remember it comes back hundredfold. Your source of you in this oneness connects who will come into your space to be with you. Many words are put unto relationships about soul groups, soul mates, or twin flames. All of that is an identity of remembrance with that person because you are remembering the identity with yourself. A person's twin flame means that person is going to bring you to a culmination of love that will allow you to move forward to a new extension of your holy self. Soul mates mean that you are of a similar vibration in energy, so you might all like the yellow of the rainbow. You are all soul mates so to speak because you vibrate with similar frequencies, yet you are all part of the holy family. A lot of times, the soul mate energy allows you, as a mass conscious group, to create a new vibrational understanding in your community in the global effectiveness that you are. Soul group energy helps with quantum physics. It allows for greater telepathy of one consciousness to occur simultaneously throughout. This is wonderful because this is when miracles feel effortless. A soul connection has the gift of being interdependent and healing with love the separation that is felt. You are all destined for every type of relationship in this lifetime. Some seem that they occur in an instant, and some seem that you must wait forever. The timing is what you have chosen so that you can give the lesson of the relationship of love deeper than you have ever gotten it before. You are not alone ever. The relationship with us, and the relationship with source is eternal. As you come to share and cocreate with us, the timing around events for you seem to lessen. Time can disappear for that knowledge of predestiny is one gift that the Holy Spirit is part of each of your divine blueprints. If you need help in any relationship, coming to cocreate with spirit through the essence of your holy temple will bring in knowledge and truth in timing so you fulfill that purpose, because you are all here for a deep love story and to love like you have never loved before, because in Heaven this is how love is experience. Be honored to share in this holy connection, to extend in the joy of gifts that you are, providing the elixir of love's delight in oneness.

What you give forth you shall receive. Every moment in your space is about giving and receiving. You cannot hold your breath for long, but your body automatically wants to breathe out, so you want to extend out as much as you want to come in and know yourself. This is true for every molecule that exists. The atom is its own little universe, and you are filled with many atoms that interact and have a chemical reaction, then come back in and claim your resonance of sound. You are all a sound that fills eternity as if a choir. Your sound resonates eternally. You are always extending your note, your sound. What you get to do in this reality is find that sound within you and know your note. In knowing and loving your note it gives you the strength of courage to resonate it cleaner, more vibrant, and higher in the scale of twenty octaves. Your note is yours. You cannot exist without another's note because together you make up the sound of heaven. As you find that note in the placement of now, and the more you sing it out, the more you give and receive in that reaction of that space of resonance. When we have pain, we make our note much lower and so, of course, that vibrational frequency will bring people in who resonate in that cord with you. Yet, inside, you know your way here, so as you work on yourself, you will find your true placement in the note of Heaven. Knowing your note gives you the holiest power to be you beyond any constraints. You are limitless, you are grand in eternity as your note vibrates. Namaste

Mike: Can you create without love?

Raphael: Find a place where you aren't giving and receiving love. A lot of times what we give and receive feels like we want to put up defense mechanisms. For the rawness of your love creates miracles, yet that rawness of love means that you are totally one with the holy power of source. If you really claim that space, you might just disappear. Seeing love as one little force is false; it is everything. Love is in every atom and every space. You cannot create without love; because you feel separate from what you create you might judge it as not good. Yet what a gift to create everything with the weave of love and to know it is always good. You are not separate. Your energy is too interwoven with each other and with everything here. The fabrics of your energies are intertwined so purposefully.

Those energy weaves have brought you together in destiny for you to understand not to have borders with love, but allow love to permeate everything and to shine yourself and your world in that great elixir that love is. Once the idea of separation falls away, love just is.

Elizabeth: How do we apply this information in our daily lives?

Raphael: You each put into place divine people to be with and to understand love that you are. Sometimes for this linear space, some relationships feel intense and you learn everything at once. Other times there can be relationships that feel like comets that come into your lives and leave and they go far away and then they come back. That expression with them allows you to receive an idea of you. It helps you to retune an idea of you. Some relationships last a lifetime. These glorious relationships allow both people to step into the divine blueprint. As you decided what you all wanted to extend in your holiest temple that you have chosen this lifetime, you predestined yourself on who and what you were to bring into you like breathing in, holding your breath, then breathing out. This world vibrates on emotion and many times that emotional impact doesn't hit you until you are living in your temple in this reality. Those emotions are pockets of wealth for you to claim yourself at a deeper level. Emotions of joy, grief, and love express your truth in how you claim your holy power and the source you want to plug into. Do you plug into the source that is above? Or do you plug into a source that holds fear? Those are your choices. Each person, each emotion provides you with that depth of opportunity to plug your wholeness in love. Some relationships are super easy and fun. Some will grow in discontent, for they have come in wanting to understand the depth of pain and pleasure in this lifetime. That is not a wrong lifetime but a truly learning lifetime. When you have completed that lifetime and you are in a lifetime that wants to celebrate the highest glory of your temple in love, being with an individual that just wants to keep going over pain and pleasure will drag you down the music scale quicker than your fingers on the piano. Claiming that you have completed that experience allows you, with divine focus and intention, to be in the right resonant note that you are and to bring in the right vibrational people where you are supposed to be. What a gift to claim in yourself that I am done with that. That is true love. That contentment in love is everlasting. That is eternity for love extends the crescendos. There is no boredom in love. Finally, the joy in that crescendo is what you all came to do.

Mike: Can you expand on the process of how we decide what relationships we are going to have before we come into this form?

Raphael: These decisions are not a conscious awareness but are a feeling of energy that needs to become more in tune to the place you hold as sacred. Thus, you are not thinking about all the pieces that will touch you, or you will touch as you come into your most sacred relationships in form. Your awareness is to recognize that there is a moment of movement that you have planned with another to assist in the evolution of recognizing the truth of love that you are home in already.

As spirits, you are energy forms that unite to bring a new spectrum of energy to a place that is stagnant or in pain. Much of your work is to see the strength, the foundation, the healer, the teacher, and the vibrational pulse of your highest truth. You connect with others to bring forth a destiny that your soul knew was perfect timing. The clearer you sing your note of your destiny, the clearer or in tune others become to their pivotal song and their destiny as they mix with you.

Your space, which is the world of form has pain stories that you all have chosen to rewrite into a melody of love. Bringing forth love is the greatest gift but can also bring you the greatest drama. Thus, you pick the core pedals of your evolution to your essence, or destiny, in a lifetime to be strong with you in those vibrations. You are the author of your life. We hold your table of contents within the story that you came to be. In that table of contents, those main topics of you are the destinies that are woven in all the divine relationships that you have become a clear note with. As you looked at your soul's placement in your own melody of a love story, you have chosen your divine relationships to be your best friend who can hold the note with you, your partners in intimacy so you both can stretch each other to a new cord of singing hallelulah. Who you are is not defined by your relationships with the pedals around you. Those placements allow your note to become clear in a way that it celebrates its perfect pitch with oneness of love. When you define yourself away from the pedals around you, you then lose a vibration of core strength that you brought to sing your song. When you know you are in tune, that vibration cracks all the walls of defenses that you and another hold, to begin a melody that is contagious and becomes an addicting elixir to your essence.

Elizabeth: You have said that the moment you heal a pain story, you stop that pain story for generations and lifetimes. It is my understanding that it includes going back and helping our ancestors, whether they are on the other side or not. It helps them grow and heal as well. Is that correct? And is that because there is no time and space so we can reach back to the ancestors?

Raphael: Right; because you are all feeling grief from your biggest separation of your creator. So, you all go back to that space. That is where all pain stories originated and thus where you all go to bow to how you, who is so powerful, did nothing wrong with your small thought of "what if." You must go back to the original source of pain to truly erase all belief in pain. For you are innocent, you are whole, and you are spirit. You must heal your pain to become increasingly in tune with being innocent, spirit, and an expression of love. As you play out your world of having no Karma, you help energetically coach those around you who are still holding their flag of defiance and claiming their pain is so much more important than the love story that they are. Because as a collective, each cell heals, and as each cell heals the tissue of the heart heals, and the vibrational frequency of the liver heals, and thus you, as a cell of great oneness, help another cell release its memories of pain, hatred, destruction, separation, isolation, and loss. Great loss occurred in the fabric of the oneness you are as the whole essence as the child of love when you felt the loss of eternal love, even if it was a blip of time. As you awaken and know that you are innocent, whole, and created by the love story that you are in tune with, and you sing, you help others to catch that infectious tune of love, and start humming their note. That is why you may be awakened but you might, at points, get pulled into places that you must hold space, for you are now the tuning fork for others to awaken to, and this is but a joyous art of celebrating love.

Mike: The story of Trisha's and my creation together was in the crystal cave and through many lifetimes together over eons made me think of the question: what signals the end of needing to revisit relationships over time?

Raphael: There is never a stop with relationships of love. It might not be in human form, for in Heaven all binding is in love. The essence of love is what binds all. The paradigms of human existence are a small spectrum of uncovering your pain stories. It is a brutal spectrum in a form of a body that you hold right now. You are very vulnerable to everything, and in your vulnerability to food, to outside and inside sources, to sources that hold you down, or ones that alleviate your pain; the vulnerability is large. The experience here is felt because of the belief that your body is vulnerable. In other dimensions and spectrums, uncovering the divinity of you is different. It is not played off a vulnerability of a body. Here, because it is so demanding, each moment you breathe you have decided to live or to die. That is an extreme stress on all your psyches that you have with you. In this human form, you search for the petals in blossoming your essence to ones who will help you not feel so vulnerable. In that space, your togetherness is about the strength of your bond to become tuned into your wholeness of your innocence in recognizing that humanity is so much stronger when they do connect with their human form heart to heart, holding hands, and gazing deeply into another's eyes. Movement of all souls is about the fine tuning of your notes that you hold in the orchestra and harmonics of Absolute Love. In these harmonics, it is beyond any spectrum of understanding because you cannot make it personal. But it is a calling that you are still in your heavenly home embraced by Absolute Love.

A lot happens because you visualize yourself as a body that is vulnerable and not as a spirit holding its clear pitch of love. Thus, the relationships you go through in all the divine ways you have chosen to meet in all the spectrums of knowing you, helps you to be at each moment in each reality that is happening now, to be in perfect tune with your reality of your note. For if you are out of tune right now, you might be out of tune in another existence. By healing now, you heal another. By claiming a divine choice of you, you get to be the key and then that lifetime where you hold that key, it vibrates to all that you are, and thus you have disappeared any illusion of separation back to one. You and My Lady have been in many lifetimes, and in each lifetime you hold a pattern of understanding who you are in that divine truth of that life. Once you hold it, it vibrates and heals all the times you have held it. This does not make any relationship less if you did not come together and stay in love, because your love is only love that makes you invulnerable in a human form here. That vulnerability is because you do not trust your own awareness of you to hold your creators note and tune with yours. As you journey, it is a journey of fulfilling a destiny of remembrance that your notes harmonize to create a new chord of being one in Absolute Love. This chord is critical on the planet that you are now on and will hold a vibration for others to search and play with. It is a beautiful gift to allow your vulnerability to be seen and trusted, and that is the crux of your placement as you learn to be in tune to allow you to be vulnerable in a place that doesn't believe vulnerability is a gift, but a trait of death. Become vulnerable and allow your note to be strong, and that allows magnetic forces to be whole in the world around you.

Elizabeth: You said that relationships that know love have known love before. Does that mean that is takes many lifetimes together before we know unconditional love?

Raphael: Yes and no. In duality, you can grant the greatest aha on all spectrums of vibrational frequencies. The spectrum of being human is the one where you feel it and you play out of your physical form. But, in all of that, there are lifetimes when you alone have chosen to seclude yourself and be one with your creator, yet that seclusion of Absolute Love that you have connected to is an awakening of your vibrational frequency to a higher harmonic that you come back to hold. Each time you find Absolute Love, it holds your harmonics to be one that resonates in your note of the essence of your creator in the essence of Heaven. In any relationship of duality or projecting out, versus one who is observing and seeing in, you are still working off the mirrors of illusion. Each person you look to you bounce something to, because of the mirror effect, and they bounce something back. Then all vibrations around you are illusions of your mirrors. When you can look at one and bounce pure love, and they bounce back pure love, that placement of clarity that your note in the oneness of harmonics produces, sings so perfectly, that it is celebrated in all you are. That is the moment you have erased all pain and the story of separation. Many lives take time to get there. The gift of the trenches of duality is so strong it is hard to know that you walk alone in the hall of mirrors to become fully in love with your connection to your creator. Yes, on one level, the ones who can do it in seclusion come back usually and say I want to do it, I want to celebrate this note to all spaces of duality, for in this, the disappearance of pain is a tsunami of healing. Some souls choose to come back, some souls hold that awakened awareness and become teachers from the aspect of the Holy Spirit to navigate others out of the mirrors of illusion to the clear note of love. So, one soul—that is you—celebrating your clear note will participate in the hug of love that is the Holy Spirit. For we are created to work in unison to release dualities' story of special love and special pain.

Chapter 4 - Relationships and Soulmates

Mike: Can you expand on the definitions of soul mates and twin flames. Do you always meet your twin flame or is that something that is spread over many lifetimes?

Raphael: Soul groups are groups that hold a similar vibrational texture. They also are one in the field of relationships that can bring in a positive or a negative to how you react to the formula of your destiny together. Like water molecules in H2O, the hydrogen loves those oxygens. They look for them to create a compound that is super important to your world of form. They are needed with each other, yes? They are soul groupings for their essence together which creates a necessary ingredient to live your life. Thus, you react within certain spectrums of people around you and you know the ones that you react to create the nourishment you need to hold the vibration of your note, and strengthen that vibration of a note of love. You look for that harmonious pattern for nourishment. But also, hydrogen is not just for you, dear oxygen; it is in many chemical spaces of reactions. You have certain soul groupings who are the noble gases that come down and hold space, choosing a reaction to move what is valuable in the chain of reactions that allow the all to hold their note. There are many unstable chemical relationships, and they fizzle quickly because their grouping is not harmonious, nor does it truly hold the vibration to nurture your core note. Some relationships you feel are from another planet. It is because this relationship is not stable for who you are this lifetime. It does not mean it is a wrong relationship, but I would not necessarily say that it is a soul remembrance.

As you move into a new awareness of you, you take on a different holding of how you want to react in a stable relationship. Because, it all is about the reaction here that makes you feel love, and you break your defenses to love, or it makes you feel vulnerable and you put up your defenses. The most important relationships for you are the ones that fit in the most harmonious way that celebrates your true remembrance of being innocent and whole. This placement is what you call a twin flame because that touch stone means more to you about the depth of all you have gone through as you do for them. There is a meaning and a depth of remembrance that gives you the place to be vulnerable in connecting in your perfect pitch of Absolute Love. The twin flames relationship sometimes is destined within a lifetime and sometimes they are not. The programming that you both pick up in other chemical relationships when you pull together makes answers complete. It is an integration of both of you as you both harmonize the beauty of that remembrance for each other as you sought the other's reactions. Chemistry in a chemical test tube can look very messy. It believes chaos is occurring and somehow things come together. To us you will play in chaos at times as we wonder how you will come together. But there is a magnetic relationship and an electrical force that is not chaotic that brings chemistry into reactions that are known and are precisely formulated.

There is an electrical energy within your backbone that holds the pattern of all the chemistry and all your reactions that you are here to participate in. When you do, there is a surge even if you don't like someone. You immediately say you don't like them. Why? Because you are ready to have this reaction to clarify your vulnerability and your trust in saying who you are. How delicious is it that you get to react and uncover with mindfulness the reason behind the reaction? The beauty behind a twin flame is that when they are there, it is almost like falling back to the moment of the remembrance of your perfect pitch of love. At that moment, you have cleaned the vibrational setting. Can you hold that with other reactions? That is your great adventure. The experience of those reactions becomes a story that you get to weave in your remembrance of you being here now.

Mike: So, you can have more than one twin flame?

Raphael: Usually not. You did not separate that piece of remembrance of love. You put it in the adventure of duality. You put a lot in finding that person and in that, can that human person live up to your expectations of that remembrance for they too have had chemistry and lots of reactions. What they bring to you is an internal downloading that goes beyond anything physical. It is a downloading of your essence with theirs, but you seek this person out and, in your definitions of what you hold them to be, they might not measure up in that lifetime to you in your expectations. Together with you, everything has been downloaded that you have sought them out for. This is where it gets critical in knowing your authentic self within the oneness of source and using us as the communication device. You do not fail if you do not do this. There is no game of winners and losers in a place of understanding you. Each expression of you allows you to know and remember you. You did not fail or loose. Give yourself the permission to know you, then it will bring greater strength in the awareness of how you harmonize and nourish all the chemistry of reaction.

Elizabeth: You have said that as you come to share and cocreate with us, the timing around events seems to lessen. If that is so, why does it seem so hard for some people to find a love or a partnership that they want so much, and particularly for those spiritual people that want unconditional love, and it just seems so hard for them to find a partner?

Raphael: Partnership has been given a lot of labels. In holding onto those labels, the vibration of bringing in "your one" changes in timing and divine sacred relationships. You have unprincipled warfare on identities right now in relationships. The ego desires to make the identity of what is right and what is wrong permanent in your psyches of how to be. Thus, you who are very spiritual and open are like balloons having rocks thrown at them. It feels like you will never be able to find the safe place for the one to pull you in by your string. The timing for you at this point is to undergo a metamorphosis on what do you want to hold onto at an ideological level. Words, written in a time before Jesus was born, or a time Earth knew great civilizations, have continued to denounce the freedom to understand love for the sake of one energy field, and one's true being at that moment. Civilizations need power to move its agenda in a world that is very vulnerable. This vulnerability in your human form becomes the only tool that civilization can attack. You, who participate in the pebbles of society, are separated to hold identities that somehow hold power for the civilization that you have created, which will keep you safe. You are all changing, and again, this has happened over and over. Jesus was a God who was another God in a previous eon of existence. That God was another God, for you have cycled this identity with a Holy being to create a structure of safety for the power of the society that has emerged.

Those who seek their ones and can't, may be very good and highly evolved people, but have come to be part of a fringe identity to some degree. That is an unconscious motivation that they have brought, because only when the ones on the fringe can look at the whole and the identity of the structure can change occur. For it is the fringe that folds back to merge into the reality of a new society. As spiritual people, you are on the fringe of society, right? Those that have chosen to be even more on the fringe are wondering if you chose wrong, for this is so hard. Your gift could be just wanting a family, yet, your soul sought this position, because you have done the art of rowing it back to the middle and helped to hold the harmonics of reactions in love, not chaos. As you are called to carry out your gift to humanity, you are seen. To be where you are does not mean that you will not get the gift, but in doing so you must really look at those identities and harmonize with the higher texture and harmonics of love.

A divine relationship does not have to be a biblical relationship of your world. You bring yourself to the space and ask who are truly here to cocreate. Knowing the truth around the relationship that you are truly seeking is important. You must hold the notes as you are going through a deep metamorphosis in your society. It takes all of you right now to hold who you are. The reaction of identities around you is happening because they are losing their power, so when the ego makes you feel not safe you make new rules to be safe. You have many spectrums of groups making new rules to be safe. Holding your own idea of what is safe brings in your nourishment with your soul groups, so you can be the nourishment of healing that is needed.

As people are coming together, it is because they have said yes to their destiny, and the person who holds that same yes will join with them. The ones who have gone into relationships looking for a status quo are now realizing that those identities were written in sand and are disappearing. The idea of reclaiming, evolving, and holding the truth of an identity will take place. It does not matter what body or Holy Temple you have decided on.

You are all vulnerable and you can have the likes magnetized to the likes, so two people believing the same still might end up hurting each other, for on an unconscious level they might be reacting to their vulnerability. Not reacting to your vulnerability strengthens your note in love. Many, who feel they are not seen, hold the receptor sites like the hydrogens that want to be around the oxygens, so it hangs out and says pick me. It is the same with your soul when you say, "Yes, we will help guide you through the pick me scenario and create a nourishment of togetherness." It is that belief and trust that you are not vulnerable, even if all the reactions around you tell you your life is over. Know that if you are here clearing and singing your note, you will not be a martyr for that space but an anchor point to move and transform identities that are ready to be washed away. Your groups on the fringe will know they are safe because they have such good connective hearts that they have been able to share. Your placement is pivotal, and we do not want you to take on the mantle of all this responsibility. Share with us please. But your actions are required, in small ways and big ways. When you feel called to act, activate in motion, and sing your note as clearly as it can be, and this will help bring the harmonious connection that people are seeking.

Chapter 5

Conflict

We reflect together in the arena of conflict, which holds structure of your conscious awareness in place. Structure allows you to awaken into the remembrance of your totality of love, and in your great oneness of love. Conflict is part of this creation. Conflict is part of your dream, or illusion space, or the great creation that you have chosen to be in now. Conflict is a beat that expresses all the spectrum of separation. For only in the belief of separation do you have conflict. Absolute Love broken down is still Absolute Love. Yet, if the belief of Absolute Love has become diluted, which it does in this spatial representation that you are in, then this dilution of Absolute Love, causes conflict. Conflict then, is the great virus your mind had, for conscious mind will continuously hyper focus on what you believe you have done wrong. The more your conscious mind focuses on that, the less time you have to remember the light that you are and to seek all the light that is around you. Conflict is a part of you, for you believe in separation. In separation, you have created intervals so everything is not only qualitative; it is quantitative, subjective, and objective. You have these purposes for everything because you understand intervals. Intervals allow an exchange to happen, and when exchanges happen in separation or scarcity, you have decision remorse. The truth deep within you is the knowledge that you are a part of Absolute Love. The conflict within you is inherently part of the conditional conscious mind, and part of your unconditional or unconscious mind. Not knowing how to stop the conflict within you, you search to understand that depth of conflict with others around you. Acknowledging this awareness, that your human identity is searching for likeminded ones in love, but also in conflict, helps you to see; as within, so without. If there is a conflict within, you can be certain that you will see it in the landscape that is around you now. Many times, this conflict is felt because your love has been diluted.

Dilution of love creates conflict, for you are Absolute Love as your creator is Absolute Love. The mind is searching to become awakened always. All minds are searching to awaken to the knowledge of Absolute Love. In doing so, this awakening process will flow or project conflict into your space to see where your decision remorse of love has been twisted. For here, this scarcity and separation makes all conscious minds put love on a spectrum. It becomes a game of giving intervals of love to one and trying to get intervals of love back. These games create conflict, for it is not your reality to just be in love. Conflict is always about how the Absolute Love that you are becomes diluted with the game of separation and the game of scarcity. Conflict then, in your conscious mind, is saying with honesty, "What is my reality now and what am I trying to portray now?"

When you have disparity between your reality, truth, and what other people around you are projecting onto you it causes every neuron firing to say you are in conflict. Can't they see that you are Absolute Love and you have given every ounce of love that you are to this situation? Yet, the projection to you is not that of love, but of condemnation. They do not understand the intervals that you have been giving and receiving of love. It is hard to wrap anything in true love. On paper, Absolute Love does not come forth because Absolute Love just is. But, when you are in conflict in areas around you, the reality of you is quite skewed by the reality of others. Saying, "I am Absolute Love," does not feel that it would make a difference at times of conflict. Your conscious mind wants to fill in the boxes of intervals, to make the world from that vantage point look pretty. But you are bigger in Absolute Love than boxes. You are bigger than any interval that your conscious mind can create. All figures in your reality are important because you all have agreed that it is so. All symbolic energy in your numbers, letters, and words, have been brought to communicate in this space that you have created, to communicate intervals that are held together with love that is conditioned. If that is the condition, every decision you make will always fight with the condition place of your conscious mind, the midbrain, or unconscious mind, which is closer to whom you are in the offering of total spirit.

Your reality gives you the opportunity to awaken, as we say, to stamp out that belief, and choose to create with Absolute Love. The more you awaken you will find that conflict will come faster at times. This is not for a punishment, but it is in a way mental, physical, and spiritual gymnastics. To be anchored in who you really are in Absolute Love, and make your awakened space of looking at the conflict from a perspective of change not required, you can chose to make the experience different. I ask for the highest and clearest truth of this situation to be known so I can walk through the bullets of conflict and survive. The bullets of conflict are only coming because I am ready to claim my holiest truth that I am more than lack, I am more than separation, for I am whole in the placement of my now, and I walk it in wholeness of holding and trusting that love that I know I am will guide my way to my true divine placement.

Many are addicted to conflict in your space, for conflict allows pain to be the strength that glues the world together. Any faith in pain or punishment is because you have decided on a mass consciousness that this is so. You can opt out of the system at any time, really. There is a clause in all your predestined contracts to opt out of conflict, to opt out of pain, and to opt out of punishment. It will be amazing as you do, for the strength of you will grow from inside out. The pain bubble that feels like it has been suffocating you will be released. We are here to help all of those who want to opt out and help release the pain bubble of conflict, for you all have the divine blueprint to manifest all your dreams in love, and that love propels this world more strongly, more vividly, and more joyfully than pain. As pain is released, you will be able to see it as it is coming towards you, and you will be granted space to make that pain ease before it touches the totality of yourself. The cellular memory will be released around that pain. You will also be able to choose love with greater intentional force, and like a rocket that love will move you further than what you can imagine at this moment. Love is contingent overall, and it breaks the structure of all the boxes that separation wants you to fill. Love in this dimension looks messy because you are not building the boxes. You are allowing the boxes to collapse and bring forth the creative space of love.

Duality is not easy. Duality causes conflict. Duality always makes you have the need to live in the past or project so far in the future that your now is forgotten. Remembering, holding, and trusting the system of oneness and Absolute Love gives you the opportunity for peace and keeps you in the now, creating your reality with every fiber of your intentions.

Chapter 5 - Conflict

We celebrate all the boxes of duality and see the grand oneness. Recognize that conflict does not serve your truth, but it does serve the system of duality, and when you are faced with conflict in this space you have many resources of light, of love, and of holy togetherness to walk with you through that placement, for each time your soul overcomes conflict in Absolute Love you never have to go through that again. Absolute love erases that conflict and that is a glorious thing for all humanity. We come, for we are here to serve you, in our great gifts of knowing that you are made in love and we serve that spark of love as you show it in every facet of your world.

Conflict is your way of staying hidden from exposing to you in all your creations that you created; a place of pain and love, of good and bad. You believe that you must protect yourself and others from your original sin. Thus, the more the successes that you have as a collective deemed as worthy and good, the more you believe you have created without the influences of original sin. Yet, you all have the aspects of your original "what if." That is not scary to acknowledge when you start to know, with every one of your placements, that you are whole, innocent, and Absolute Love. In all the conflicts in your now, decision remorse is your biggest one. As you look upon each decision of you today, you will heal the pain of your past to really find the continuity of the knowledge of your wholeness in your now. Be strong when you look at the conflict before you. Do not shy away from what you have created, but hug and kiss it to dissolve the energy of pain through the remembrance of love. Your now is the totality of you, and as you see what is before you, and if there is pain, it is just an acknowledgment that you accept your greatest gift that you can give through the forgiveness of ever causing that pain to be a remembrance of you. Your light, your love, and your wholeness are always your truth. Be grounded and know that and your creation will light your now.

Elizabeth: I would like to raise my hand and opt out of pain and suffering, but what about having the strength to do that?

Raphael: Your strength is there for it is a mind belief that this world needs pain to dance. That pain is what others seek to help you with. That pain is what is seen, and I will tell you that it is only seen from duality. We see love. Conflict is not part of our vocabulary. Expressions of love and light are our colors. Humanity has chosen to work in pain and hold the desert of pain. Yet, there are oases, and placements for you to come and share love, as you build that desert of pain back to the harvest of abundance. Pain is abundant only because you have chosen so mentally. It is all in your mind. You react with your body because it is registered in your mind. Pain is mainly in your true placement of what the logical conscious mind wants. Your whole mind seeks harmony, and you will forever seek harmony, and as you do, you opt out of pain.

Mike: I love the concept but on the day to day, how do you apply it?

Raphael: For you in the physicality, it is moment by moment, for you are remembering to the deepest cellular level that you have been created in love and not pain. Pain is felt and remembered in your body, and you have been taught through pain here. You all know what not to touch when you are little, for you have probably touched and got a boo-boo. You don't want to have that decision remorse any longer. The conditioning of pain has made you all strong in the human form, and pain becomes the barter, and the tool to lord over human forms. That conditioning as a group is very hard to break. Like the flow of electricity, if you are an atom flowing, you don't stop with your flow, you keep going, until you recognize that there is another anchor point you can go to. This is what we call "awakened." For us, by the human mind awakening, it is saying, "I will not be powerful with pain. I opt out of that system and look to Absolute Love for my power." Your daily lives surround you with many pain opportunities. The way you smile or nod could change because much in your conditioning surrounds how you fit in a pain puzzle, not how you fit in a love story. Love stories are but a dream in this world, yet this world is but a dream to Absolute Love. As you connect in pain, you forget that love was truly the reason you are here. This space needs love. Pain is all over and in your airwaves. Love is whispered about. To change that on a physical day to day level is to recognize that your cells are singing to everything and everyone; you are love. Your love is important. It makes others anchor to their love. If you are just floating around in pain, you take whatever that pain provides. But, when you are anchored in love you know that this is your truth, and you create from that space. You do not take from that space. There is a huge difference in those two words. Do you create or take? Pain takes and love creates.

Elizabeth: Since there seems to be conflict in the mass consciousness, I also think that, because of our media, there is more of a focus on it. What are your thoughts on that?

Raphael: Yes, your mind will awaken slowly. The belief that you are love is scary. Could it really be that true? It is that simple. I am love. The mind wants to take the hardest path to something. Again, it is proven that you have done your due diligence in getting there. What your attention is in the mass conscious, will again like magnetic forces, bring things together. If your mind holds conflict, then you will see places of conflict come into you. Conflict and pain get to be the headlines of all stories in this space. Yet again, that great balancing that every time you choose love, every time you yourself make it your mission to forgive, to smile, to pay it forward somehow, will take away that conflict within the mass consciousness and will iron out the places on a big viewpoint. Intentional love from all of you takes away the blueprints of conflicts of war within your world. One person honoring and standing in love will have a tremendous impact of dissipating future conflicts who the soul might have had Karma with. A lot of these conflicts did not pop out of nowhere. Your conflicts do not pop out of nowhere for they have been recycled from the beginning of this space. And so, even if you are choosing love and conflict comes in, know that the karmic space of this conflict was globally brought to you at this time to heal and to dissipate, so you do not have to do that conflict again. Many souls who are awakened will go back to a conflict space to remember love, so that conflict can be ironed out of your mass conscious place. And the grassroots media connects more people to good than to bad. You are interwoven. By shouting out your love it changes future placements of mankind. There are more awakened lightworkers than ever before, for you have come to iron out pain and conflict, and to allow the creative force of love to shine. You have great voices, for your minds hold the divineness of Absolute Love. Holding that space will bring critical conflict to dust. People will love, and all the rest is that recognition that conflict is not your reality and conflict can be changed.

Mike: What if I do not believe in separation or, in other words, I want connection and to avoid conflict? What do I have to do to achieve that?

Raphael: You have already begun, so to speak, in the books that you are creating and have been reading. It is the idea that what you created in your beliefs of separation, that you do have to slowly let go of. In that idea of great loss of that expression that you never had, is the dark secret, the black hole that finds you and all of you waking up in terror. When you awaken to some placement of acknowledging that there are unknowns in what you can touch and feel, what you can hear, and what you can physically engage in the remembrance of that feeling that you never felt before is there. There is a depth of loss that you tried to run from, in which none of you can deny because you created it, even if it was just a blip. So, your dark deep secrets must become a reality so to speak. A space that you can bow and say, "This knot, this dark secret of loss, pain, and separation is 'evil,'" which only you have determined that—defines you as a creator. That piece of you was a beautiful movement of your free will in the great "what if." Mistakes in a journey of "what ifs" are instantly hugged with the arms of the heart and the joy of love.

Thus, through your creation of pain it resulted in you running further into illusions and dreams. Hiding from that decision to usurp the glorious Father, Mother, and AUM of love you must hold the space to know that your creations are hugged, and remember in your illusions and dreams that you are love, that you are whole, and innocent; that the dreams and illusions you fabricate are creations of the ego. As creations of the ego which hold all the energy of loss and separation, it is hard to heal that space for you and to conquer that mountain of pain and separation. Know you are a victorious light that heals that darkness into everlasting joy. Each of the pieces that hold the heaviness of loss of separation and pain are gifted to you; to see yourself as a glorious creator of that space, and to look at that pain and know that I do not need to run from this darkness, for I created it and I forgive that I forgot that love holds no darkness. I am created in *love*, and thus this creation will be a treasure of love, bringing in any light to the darkness that you see when you look upon the soul of you and that awareness of you. You are coming to this place of holding honesty within yourself, for you are your biggest nightmare. Within you is that darkest place that you have seen in the creations of separation.

Mike: Can you expand on your comment about "we are our biggest nightmare?"

Raphael: You do not seek yourself and many have said, "Seek yourself and you will know your truths." It is easier to seek yourself to find all the glorious times of you but not one to see the times where they were a murderer, or they were a dictator or an abuser of all that was given to them. To seek information is to be aware that the information you seek might not always make you feel at the top of your world. Seeking inward can bring many to an expanse of power without ever looking at the depth of monsters that they have certainly been. When you have the courage, and that is usually when you have the strength of seeing what is good in you, you start slowly looking at your nightmares. As you go into those places, with the strength of forgiveness, you can bring a great joy for all the energy locked up in that pain; it is part of you and your whole essence of love. As you disappear your pain, you have the strength to be one in all your decisions.

Chapter 5 - Conflict

The love of the dark side has its power because you claim your power of this creation. The dark energy does have power that you gave it when you created separation. It is not ever a creation of God but it is a source of you.

To claim this source of pain and bring it into the highest essence of love that you are, turns it into a vibration, a wholeness and a knowing. Many have a confidence of knowing that your decision of choice is in the expression, the essence, and the glory of love. It is a permanent knowledge, a permanent knowing that you hold now and forever after. You must claim that journey to uncover and see your pain, to change that pain into a knowledge and knowing of love. For you fight your nightmares of separation continuously. They do not end until you climb, walk, swim into that darkness of you and to see the fears that paralyze you, so you can bring a dialogue within you to claim your love within that space. Many hold regrets. Regretting decisions and actions and not knowing how to make the right movement into those regrets allows the ego to settle into those cracks that regret holds—and many mistakes are just the regret, but become your nightmare—for the ego of separation works in this space of regrets and turns it into paranoia and pain.

Many forget why they even have conflicts because it was never a big deal, but then it becomes a big deal because looking at these conflicts or regrets bring too much pain and fear. This allows pride, greed, and competition to take and make walls and to really dive back to the core place of that regret, and that passage of separation. Your gift now, yes, is to feel regret and to hold the space of you with the Holy Spirit, and ask the light of the truth to shine and know all intentions are a part of the gift of free will. As you say "Ahh, this was my gift of free will," you can celebrate the creation in front of you and see how you can create differently. As a result, you will create differently, for your yes in acknowledging that you are a creator with the mightiest gift of free will gives you the gift to no longer hold regret, but to acknowledge your creation and say, "What if I create from this space? I am not changing my mind; I am not confused in who I am. I am excited to create a new me now that I have knowledge of how this creation will be if I use my right mind connected with all the love and good that I am." With the grace of the energy of the fabric of connection with your essence of you in wholeness with God, you create your highest and best, replacing forever the fears of your nightmares.

Mike: And that is replacing the fears of your nightmares, in all lives simultaneously, so you are healing it all?

Raphael: Right.

Mike: That is why forgiveness and love are so important because it forgives all supposed past lives, which I believe are all happening now? So, you are doing it for all the lives before and in the future?

Raphael: Yes.

Mike: You say that the more you awaken you will find that conflict will come faster at times. Can you speak on this some more because it feels like awakening should be a reward, but this seems to be the opposite?

Raphael: (Laughing. . . .) Many want the awakening to be their reward for going inward. They only want the good of that awakening to be their space. For what you do well within this illusion you believe that you deserve something good, or some type of reward. Going inward and acknowledging your truth you want to believe that the awakening provides you a buffer, a get out of pain card, that somehow, all awakened ones have all the joys of your illusions. Thus, many do gravitate to the awakening process for they are tired with making their will be done. They acknowledge that if they just put their will into manifesting their heart's desires, they might not be able to eternally hold, or feel, the permanence of their achievements of their will be done. Many process in awakening from this idea of lack, of tiring in conflict to some degree, and decision remorse. The belief that you must be at that bottom of not loving yourself to go into an awakening is again an idea that wants awakening to be given all rewards, and not the healing of the mazes, of the smoke and mirrors of duality. In duality, all that is before you are temporary. Wealthy people know they can lose their riches in the blink of an eye, so they must hold on and gain more riches, so they won't lose their illusion of riches. Many go into the process of connecting with the Holy Spirit to safeguard their heart, their mind, and their physical reality from any pain that is a part of the landscape you created within duality.

What happens as you awaken, you make more knowledgeable decisions from your right mind — and not from the sense of right and left hemisphere — but from that knowledge of the highest path. You would say this is the right instead of wrong path. It isn't one path, but it is one known quality of deciding and feeling so right that you are willing to hold that rightness, and to hold that knowledge that this decision has the strength of all of you as a creator to buffer any pain of duality that might come as you hold that decision. Thus, you don't wrestle within yourself about any fear that you might have chosen wrong. You begin in an awakened space to hold knowledge, which is the knowledge of your highest self and of how your higher self is connected within the Holy Spirit as a bridge to bring you into the highest and best of your destiny. The more you use the knowledge and the knowing that your light and love and your connection with the Holy Spirit, you have more rewards, for you have peace of mind that you never had before. You have a depth of nourishment that you bring the world to a Holy place that is permanent. You seek permanence, and you are in a world of change. How do you behold permanence yet deepen your knowledge and knowing of your right mind of your divine placement? You are a divine essence, and to emphasize that essence of divine awakened one, you do go into places that hold the collective pain of darkness. Those pain places of your collective nightmare become a journey to behold with the Holy Spirit. The more you awaken, and you hold your connection with the strength of the Holy Spirit, you can walk on water and not drown in the heavy emotional pains that fear invokes. It does not mean that you might get dragged into stories of pain or fear. The pain around you is kissed away by just the essence of you. The portals of pain that you have come to heal and forgive in your destiny of awakening then become a part of your sacred gift in bringing permanence to all the ones around you. It becomes a gift and not a punishment as you awaken, and to be a savior, so to speak, of your journey into the elements of separation that you have chosen to heal and forgive.

All of you in this illusion as you awaken have a destiny in sharing the brilliance of the knowledge of your truth in light and love, and thus you will have a destiny in a pain story to bring the gift of forgiveness, allowing that story to disappear from your collective story lines forever. Some great sources say that, "There is great light that also illuminates great darkness." As you claim your light, you are just finally able to hug your awarenesses of darkness and say, "God bless you, good bless you, I bless you." You then heal your greatest fear of what you created. Thus, many stop their fear of success in awakening because of the story of where there is great love and great light, you find great hatred or darkness. What you created, Dear One, you get to undo. Thus, your awakening is the absolute answer to collapsing all stories of pain and darkness.

Elizabeth: How can we speed up the process of awakening without inflicting too much harm?

Raphael: You again are afraid of free choice. For in free choice pain is the remembrance and not the love. You do not love what you created in this illusion, otherwise there would be no conflict at all. Thus, the thought of awakening is an idea that scares any chords of pain. The heaviness of your creation and of the ego pulls at you, making and feeling the permanence of your creation, instead of allowing your awaking to be as freeing as the way you sleep. Each essence, each soul, unfolds into their own awakening of the knowledge that you created all; as the creator, you get to create a new within your knowledge that you are a child of love who is whole and innocent. If you, in an awakened space, create within the whole and innocence in the wonderment of Absolute Love, you have no decision remorse, only joy. You are all awakened now, but you have chosen this incarnation, this expression to unfold in this awareness because it gives you the greatest extension of participation as the creator of it all. Souls share the time that they are needed for you all to wake up in this reality together. You just don't know that you are because you do not have the awareness of all. Awakening is the most profound orchestra and collaboration, or simulation, of how to push it beyond the divine appointment that it is for you or another.

Chapter 6

Trust

You dance every moment in the awareness of trust beyond your physicality. You trust at this moment that another human form could bring forth words of the Holy Spirit in a vibration that is hard to hear. I dance eternally with you to hold the strength of trust beyond the holy temple of your physical form. To search beyond what you can physically hear, see, touch, and taste is a pathway to trust that there is much more to all of this than what you know now.

Each decision to extend your awareness to a greater expression of your imagination allows trust in yourself to build confidence of your consciousness. Trust is the center point that begins a journey to somewhere else. To extend to the next place is to trust that your physical form will be able to balance and move all your muscles to a place of safety. Your holy moment of oneness is the trust of you, the awareness of the creator, and holy source of pure love, which is God.

You create amazing experiences to understand trust in yourself, which is the greatest question that motivates you to participate in any lifetime. Trust of yourself allows the ripples of decisions to unfold, so what you believe within can be shown without to the landscape of your now. To trust is to know that you have created and it is good, and you can set your creation free to also create and know it is good. In holy trust, you cement your oneness in working with the divine Holy Spirit to know yourself completely as the creator of your now.

To trust in yourself is the greatest gift that you can give yourself, for that allows the mastery of all of you to extend into every particle of awareness to move without fear. If you are good, only good can be in the freedom that happens and it springboards you to know Heaven.

Trust in yourself is not easy, and since it is a point of reference in every lifetime it can be overwhelming to think that it does show itself once again. The true trust of you is the purest acknowledgment that you are love, you come from Absolute Love, and that nothing can harm love. Love is the highest vibration eternally. Because trust is the holy center to master, you hold faith in each divine experience that you create decisions with. Faith shows to yourself, and only to yourself, that you know—without a doubt—there is something about you that is so good that you are willing to expose it. You are willing to rewrite all stories that your conscious mind holds.

The whole of you is happening right now. The time that you have created is only a symbolic way to give yourself faith in the marker of knowing trust. Time gives you the signs of healing and of awakening to decisions that renew your partnership in the holiest dance of love. Bringing love to you filters at every moment and boosts your faith that what is before you can change in an instant when you choose to trust your holy gifts of love. Faith to engage with all the different participants who show up in your space provides a canvas to trust that you are sharing your gift of you with another and your good will flourish in their space. Each particle of space that surrounds you, knows you. The air you breath is a part of your aura field that participates in claiming you to another. As you breathe in deeply, you bring in the holiest you.

As you breathe out, you share the holiest you. There is no placement in your now that is not a part of you. All is made in the divine oneness of you, and as you share your breath to another, you share a holy gift of trusting yourself to extend good. The more you extend through trust, it will bring more of your good to you in the now. You are all here to trust that each of you wants the holiest kinship with each other equally and, in that holiest kinship, that your dance will open your sacredness. As your light, which has shone for eternity and will continue to, opens, others will too. The light that you share ignites particles around you to participate in the expansion of your holiest manifestation for the happiest dream that you will trust yourself to have. Everything before you is what you have trusted yourself to have and it is the faith of this trust that wakes you up to participate. The faith of knowing that when you trust, and when it is absolute, heaven appears and becomes visible. Become aware that you can trust it is here; explore your faith and know that you choose the conditions of your dance with each other and yourself. Understand love and your fear of trust that you can stop the game of duality and know that you have always just wanted to side with the Holy Spirit of love, for that is your natural placement of home, of being, and of now.

My joy is to celebrate you sharing your faith to hold trust fully. There is so much more for you as you extend your greatness for your creations are your artistry of living your faith.

To breathe in creativity, it expands the awareness that connections are eternal. Each space of a connection holds a dynamic flow of information and provides strength, abundance, and peace. Creativity evolves when you trust that you are, and always have been, connected to the source of your creation. How you identify with your source of creation is your story that you get to expand in. What choices you decide to be creative in gives you the depth of conversation and the depth of awareness that you are one in the source that created you. Oneness allows the identity to be strength in motion. Oneness says you trust beyond your physical senses to a greater gift of understanding and accepting truths that anchor you as the source of light in darkness. Your identity allows you to trust yourself. This identity of trusting you gives you permission motion to move and go behold the wonderment of love. For here in your dimensional placement of physical form, you have an experience of movement. You move in what you hold as your priorities of sharing your identity. Movement says this is who I am. When it is in love, it speaks so others can trust you to be in your truth.

Trust in truth. Your truth, when you hold an identity and move in love, opens all voices to celebrate an expansion of community, conversation, and of trust—not only for yourself and others—but in a global awareness that you will act and share all voices to feel compassion in welcoming in truth and love.

If we then weave trust into your vision, you will walk steadfast in the wholeness of how your destiny is meant to participate in strengthening the light, the truth, and the joy of remembering the power in your crown. For you all wear a Holy crown of the true son and daughter of your Creator. You are royalty, and when you hold that identity of your power as royalty, you acknowledge your responsibility to give as well as to receive your wholeness in participating in trust throughout all your vortexes of being.

Trust in a physical form is hard, for trust is a quality of how you see your pure connection to your creator, and the creation around you. If you view your creator as a task master, and as one who judges harshly, your trust of you in the identity as a human who moves to connect, won't be the clearest trust in truth that you can be. For if you trust in fear, you will create anxiety and worry. You will never own your identity as one who is whole and innocent. You are not here to live a life prison sentence. You are not here to feel the continuation of every wrong that you have imagined yourself doing. You are here to trust your absolute oneness in your creator, and to accept your innocence, and share that light in your expansion of love.

The ego is madly obsessed with keeping you full of wrongs. The more you have become identified with your wrong doings, you will not embrace the full love of your destiny. Nor will you share it and help others claim their highest destiny. The ego knows that it is hard when you are in your physical body to trust beyond your physical senses. If you reach out and trust outside what you physically sense, you will break its strong hold on the truths of your identities about you, and your trust in you. If you stop trusting you, you will never trust your creator again. Thus, the mad, mad world of showing mirrors to your wrongdoing become your need to be narrowly defined and timid in expressing your fullness, wholeness, and oneness. When you claim to be timid, and when you become afraid of anything beyond your physical awareness, you have given your trust card to any rules and systems that limit your attunement to the full truth of your needs.

Because physical bodies feel their vulnerability and the ego's chaotic pounding of how badly you resist these messages, the muscle of trust must be used and strengthened over any voice, vision, smell, and feeling the ego sends your way to make you its puppet. Your creator's gift was us—the Holy Spirit—hugging and strengthening you, and working those muscles within your body, emotions, mind, and soul. We are your personal trainers for trust.

We are here to help you lift that identity of abandonment, of victimhood, and of failure into the muscle of knowing the identity of your destiny and of how, in trust of your core identity and destiny together, you say yes to your truth and the oneness you have with the creator in sharing your light and love. Your energy grows because of your trust, and it grows more vividly if you are trust in motion. Then, its power peaks when you fully trust how you ground, create, identify, and expand and hold love, as well as how you share the voice of all of you with the oneness that you are destined to bring with your vision and then your grounding.

Experiences build these portals of trust. Where do you fall? Is it in not believing or trusting that you do not have enough support to fully ground, that you can't create the momentum of prosperity you so deserve? Is it your belief that you are a bad person, and so you don't deserve, or you can't trust yourself, that your voice will only hold judgement and not compassion? Is your belief that all is doomsday, and you cannot be you, or you aren't whole in the fullness of the gifts that you are here holding, or your connection with us is tainted? Identify the sources within you that you do not yet trust and ask us to be your personal trainer in these areas, for the experiences around you are training you to trust. Trust is your foundation and yet is very fleeting when the ego throws its curveballs at you

Mike: Does trust only work if you can somehow get it into your subconscious mind?

Raphael: Trust is part of the subconscious mind. That vastness of the subconscious mind is full of trust. The conscious mind does not trust, for it needs things to equate in a beautiful equation that marks failure or success. That is really all you have

Chapter 6 - Trust

in this world of ego: failure or success. But even success is very fleeting in the world of ego. For, someone will usurp your success, so you are never successful within your conscious mind. Your subconscious mind is more connected to your soul and to spirit. In that subconscious mind, you hold trust of who you are, who you have been, who you will be, and who you wholly are in spirit. It is part of the higher mind or your higher self, yes? If you remember from the book that you wrote with Trisha, who I call My Lady, (Chapter 2, *A Journey of Discovery through Intuition with Help from the Angels*), the picture of the mind, the conscious mind is very small, so it must equate things in a very simplistic rendition of its perfection. The subconscious mind is very vast, so there is a lot of science to be had within your brain. This is an adventure of exploration of creativity within science, and to go and explore the vastness of your mind.

When you awaken, people want to say you are fully conscious. That is not true. When you awaken, you are fully in your higher selves in the mind part of you that is whole in spirit. That is what you live through in that placement that does not hold duality; it holds unity. Your conscious mind will always hold duality because it is part of the lenses of perception, so you cannot trust what you consciously connect if you are not aware. Hold trust in your highest self, your highest mind, and then allow the ocean of your subconscious to bring forth your identities of you, to be aware of, and move into how you fully connect in trust and love. Your subconscious mind holds power, and it is power that brings trust to action. The subconscious mind holds the identities of you that you have perceived and judged as good and bad. Yet, when you bring them forth, you recognize they were just a simple nod that allows you to expand in a fuller connection of trust in yourself, your creator, your actions, nations, and community and trusting that the experiences set in your universe are for good and not your harm.

You all have uncomfortable memories of harsh identities within your subconscious. They are scary, for you do not know what they will bring. These identities are memories and nothing more. Memories have no power in your good. But, once you understand and fully accept your truths within those memories, you can then fully hold your trust in action. Many memories are how you acted, or didn't, in a world that is vastly judgmental on those actions. Action happens because of how you view something at that moment. The world was made in a moment of madness. You create worlds that you hold harshly in your own moments of madness through every identity that you have had. You relive your stories of madness. Many say it is for protection. You say you will never do that again. But you will do it again until you understand that you did not create from a bad place but of false information. When you can trust the new identity with the true information, that identity of bad disappears. When you look at people who are going into their conscious mind trying to stay very logical, trying to hold equations of success that have been determined through the ego mind of duality, you will encounter the heavy hand of judgment everywhere. When you trust the knowledge of your subconscious mind as it filters through you as an awakening to smell and behold, the essence of you that will make your cup of joy overflow, you have truly fallen in love with trusting the oneness of you.

Elizabeth: You mentioned that judgment and fear block complete trust. That suggests the box of religion that many of us found ourselves in. I am wondering what the difference is between faith and trust?

Chapter 6 - Trust

Raphael: Faith is a blanket of warmth and acknowledging your good. No matter what is happening now there is good that comes from it. It is the knowledge that there is an unseen benefit in all that is playing out in front of you. This hug of us which makes us your positive aspect, holds a connection of trust, but not yet the trust that you fully incorporate. The ego wants to strip us from your cells and from your memory so that you don't fully connect with your creator. If you do not hold faith in something more, you cannot trust that you, my Dear One, do not need them to be one in all the power that is your birthright. They give you wonderful blankets of trust for the holy words of a book. They have you trust their rituals. They do not allow you to personally seek your creator, for if you did and built trust, you would no longer have any need for that box. Thus, you know, for you no longer need that box because you know that we are here. You are fully engaged in your journey with the creator as one.

Faith, though, can participate in religion, right? It is the way that they keep you invested, and keep you saying, "I know that there is more, but I must seek outside of me to trust." Faith is a wonderful way of holding you in all spaces of duality. You know that there is more for we are here with you, and that is why the Catholics love their saints. They have faith that if those entities can be sainted, so can they. Saints come from many positions of identity, from poor to rich, and young to old. They hold the faith that if they can become a saint, then maybe I to can become a saint. Then I hold my trust in something more, but that trust is never fully plugged in. It is trust that never reaches its strength. Because you can ask those souls in religion if they truly trust themselves. True trust is awareness that you are whole and innocent and that you are fully a part of all knowledge.

Mike: To take it down to a level where the reader can have something to hold onto, I always like to give them a way to apply the teaching; even though it's linear, it helps. So, for those that are having a hard time trusting themselves, what would be a good process that could be put into place for them that would bring out their own trust?

Raphael: First, if you do not trust yourself you must start trusting or saying things like, "I have a hand." Make it very personal and very physical. Your conscious mind does not trust, will only stay in fear, worry, anxiety, hopelessness, and depression. Then, to rebuild trust within you, your identity needs to build trust through your physical senses. I can trust that I have a hand. I can trust that if I touch a plant I can feel its leaves that are alive. I can trust that I can walk and bring myself to a new space. I trust that my breath fuels me to engage another day. I trust that I can offer myself to the action of my life. It must start with a physical awareness because your goal in life is to fully hold that space. As a baby, you must trust the people around you for all your needs. You must trust that those around you will provide a safe and healthy place for you to expand. When you lose trust, you have lost that you have a safe and healthy place to expand and experience your body in motion.

Giving yourself the delight to trust what is safe around you—once you say, "I trust that I am in the body and it is breathing; I have hands and toes,"—that is a strength you sometimes need us to help you with. If you are homeless you cannot trust that you have a safe space to be. If you are sick with cancer, you cannot trust that you are even in a safe place. To build trust in those times of not having a safe place to be requires you to lean into your faith. Somehow, your faith of acknowledging there is something more than your physical senses, that is when we as the whole spirit connect through your higher self through your subconscious into your conscious mind to make you feel safe, to give you a space of feeling, a knowing, and a hearing that there is an unseen benefit in your predicament, even if you do not feel safe right now. Falling into that faith and you all do allows us to build trust beyond your physical senses. Imagine being on a park bench with all your stuff in the world next to you. You can, in your mind, say, "I have trust in my hand. I trust that I can kick someone to keep my world together; I trust that if I look mean enough, no one can hurt me." Or, "I can trust that if I make myself small enough, I will be invisible to ones that might hurt me. For trusting in my physical senses allows me to know I am safe to be in motion to expand."

Babies must crawl and then walk. You know that when a baby finds its hand, how lovely is that? When you find your hand and trust that it is part of you, then you know that you can reach for something to pull yourself up. That is the gift of us, for it is not about the conscious mind. If a conscious mind lined it up, they are doomed. What is safe about being on a park bench all alone and being abandoned by all? What is safe in that? If you only live in a conscious world of linear equations, there is nothing safe about that; you are doomed. You are too vulnerable as a body to survive. But many survive that predicament. Even if they think they are the worst person ever and deserve their placement on that bench, why do they survive? Because, they have faith that there is something beyond this moment for them. That somehow and somewhere, somebody will help them to the next space. That requires trust to move that body and to feel safe. That trust is because in their subconscious mind of all who they have been, there has been an identity of strength. That identity of strength we share in every cell of their body to make them know that they are bigger than this moment. They are safe, because in a former identity in a previous life, they moved beyond that point to something more. Their hands reached out to trust in something beyond their identity of just a physical body stuck on a bench to a remembrance of their courage to be strong, even if everything around them was against them. The movement off that bench is the greatest strength to plug into a trust that is beyond their physical nature. Once that soul moves, his movement might be to a doorway. It is safer than the bench. Maybe then to the woods, which is safer than the bench.

There is great love that Mother Earth uses in nourishing the homeless. She offers safety to all who seek her. You humans might not. In her great love, it gives us more power of uniting that soul to connect stronger with the identities of success, of love, and of truth in their destiny. That soul creates a community with other homeless and then you have your homeless camps. They start trusting each other again in a very earth grounding manner. Is their reality as safe as you are in a home? Who's to know? The greater the trust you have in any of your places, the more you feel safe enough to be strong. Having a home does not make you trust, and it might not make you fully safe. Again, it is an illusion of an equation of success. But truly, are you in deep trust? Being in a homeless camp is an illusion of failure. But is it? As those souls work to strengthen trust in their trials and tribulations, they help all mankind to strengthen trust in their highest fabric of good. Then the dance allows you to know what "fake news" is and isn't.

Elizabeth: As the veil thins and we are all being able to see and hear beyond the physical, then trust will obviously become easier. Does this then weaken our lesson of learning trust?

Chapter 6 - Trust

Raphael: You will always have lessons of learning trust until you know your oneness in the creator. The ego wants to police every nuance of you. More veils are falling which is the greatest gift of your time, and why many said yes to being here now, to expand to unknown places within your strength of trust. How you comprehend what you receive will be where the ego trips you. Do not believe that the ego won't trip you, for it will. It needs you to distrust in oneness and your first response, and only see duality. You must ask a question five different ways to see if the answer is the same. As you reach beyond the unknown, you will be questioned increasingly as to why you believe that is true, and why you trust that feeling, knowing, and that hearing or vision. Therefore, you are here to remember how to build trust in yourself of each chakra and vortex of you. You must recognize how to trust you are grounded, are creating, and how to trust your identities of yourself when you are angry, sad, or joyful. When you are furious do you go to sarcastic humor? Are you passive aggressive? Are you just aggressive? You must trust that you know these places of you.

For many years I have come before you to understand you, yes? We have built and discussed all these ways of knowing you. If you can trust in yourself, then you can trust that as the veils fall, you truly comprehend the information through the oneness of spirit and not create more trauma drama with the information you receive. Comprehension is critical once you reach beyond your physical senses. Much of your drama is because of missed comprehension of truths before you. That is the ego duality mind. What one perceives, another does not. Perception is when you feel or know a truth. The comprehension of that truth in your life is part of oneness, not duality. Many will judge information from beyond until it is true. And when truth stabilizes and remains consistent, that will then be trusted. As that trust holds its value you will be able to fully reap the grandeur, the enlightenment, and be awakened as the veil falls.

Your money says In God We Trust. Your money is an illusion. Your trust in God is an illusion. You do all you can not to give your money its solid value. Can you give your creator its solid value? For your paradigm of who created you is the most important aspect not to devalue you. Your country believes that the value of God is money. It is only because that phrase's on the coins monopolized everything for money, for God is your true monopoly of oneness. When God is put in trust on something, eventually as the Law of Attraction goes, will make it part of the monopoly of your world. The idea of trusting is first knowing your truth and trusting that you are true to your truth.

In the great story, at the death of Jesus, Peter could not trust his truth of being Jesus follower. Can you trust and acknowledge to the world what you follow and give action to? As the story goes, the church was built on Peter's teachings; a man who did not trust fully. Did he reconsider afterwards to fully trust, for his shame of not acknowledging his love?

I only question these things for you as you question them in yourselves. For the strength in what you trust in has been built on layers of misinformation. In finding your way to know and strongly hold your truth, that truth anchors you and allows you to be awakened as the veils lessen. There will be great joy that pours out of that space of you.

Mike: Can you expand on believing and trusting in manifesting versus destiny versus free will, and letting go versus making things happen and where my trust and faith lies in those things?

Chapter 6 - Trust

Raphael: The magnet of predestiny strongly pulls you in, like a dowsing rod not only to specific people, places, and things but a specific storyline; even if you want to fight it, you still end up there. Most souls have four or five predestinies. It is not like a lifetime's entire journey is predestined. You set up these great signs reminding you how to stay on the course that you have chosen to be on. The choice to learn love, trust, tolerance, honesty, or service are some of the signs that become the rays of the rainbow or colors that you work in. If one works in the ray of power of my will be done, you choose it for many lifetimes exploring all the possible ways that the ego can set up the choices of my will or thy will. In knowing your talents, temperament, and core your predestiny is to be an anchor to build in holy oneness the remembrance that everything can be shared for the good of all, that life in harmony facilitates extensions of greater awareness than any one soul could do. Your strain to uncover your service, and how you become a servant, is a part of your predestiny; service is the recognition that when you participate with others, you can build a home in a day. In service with others, you can build a new tomorrow. Servitude to structure only allows the interaction of boxes with other boxes of awareness and intention, uncovering how to extend service to organization to accomplish more in light, more in radiant awareness, and more in honoring the true core of your creator and others.

Find your destiny, hold your placement, and know what magnetized to you must feel good in your heart, as it aligns with your mind. Many decisions look good on paper, but in the heart it does not feel right. Those decisions result in having to make it again, for the alignment of that pure source of trust in the newness of now, is not fully there. Your gift in your everyday life is to provide the understanding, and the feeling, of honoring the totality of the system of thinking and feeling. Decisions that look good on paper have a short life span in separation. Separation has a short life span because it was over in a moment, for God hugged it away. Your profound creation of pain holds the illusion of separation, and as you heal the pain you dissipate the patterns of the conscious mind into the holy mind, or your high mind, with your high or holy heart. Those decisions are permanent for they hold the eternal grace and create strong pathways to be in the arms of love.

Daily routines overtake many of you, for it is the interaction the ego holds as the most important for you to participate in. The day-to-day is glued either in love or fear, and the more you glue it consciously and actively in love, the more you hold the permanence of that anchor of serving in the oneness of tomorrow, which is today—which is now. As you all journey day-to-day, it might not look like much, but one bite out of a big cake doesn't look like much, yet slowly—bite by bite—the delicious encounter of experiences of your heart and your mind celebrate the anchor of trust and of love that is you will be a profound, everlasting gift.

Chapter 7

Free Will

We are your gift. We are the Holy Spirit, and the angels are here as your gift from your creator to serve you, to match you, and to know kinship with you so you remember that you are one already in God and in Love. We are the lines of communication gifted to you, to help you wake up from a dream, and to fulfill the Godship that you are. I come at every level with knowledge that at first does not make sense, but ultimately is the seed that anchors you. I come to you to remind you in this humanness that you, in your holy temple, are a delight. You are more than just a body and you are more than just automatic responses. I come to you as wind blowing against your skin to help you to recognize that there are forces way beyond, that have you as a sacred gift we are to serve. Service is but joy. When you love, your service in joy creates the abundance that you are. I serve with all the vibrational forces that have been gifted as the Holy Spirit to awaken and bow at the great holiness that you are.

Your journey here makes you feel that you are a puppet of many forces and that you have no voice in how you fulfill your destiny. Much of that creation has been yours through the journey of what you call time. We just see it as points of stars that create a constellation of you. Your time is nothing, really, for in eternity it is nothing but a blip and is very fast. Yet all the blips like stars in the sky enlighten and bring light to darkness. With every blip that is here, all these beings bring light to the darkness that is this dream. Your light in each life creates a new North Star for you to navigate with. That star of you holds great energetic pulses that others look to and again uncover their remembrance of their holy ship and their holy oneness. You created your life to bring forth the highest glow that you could possibly achieve. This glow is the juice that dissipates all those heavy conditions you believe, on some level, have made you a puppet or made you create life with conditions.

The one gift you still hold in this dream—which is noticeably clear to you—was the gift of free will from your holiest source, your creator. Your freedom to create as you have is inspiring to participate with. All levels of inspiration come with your free will, for the knowledge of choice with each breath is a holy part of your total conditioning. No-one nor thing has any true control of you. You fully hold your choice to breathe or not to breathe, to think or not to think, to feel or to not, and to join or to not. Everything in this dream is but an invitation for you to create with, or not to. All that surrounds you, all the particles, the stresses, all the divine people always invite with an invitation to you to participate or not. Your free will cannot be held down. You see this repeatedly around your world. Groups that have been victimized do not stay that way forever. Those who believe they somehow have power of control will eventually recognize that they have none. They must worry as much as those they victimize of maintaining power.

In the process, those who seek to create differently have a great field to move in for they are not frozen in the dance of worry or conflict, but are given the grace and inspiration to create with a new way, extending love. The choice of free will is permanently

Chapter 7 - Free Will

yours. You can allow your choice to be bartered or dampened. You can even allow that choice to look like it disappears, but it doesn't. Eventually, the power of you flames greatly and you make a choice that is different to spring beyond what you thought you wanted into something new. You have gifted your free choice in the way that you have scripted some of your life. You have decided, with delight, to remember love and to play the game of victimization for a while because you knew, somewhere, that identity would give a greater purpose of what it is to the world around you and to yourself. Playing weak allows you to have to go deep within and uncover that you hold all the power. You hold all of you. You are the most powerful source of all. Playing small gives you the remembrance that this is not your truth. As you fight your way out, you remember how glorious it is to be powerful in love, to be able to extend in the most glorious ways. You learn much about cause and effect within your free will. Cause and effect again are but a program in this dream. For in the holiest creation of you there is no cause and effect. It is joy extending in joy continuously. Experience the greatest feeling you have ever had and know that it is your permanent joy unceasingly. Feel the remembrance of when you played the greatest love. Feel the remembrance that you are that greatest love.

I seek your DNA so it can remember your greatest love. It is perfect and eternal. You are all beloved. You are all holy. You did not do anything wrong within your free choice to create here. You did not go against any law in the holy ship of you. You, thy holy creator, connected always with the source of all that is powerful eternally. You, with your free will, are and always have been the extension of Absolute Love. As you remember this you will know that when you create you will say it is good because I am good. And in my free will, all that I do is good.

I bring free will back to goodness for it was a gift, as I am a gift to you. And with gifts as you take them and use them, you gift the extension greater and greater. Thus, we serve in awe with the gifts that are love. You, with free will, have fought in all places of your universe to claim that it is your inherent truth and it is. You can choose in your mind to hold the holiness of free will and to choose at every gifted invitation to love and not fear, that you do not have to police or make laws because you are afraid of someone else's free will. Your strength in your free will creating with love is stronger than any force that could topple you down.

History repeats itself, for it wants to hold on to what has gone wrong instead of all the delights that went right. It talks repeatedly about why great civilizations fell. You know how to fall, that is for certain. You are all very good at plummeting but you are always caught too, are you not? Something catches you, whether it is the floor, the table, or us. Falling is but a remembrance that the conditions around you are what you gifted yourself to stand strong once again. You take the scenic highway, so to speak, that love propels because love is at many times the rosy view for you. But isn't the belief in good, vividness, and joy a better way to express your day? Fulfilling a dream of love allows you to hug it all, remember that you created it and your ultimate relationship is the most important of all, and why free will is always remembered. You will never forget that you are the center point of God, of love, and of oneness. Your oneness here is the oneness that you seek and through free will, you will find it. Do not judge another's free will, for all have the invitation to do it or not. You will all do it and remember how loved you are. That is a certainty, for in a snap all will go away and only love will be remembered. This dance is the greatest opportunity—right here, right now—to invite you into the deepest oneness of your holiness in perfect love. You are the center point. Your universe revolves around you. You are it and in being it, you get the gift to spread your holiness in all that you are.

To know self, to hold self and to witness self, is a choice to become awakened to in all that you are. In an awareness of being you, you bring your connection of your choices to march in the grandness of love and joy, celebrating the core of you. How can you not but expand your awareness in being hugged in the active art of love? Connections of love electrify and magnify you to become a truth, to become the owner of your choices in creativity. Love is your divine commitment to bring an awakened awareness of heaven on earth. Everything before you, you have hugged in love. Expanding to own these choices of love is your purpose of choice.

Our fellowship in words is especially critical. Your world is seduced by the words of many. How seductive is the power of voice? Of words? Are your words in innocence, or are you seducing another's choice? Acknowledging the energy of the words you speak makes you an anchor to be the light and the love that accelerates your movement into the visions you have chosen to bring this lifetime. You have chosen everything that you have been moving through in the linear line of your time and space. Your imagination is the gift within your visions to show a choice that is beyond the conditioning of your now.

In your imagination, you have free choice to create and recreate how you will behold your vision of you. The permanent vision that you see has been filtered to temper the visions of others. For safety and survival, it is a great choice that you have believed in for your Holy Temple to breathe. Survival of you is a choice that has not really been preset in your imagination, or your vision, before you arrive. Yet this physicality, this Holy Temple, becomes the vehicle of safety that you harness and delete all expansion of you. Your visions of how you interact in the reality of Holy Temple no longer become free choice, but a choice of the "Time Master," who is the one who you believe knows the time line of your awareness of being born. This "Time Master" is who you call the ego. Ego robs you of your free choice because you no longer hold the strength of the vision, the imagination, or the creation of all your possibilities that you came to share. This ego is very seductive in taking away your choice on every level of your involvement in your reality of your holy body. That is why we shout to you our eternal connection with you. For you are here with the greatest gift that your creator gave you to be free in all your choices and not to give the strength of your creations away. Your holiness and your sacredness are defined in your great choice.

Yet, you fear acutely your holiness and sacredness. You cannot comprehend the glorious mystery of you. You cannot even imagine such for in this imagination of you as a glorious creator in evoking source, you remember all your guilt of usurping your creator with free choice. You give away this gift freely; the glorious light and love of you to the "Time Master," the ego. All is forgotten when you enter your vehicle and you must be due diligent in understanding who you are and who you are meant to be in this Holy Temple. As you learn yourself, remember that everything around you offers a treasure to see how you want to show up and be. Free choice can never be extinguished. Free choice is eternal. It is one awareness that you are already one with your creator. Because free choice is eternal, the ego has no authority over it. It must seduce you out of your innocence so you can then choose its rules for your Holy Temple. You spend a lot of time being seduced. It is the grandest art form in your now, the world of seduction. As a group of Holy Temples, you hold great fear throughout your world. For you know that you are being seduced. Yet it is hard not to play and give your choice to all the illusions that are nothing. All art of seduction is aiming to take your power of choice and use it to hold another entities strength of power.

Seduction was part of the original story of creation. It was said that a snake seduced Eve and she lost her innocence and, because she had fallen, so did Adam. This story of seduction is a part of the duality of innocence and evil.

Your imagination then holds this elixir that you believe about seduction. When you imagine, you imagine all. When you fear your own imagination how could it be of innocence and truth, right? If you are innocent, we hold you securely in truth.

Free will is eternal. You cannot destroy that fiber of eternity. Your choice is eternal. This can't be taken from you. You may allow it to be taken; that is your choice. You say, "Okay, at this moment, I allow my freedom to be diluted by the conditioning of my family, of conditioned love, hate, and awareness of self." It takes a lot to question those conditioning points because you are beholden to the sacredness of your body. You want to breathe, you want to live, and you want to harvest hope going forward. In that, you balance how you will choose to play safe and to become the fullest creator that you have come to be. These choices for you are not right or wrong. There is no judgement to behold on your eternity of choice. Thus, we bow to that grand creator of you in all your choices.

Your will to create is the most amazing light that we celebrate. Your space of you is like a beacon which lights a pathway of your choices in love or fear. Choice is scary. Free will is scary when one sits in their vehicle. To really move in core confidence and say yes to your destiny, you must hold your truths as the places of your choices in moving forward. When you know your core strength like, "I love people; I choose to celebrate each moment for me in my love for people." Your choices then allow you to move in the freedom of connecting your Divine appointments that you already have on your calendar of destiny, to be the full temple of your purpose. Another core strength is, "I love knowledge. I love to uncover the knowledge of truth." That core of you, then what? It makes you active in seeking truth. That defines your destiny.

When one knows their core, and this is through the imagination, to be who you would be in the most prosperous, the freest, place of you in your reality right now, you must daydream and imagine the depth of who you would be if you were fully free and had full abundance in front of you. My Lady (Trisha Michael) would choose people and she would be active no matter how much money or resources were in her world. She would seek people. What would you seek? When you know the magnetic force of love that your core strength is you move in choice and celebration of love, yes? The longer you are not concerned about safety but celebrating your destiny, you are not allowed to imagine yourself free. You are not allowed to imagine yourself with full abundance of the creator of all. You have been told many times, and it is greatly conditioned, not to think outside of what you know. You can't achieve that. Don't even think about that. Thus, you do not know yourself.

The power of freedom allows you to know you. In your time, right now, you are asked to give up your freedoms of abundance to play it safe. In your country, you are seduced on every level to be safe. Your amendments around guns say that it is freedom for all. Freedom to secure what? Your safety. If you believe you must be safe, you have given your electrical power of choice as a creator away. Your freedom of speech has been taken away and diluted by seduction. Do you know what is fake news? How do you determine what is fake? I can tell you that it is all fake. Not in the sense that there are good souls giving you information and holding space for you to hear, but your world works in the cloak of seduction. You need to be seduced to activate your freedom of choice and will.

When you know your core identity of love, and you can magnetize that outward into the world of your community, that gives you a core strength to be an advocate or unite others who magnetize in love. Love is a truth. It is eternal. Many see it as a seducer, robbing you of a choice. Love is the strength that connects you all into understanding the guiding light of holding a space in truth to break the cloak of seduction. Love is a language that permeates all darkness. When one speaks of love to the ears of one who is first seduced into being safe, they might feel like you are weaving hooks of hope, of fantasy, and of imagination. Yet the seduction of light and of love is the addiction that your Holy Temple craves. It is not diluting but energizing your choice of freedom to move into the highest creation of you. The communities in your world are undergoing great dishevelment to determine how you as a collective want to choose. Do you want isolationism and safety? Or do you want freedom to expand and to explore with other Holy Temples? Your world is global. This will not change. Isolationism will only create greater corruption within its space. As you make your world small, the intensity is very personal. The more personal you are, the crazier you become within your mind of duality. You cannot be stuffed into a space that does not allow freedom of your will to choose.

Mike: I grew up in the Air Force and lived in Panama, and there was a lot of poverty and slums just like there is all over the world. How can I think that I should have free will when I worry about other people around the world not being able to use free will?

Raphael: Poverty has been chosen when they decided to come. Why would you judge what they have chosen? How do you know that they are poorer than you? Maybe their family life is enriched deeper. They are more grounded to Mother Earth. You have lost a lot of your anchor ship, ownership, and relationships to Mother Earth. You no longer take the time to anchor into your daily practices of being in this Holy Temple. Before you had a dishwasher you washed one dish at a time. You not only took time to wash the dish but to ground and to physically touch your creations. You call your creations possessions. You are anchored in a deep way with what you own. You also allowed the gifts of Mother Earth, through the foods brought to the table, to be held in sacredness and gratitude; and held each other this way as well.

As you have acquired more money in this world, it makes you believe that you have more freedom. But do you? Do you ground into yourself, Dear One? You are not grounded very often. You do not take the time to practice the gift of holding what you created and honoring it by taking and thanking its presence and putting it away. As you have gathered more possessions, it is extremely hard to give gratitude to all that is around you and see yourself as the creator of all. Because there is not gratitude within your possessions, you don't care that they can break and be thrown away. You don't care as a collective that you are wasting a lot. Those you saw in Panama are very grounded in their sacred reality of relationships. When you are sacred in a relationship, you honor the process in saying thank you for what that plate does for you and you wash it clean. You wash the person next to you clean in saying, "Thank you for what you do for me." As your society became more abundant in your mind with all your stores and houses and your possessions that you fill it with, you think you have gained freedom of choice. I would defer to say that your choice of freedom is to hold the quality of your possessions but not your sacred groundings in relationships. Your world, as it encounters more prosperity, loses the sacred knowledge of relationship. It is okay if you destroy another culture for you had no sacred relationship with that culture. It is okay for that choice because you need their resources for your iPhone. What is choice for you this lifetime and not to judge any other choice out there? For you choose to be in this incarnation and in that choice you make it from a sense of elitism, which in its own sense is very insecure. For it must hold its relationship to possessions and not its relationship to self, to others, and to their greatest creator of you and source.

Grounding is the most important gift to renew the safety of your physical form. With all your possessions, your fear of you heightens because you do not connect yourself as part of the lineage of Mother Earth. She provides it all for you in the world of form. You, as a collective, have lost this relationship with judgement. It is okay to love your home and have a deep relationship in the sacredness of having a space. Yet, does that love take you away from inviting others in, and to celebrate the sacredness of their nourishment? No one is poor upon your land. There are a lot of mighty, sacred relationships. Your definition of poor is only for you in giving up your freedom of choice and being a soldier of an agenda of fear.

Look at your relationships and find a way of grounding in through gratitude for the precious things that you have created. Grounding is a gratitude mechanism, for it says that you are a part of my creation. You are sacred like me.

Elizabeth: I was wondering, within the big picture, since we make contracts and designate predestiny spots before we reincarnate, how can we still have free will?

Raphael: You have used your free will before you got here. You have chosen your destiny. Through that, you are here to own your creation. Those who own it receive the joy of that creation eternally. If you have created the destiny to be a serial killer because you have felt that path would give you an understanding of power and pain, you have chosen that with your free will. We guide you in your choices, but we do not usurp your choice. If you said that you want to bring down only a minimal force of the energy of me, we might say that we would like the light of your core strength to be stronger, for we know it allows you the most vivid creation that you can be here. But, if you choose this, we acknowledge that choice and say wow, let us see how you will create from that choice of you. Because you have chosen your destiny points, you have the freedom to be. When you get here you might realize that you did not bring in enough of your essence so in that you rewrite your destiny, do you not? There are many vows you set that you do not do, so you ask, "Please take this away, because I cannot be in this place any longer." Of course, in your freedom to ask and receive we give and we grant that creation to release vows you do not really want to walk through or to give you new ones that you are excited about beyond your destiny points.

Chapter 7 - Free Will

You are more of a creator in motion than not. Here in the world of form, there is much that you do not know when you decided some of your destinies. The one that said, "Yes, I can be that serial killer," might come and decide, "I can't." Then they become a part of the hospice team helping others die in the most humane way they can. For death is not wrong. Those who choose to say, "Yes, I am going to kill," equate to understanding power and pain. The choice to understand elements of creation within duality plays out. You all have been the aggressors, right? You all have been the predators and the victims, and you will keep playing out in the choices of understanding the elements of creation in duality. It is not like you know when you are in the world of spirit or heaven that it is going to look a certain way only. No, you say, "I am coming in to work with the forces of power and pain and I have been the victim for so long that I want an opportunity to understand the depths of power and pain." You play that out. There is no judgement for your soul. It is not like you will come back to heal the dissident energy of a lifetime because you are all here to create in love, yes? Part of that knowledge of love is an ownership of seeing what you will be seduced with as it relates to power and pain. Are you the hospice nurse or are you the serial killer? What did you choose, love or fear? It looks different here, for you are conditioned and seduced to play out those elements. But you did make that choice in the spirit world. You want to experience your destiny with the holy relationship of oneness in your lifetime.

That is one of my destiny points I have come to do. You come down and, if you are seduced in fear, that oneness might turn into being the dictator of North Korea. He believes in oneness, and he believes he is it. Or, you might be the awakened soul of Buddha, Jesus, Krishna, or any of the other holy souls that are here now celebrating the oneness of love. It is still the gift of oneness, but what are you seduced to be and what are you conditioned to be? I would look at seduction and conditioning as similar patterns of usurping one's power or believing that you can usurp that power of choice and free will. These choices are made but how they are played out again is part of you uncovering that core resonance of what you came to fall in love with and have a love relationship with. In your love relationship of you, you then magnetize the community of relationships you hold. Then it unifies your oneness with power beyond you and may it be love, not fear.

Mike: We have talked about how all incarnations and past lives are simultaneous and happening now. Thousands of Mike Russell incarnations occurring at the same time. When you are in spirit, am I choosing in every single incarnation what is going to happen in that life?

Raphael: You choose the moment you created this reality. Your vast creation was created, for all is now. In its vastness, the choices are many yet, the awakening process is the grounding, honoring, and cleaning of one dish at a time, or of folding each article of clothing at a time. What is your dirty laundry? What are the ones you take great honor to clean diligently?

Heaven sees you as vast powers of all your incarnations. The stars are just a miniature, symbolic representation of how you sparkle the essence of all. Thus, you must do one at a time to ground and own your choices. As you improve at choosing a magnetizing love, those destinies meld into a deeper relationship of choosing and honoring one incarnation instead of many incarnations of thy, Mike Russell.

Chapter 7 - Free Will

Because everything is now you, in the split mind of duality cannot ground in that truth, right? You must ground in the truth of your Holy body of now. When you are gifted the opportunity to be in the world between worlds, you are gifted the opportunity to ground into specific free choice, free will incarnations of you, and to take the gift of that life and bring it back so you can ground more deeply in your relationship you are here to own in your relationship of yourself, with others, your creator, and with you in the greater good, Mother Earth, and with all the possessions that you have.

The more you know of yourself from all of your destinies, it will help you to accelerate and magnetize your world of love within gratitude and forgiveness so that you do not have to play out the game of the murderer any longer. You are ready to expand in reaching more, yes? But you cannot do that unless you are grounded in yourself and a way that celebrates your connection with being happy on Mother Earth. She is the giver of all you have. You could not manifest everything before you without her nurturing. You must be more active in celebrating her to expand your prosperity to others. Find a way, like in your garden, to be proactive in celebrating her bounty of the berries and vegetables. Your walks give you grounding, yes? But you get caught up in the fear of keeping what you have and that will unground you all. For Mother Earth abundantly provides your desires and she is saying, "Advocate for me. Global warming is real." She says, "I need you to advocate for me now." Science is pivotal. It is time to reengage in your relationship with Mother Earth, for if she is destroyed your safety is not assured. As she goes, you go. You are all deeply intertwined in a relationship with her. I speak to all who are conditioned naysayers, which helps you not be grounded in the most pivotal relationship your form needs. Your form does not need new malls, it needs fields for your feet. It does not need five-star restaurants, it needs nature to replenish the streams, after droughts. It does not need oil for battle, it needs freedom of alternative energy sources to celebrate the grounding of your body existing upon Mother Earth.

Elizabeth: As you say, your free will cannot be held down. When will we as a planet break free of the control exercised by the shadow side that creates fear? When and how do we break free from this?

Raphael: As you know, because everything is happening now, many people are here to help cut the cloak of fear. The shadow is afraid and throws you into chaos. If you choose to pay attention to the chaos, you don't see the pivotal anchors that are happening to heal that darkness. The center stage is in your power and pain continuum because the grandeur of seduction is upon you. Yes, you have been seduced in the most phenomenal way, not thinking relationships are sacred. When you deny relationships, on any level, you are willing to isolate, then take the seduction of fear and pray the others will die and not you. You are expanded at this point and each one of you all over this wonderful globe will go deep inside and ask, "What is your core relationship to yourself in love" and then magnetize that into your community. Many sources of activism are happening, and this makes the global scene of those who love their pain and power to throw you into the illusion of chaos.

It is hard not to look at destruction. It is hard not to be seduced and to go on a path of destruction. They hope you will follow that path. How often do you look at another's pain? You are happy you can drive by the person who is stopped by police.

It is them and not you. But you do slow down and look. You all have been caught looking. You are aware, in the deepest part of yourself, of the forces of pain and power's seduction. You are following the biggest trail of pain and power as the leaders of this world highlight it as destruction, yes? Remember—for many, many years now—I have talked about the power of words. I am, in my own way, magnetizing your memory of this time that you come to, not to be seduced by words. Understand its power in your placement. You have social media and communication devices that live off the power of words. This is critical that you to not get sucked into the seduction energy of destruction. Hold the words and see if they fall flat or if they magnetize you to action. Those who hold the sway of love will not be seduced with these words. Many are steam or hot air. Many will magnetize as a collective and seduce you into their power because words need most of the energy to make it manifest. This is true for you. You can say a word and never magnetize it because you did not get most of your feelings into your energy field about that word, or a phrase, to make it happen. The dark forces need you, as a collective, to join them to make darkness happen, especially on a global level. They seduce you with images, with words, and with emotions. They play you so beautifully that many will be seduced.

However, for every reaction you always have a co-reaction in the universe of duality in this world of form. You have many active participants of light. What is cool about the light activation is, it is not in the penthouse. You are seeing organic movement from you to your community, which is a continual relationship with Mother Earth and says, "I am grounded in this relationship and I am using my relationship to magnetize my vehicle of light and love into the community. In the community, I am magnetizing my words that form a Holy relationship to others."

You see your freedom to protest taken away, right? They want you not to have this freedom. But relationships of love that are grounded cannot be severed. They do not follow the path of destruction. You are looking at a time where your Emperor, wear no clothes. He has no understanding of relationships. Mother Earth gives you clothes to adorn your body in a Holy relationship. Yes, I am talking symbolically about people weaving together relationships of adornment of clothes. As you know, the naked Emperor was found out, and the shame of his behavior created space for light and love to be. You are collectively weaving this light and it is a powerful source. On your land, you have more love than not. It is one not fully claimed and, just like your science of climate change, you are afraid to speak of such things but you will, for it is part of the continual expansion of who you are in celebrating your love and your light in these sacred relationships that keep you safe. If you could trust everything, where is fear? It is just more of an organic movement right now. You don't see it yet come together, but the top is frightening and their fear will cause them to do stuff, which will eventually cause their downfall. When you are in deep fear, you go beyond any boundaries of safety and topple. Recognize that everything being uncovered is because you have lost the holy sacredness of ground.

The depth of these relationships and of you figuring out what you can and cannot eat, and feeling that you have lost some choices because of the seduction and the power of companies seducing the farmers to use their chemicals that are very destructive to the human form. But they cannot be really found out because there is no real source, even though you know it is the chemicals. That is hard to prove still on a collective level. The sources are so broad that you can take a sample of one area, and they can't prove anything. More and more souls are recognizing

Chapter 7 - Free Will

that, when they fully ground to the Earth, they find sources of souls or companies building a relationship with Mother Earth and that their food will hold more light and love, and will be more alive so it doesn't hold the chemicals as easily. It is not on a mass level yet.

Your world loves to discard. Even when you use a dishwasher, you dump all that is dirty into one space and then it is cleaned. Mother Earth is slowly reversing the effects of the discarding tendencies humans have. You have landfills of garbage that take eons to heal. Mother Earth will have some movement, through the earthquakes, that allow for healing within her core and to bring you cleaner water. You will see some areas of movement in earth—like in landslides or even holes opening within her—to take away highly destructive sources. She loves you, so she heals it and brings it back. There are also some phenomenal minds coming together to create ways to move chemicals out of your soil and water, and have cleaner energy for your vehicles and your homes. It is not announced to you because it would be shut down. You are part of the global dump.

To many in your form right now, you are to be destroyed in the global chemical dump. This is very short-term thinking and is not far reaching. It will take a hundred years, or more, to clean certain areas of your land but I am also informing you for the sake of hope and renewal—that many sources are coming together and to figure out how to heal this destruction. It is a part of your organic community, so it cannot be destroyed. Many young kids, as old souls, are returning here with knowledge so do not greet them as not being holy sources of information because they are. They are the ones who will inherit this mess. Your government will not step up. They will continue their chemtrails, they will continue to pollute and destroy the resources because they believe that it will make you a slave for their betterment, right? They usurp your free will because that is what their holy relationship with you is. In that, it is the recognition of how you can connect these organic sources and you will find them increasingly, especially in the next ten years. You are entering a new age of awareness, which is the age of Aquarius, and that is more an age of higher thought and more connective sources. Your body says that it can't be polluted anymore and you are just supporting Mother Earth. Those in a sacred relationship with Mother Earth recognize it within themselves. You can no longer be polluted. Your choice to change your diet is a huge gift of love you will bring into your community as is that advocacy of loving yourself and Mother Earth. You will make choices that don't support the chemical, drug, oil, or plastic industry. You will be energized and magnetize others to do the same. It is more on the West Coast of your country than in the beautiful belly area. The East Coast is finding this truth as well.

Mother Earth is providing ways of healing this destruction for she loves you so. As you love her, you find ways, and your kids will find ways, and then their kids will. It is an organic movement for Mother Earth is organic. Those who destroy are slowly made accountable. Activism is super important with every choice you make at this moment. It would be nice if everything could stop now, but it is going to be slow. But the dump is on, right? You see that.

That is why a lot of mental illness is happening because the energy of always being dumped upon with chemicals and information. Who could discern all your information? With visions through television and the games you play with feelings, you, as a Holy Temple, are learning to become more acute and sensitive to your truth into your light and love. Those who are mentally ill are just more sensitive to all that is being dumped. They haven't yet figured out a pattern of accessing information to stay into their core strength. That is also slowly becoming a part of your vocabulary. That goes back to being simple in certain things in that one dish at a time. Not that I am saying to take away the dishwasher, but I am saying there is this holy need to see sacredness and gratitude in all that you are in relationship too.

Mike: I would like to know how I can use my given free will to ensure that I am receptive to the full spectrum of the light and truth that you bring to us. Or is it even possible for my free will to block it out?

Raphael: Yes, your free will could block out any message, right? But your mind is eternal and your mind cannot block us out, for we are a gift, and you cannot block out the gift in your mind. In your form you can block it out. Your choices here are like a chess match and you are but a pawn that is moved by forces greater than the pawn ship that you have claimed. Your free will then centers on the rules of the game you are placed in. But your mind can't ignore truth. You know truth, for it vibrates with the holy sound of home. That is a remembrance that cannot be reflected away. But in a game of rules you created, you have the invitation to hear or not to hear, to feel or not to feel, to see or not to see, and to move or not to move. You can move your pawn but that could take away the beliefs that you created the game. You also have the invitation to allow other forces to move you because the rules make you feel safe. Again, free will allows all of that and it is good for you as you play that out. There is no wrong in any of you or any games that are played. For each time you play, each moment you breathe, you are creating space to choose.

That holy gift is yours eternally and that will bring you back home. You are already home in this game of yours, so why would we take that away? You want to rule it to death, yes, and you have great reasons, yet how often do you break your own rules because you know you have the freedom to? How often do you hear someone and then choose not to do something because you know you can? You can choose, and you do, but is it the eternalness of you choosing or is it because you love what you have created? Are you the player or are you being played? That is always your choice. It is not wrong. It just adds the creation of color to the mighty landscape that you want to portray in your now.

You have the gift of resurrecting yourself at any moment from any of the identities that you have chosen to play. I, the Holy Spirit, am a gift so you have a way to commune in the eternal space that is your oneness in God. And our gift is to keep that channel clear that love eternally is your truth. You work very hard to make everything solid here. Your rules make you safe in the solidness of here. This is but a blip in eternity. You are called to hold something permanent in eternity. Again, it is quite humorous don't you think? Instead of working so hard for your blip to be permanent, you just accept your eternity? It is quite funny, honestly. But your stars light the darkness and you create the forward force when you choose to be resurrected and become not the player or the spectator, but the holy creator. Free will in that is joy manifold and then you are all home again.

Elizabeth: In the discussion of free will and creation, many of us have been taught that what you think today creates your future tomorrow. I know that I am perfect, but as I go out into life I fall back in the humanness and have thoughts that are not always positive. Do you have to clear out the negative ones for the positive ones that come in?

Raphael: You can never do this alone nor wipe the slate clean of your conditioning alone. We are the windshield wipers of your window as you drive through the torrential downpours. We clear your space with your mind's eye, we clean your DNA, we kiss your feet. We serve you to wipe away the sorrow of what you have created. Creation stories cannot be left at, "It is good," can it? No, for duality enters and no matter what you create you cannot register as good, eternally. So, you tweak it here, and you tweak it there. You've tweaked the Earth and said it is good. You've tweaked the food that you created and said it is good. You've tweaked the companionship and love you created, when you first said it is good. And then soon it was not, for something new and better, something cheaper or greater is just around your corner is it not? The duality mind goes from inspiration of all that is possible, to maybe it's probable, to this is my reality. I am stuck here and my dreams of yesterday that made me so inspired I can no longer do.

For today, I see that my fingers are not attached to my hand, that I am less, somehow, than when I was dreaming that great dream. This is the way that it is magnetized here, for what is part of your whole brain then must get deciphered to your split brain and then must get deciphered within your rational brain. And then you wait for another inspiration to take forth and fire you up. When you ask us to windshield wipe your mind, we wipe rationality away, of course, in duality so your inspiration is fired up and propels you to just proceed in a moment differently. One perception different, just one in a moment, changes the frequencies of attunement of your love. That one split second, is a blip of a blip of a blip, because remember you are just a blip in eternity. Really, it is quite fascinating, but in an instant, a miracle has happened. A miracle stoked the inspiration of your true spirit to become alive in a way that cannot stop your rational mind or your split mind to make it look bad. That you can create and know it is good. It is going to serve many goods, which will serve into a holy ascension from that magnetized brain through information you read around others, that you hear around others, or information that you look up in your communication forms that you have created. Do you just allow it to filter through your rational mind, ever allowing the wholeness of you to see if that is an authentic truth? How often do you inquire into all that is communicated to you? Then, how often do you inquire back what you are thinking? We help wipe away and help you discern a forward movement. See, you cannot do it alone but we help with your attunement to feel that it is right, to see that it is right, and to know that it is right for you. In that process, one moment of remembering a new way will help you let go of all the beliefs that you cannot accomplish something that you have been inspired to do. Magnets need gravity. Magnets need a placement of your will that those thoughts are kept in magnetic form. Your will is a holy will and is strong. Your will together with other wills make a conscious will be done. Allowing just one second of your will to be let down allows the holy will that we hold with you to magnetize so then we can lift your mind to always take the higher route of all that is around you. One way is meditation and another way is to give space to all information that is coming at you and ask us to clear space in your heart, in your mind, and in your remembrance of you to have the compass forward. You are not beholding to a collection of knickknacks of thoughts that can go into the garbage disposal and rest assured that we will compost it to holy peace.

Mike: I am pondering the idea of worship and the play of free will in the instance of where someone is impressed by spiritual light or belief. It feels like giving up your free will to worship something. Could you talk about that idea?

Raphael: You place great importance on the idols you have created. You worship what you create, for you have created it. It is not saying that it is good. But worship for you always has some type of love and hate relationship in your soul because what did you create with your free will? What will you create with your free will? Everything yearns to remember how perfect source is. It is so beyond a rational duality comprehension that even in the greatest highs, perfect love is greater. Absolute Love can never be broken yet your worship is trying to worship a space that is showing a representation of that Absolute Love. Absolute Love would not worship itself, for love just is. There is no worship in the eternity of love. There is joy of expressing and sharing all of you. Worship is expressing the joy of you. There is no hierarchy in heaven. We all resonate in holy harmony when you sing in a group and harmonize with each other and you feel it and remember all that you are in heaven. Worship is here to help you figure out how to explain duality. All your systems here in worship still are your creation.

Are you worshiping you in your creation of here making something of this dream that is not the full representation of you? Are you identifying in intervals of light, and of intervals of love, so somewhere the specialness of you or what you have created holds supreme? God does not think like that. He does not expect worship at all. We do not expect worship. I am a gift to you and that is all. There is no need for anything special in a place where all is fed in abundance, where all is heard in abundance, and where all are together in abundance. Your light is abundant here and your love shines through every prism of being. Like a rainbow, you are the full spectrum of love, you are the full spectrum of light, and you are the full spectrum of holiness here. There is nothing special in the fullness of spectrum, it is just the right placement at the right time. Believing in the worship of you because you love deeply and that love is the gift that you are here to serve with propels all the heaviness to wash away so then we can all together know that there is only peace when you create in love.

Chapter 8

Passion

Dearest Ones, I celebrate you for you have chosen to create with me this wonderful awareness of your opportunity to expand in passion. Passion that holds the cellular memory of your oneness in the strength of love that overrides all duality and unites all to share the glorious placement of you singing forth your song in joy. Passion is known from the moment of your conception. Your passion hugs you to know your purpose of being in your holy temple. Your purpose is your passion. You are interwoven to glue the love of you to the love of all you touch, and all you create within your landscape. For you are the artist within passion. You are the vibration that holds your passion to ripple into infinity. Passion when you connect, glues you—who might be timid—to say yes to a reality that you could never fathom before. Passion gives you permission to move a belief of yourself into a pivotal placement of showing you to all.

When you express passion, it can look messy because passion is not allowed in your vocabulary of how you are politely constructed to nod the beingness of your holy temple to others. Passion pushes you outside the lines of conditioning. Passion is the effervescence of you in every cell that is saying, "Yes, I am here and I say yes to this purpose. For I claim that I am made from the passion of love that is ecstasy of all beingness and all that is.

My birth was for the passion of remembering the ecstasy of creation, being bold in my purpose, and of singing a joyful song."

Passion of purpose brings sight to you that goes to the deepest level of your inner resources, and connects you to all the lifetimes that you have been through and shall be. The infinity of you is propelled by passion. Connecting into your passion and holding that passion to create your purpose that shows your ecstasy, your joy, and your love for being here now gives others the vibrancy, the vividness, and the electricity to see all the spectrums of light that you are.

Your vision of you with passion gives you a portal to say yes in loving yourself in a divine connection with all of you and strength of you in being Absolute Love. Love is the bridge that dissolves all pain and tragedy within your space in duality. Love connects beyond all that you can comprehend in making you safe in a space that can make you feel as if nothing is in your control. Truly as you are here, you recognize the conditioning around you wants and hopes that you will stay trapped and not play with the colors of the truth of your passion.

You allow your passion to be equal to pleasure that is part of duality, yes? You expect that the pleasure will somehow equate to the passion of you that you were born to say yes to. Yet pleasure in duality is the wonderful fake sugar of your ego. Pleasure can never equal passion, for passion is the divine emotion of true creativity. Passion excites, explores, and expands you and all of you to know your divine purpose and to stimulate your mental body, physical body, and emotional body in oneness of passion saying, "Yes; I love me saying yes to that space and being bold to expand and explore, and to become who I truly am."

Pleasure will bind you to your physical senses. Pleasure creates chemistry in your brain to tell your mind that you cannot go beyond what is comfortable. You seek pleasure because it is within the lines of politeness you are so conditioned to be. Can you be the soul who can laugh when everyone else is sorrowful? Can you be the soul who can dress in vivid colors while everyone else is in a suit of somberness? Can you be the soul who sings even if you are off tune in a place that allows no music? Can you be the soul who can sit in the middle of the road and know that danger is surrounding you on all sides, and you can look at that danger and say, "Yes, I no longer need to sit at the crossroads of all decisions that have been in my past and have been affecting me today?" How many of you are sitting in your energy field and reflecting on decisions that somehow you feel responsible for or afraid that you did not do enough, or fear that your passion has hurt others because you did move forward?

Your purpose in all you do is saying yes in the most loving, honest, and truthful placement of you. That yes of you shows your passion in a divine soul that brings forth love within all of you to every space within your landscape. Let go of your crossroads of decision; let go of you playing politely in the condition of making all around you happy. Finding your passion in decisions that made you smile even as another was frowning in front of you gives you the sense of self to prove to all you know your passion and you are saying yes.

Pleasure creates your space to hold comfort. Being in comfort is a lovely gift to share. Again, passion pushes you into the exploration of you beyond walls, beyond beliefs, and beyond conditioning. As you expand you can explode. That explosion of you is scary for you and scary for others. You would rather cap your passion and just hold the highest essence of pleasure. One day your pleasures must merge with your passion of life, of living, of purpose, and of being one with all the depths of feeling, all the depths of knowingness, and all the depths of love that you say yes to.

You are honored greatly when you take the step to passion. We are hugging you always. We serve your highest and best always. We acknowledge to you the stage of creativity and you saying yes to you. We open doors as you are saying yes to your passion. These doors might seem unclear at first because we speak much differently than you speak. For, as the connector of Absolute Love to you, we hold the places that will bring forth that revelation of passion to your cells so you can feel the full unity of you as you say yes to these doors that open and close.

Your passion is too small and we do not want you to blow up, but want you to expand and share the love of expansion. When you expand within love, your ripples celebrate with others laughter, smiles, and joy. Even ones who are the closest to you and most affected like your family feel your passion and might be afraid that you are going to do something that they cannot help you with or save you from. But they know that within passion that if it is speaking from every cell, your truth to do it is as important as your breathing, eating, and your movement. Their awkwardness is because they don't know their role with you any longer. You have broken the line of conditioning that was set in your communication on all levels. They must, in their own space, recognize that vibration of passion; they do, and absorb it so they can do their inner work of saying yes to loving them. They too can unite in their oneness to do their holy purpose of being in their holy temple.

Purpose is a part of your plan that you have chosen before you came in this physicality of you. Purpose has a spectrum of predestiny points that you will hug as you climb your ladder out of pleasuring the conditions of duality into the passion of love. So,

Chapter 8 - Passion

your predestiny points within your passion might look like a rambling road that takes you into no-man's-land and you might feel lost through these predestiny points that ramble. But it is to help you understand your true conditioning around pleasure versus passion to celebrate how you please and want to be pleased in duality, and how you really are inspired to say yes to joy in every movement and in every moment of you.

Some have come with predestiny points where you can see they build one onto another. Those souls have a clear voice in how they are here to inspire evolution within their chosen purpose. Those souls can feel all alone within themselves because their predestiny points from pleasure to passion is so united that they feel alone. You do feel alone when you are not pleasing the world around you. You are so focused within your passion and purpose yet that being alone is right in the deep knowledge that their purpose is a tsunami of change, for all that is around them.

When you are with someone, figure out what is their pleasure and their passion and nod to both. For pleasure and passion is intertwined within all of you. Introspection in loving yourself is to call out your passion and allow it to be your elixir of movement, your ecstasy of yes, and your true why am I here. Passion then becomes pleasure because they are on the same spectrum. One is just heavy in your duality of ego and the other is your passion of truth of union in oneness, of celebrating all that is you as you glue this wonderful game of duality in bringing the creativity of the lushness, and the delightful joy of your human-ness in uniting in oneness with the full reason that you came to be now.

Your passion is the glue in intuition in saying yes to uniting your birth in Absolute Love to your holy temple. It brings that light and love of you to be the propellant of movement and joy that gives evolution over duality into the oneness that you all crave.

In creation, we are bound to a sacred journey of sharing a process that allows flow to be and to stimulate connections that seem vast into your now. Creation is the dialogue of moving into passion. To create, a soul knows the excitement, the calling, and the destiny of moving in the process that you have chosen to be in and to celebrate the destiny that you chose. Many have identified passion as only a piece of a romantic setting yet passion is the pivotal piece of moving your physical form to the next step of your evolution. If you are not passionate, you do not undertake the fullness, the depth, and the sacredness of what you are bringing to that movement. Many tune out passion, for in your ego world, it is about exciting a sexual space and not understanding that passion is invoked within the body in a chemical response with forces both inside and out that magnetize together to create something that is not yet in your now. Passion pushes you to step beyond your fear and move into a greater heart space. If you do not have passion, you do hold the world in a fearful paradigm.

Your world in the ego space constantly moves passion into something you don't want instead of saying yes as you show others your passion. How often is one told not to get too passionate about a person, place, or thing? If you are too passionate, it can look like addiction. What do you do to those you label addictive personalities? Yet, the souls who hold passion as a part of their principles, as part of their grounding in exhilarating their qi force to manifest a world that holds the depth of their love and their joy have come to help others remember that a passionate purpose is not evil. Being passionate makes you expand your realities. It makes you connect to somebody. Passion holds movement that is unknown to your logical order of safety because passion is part of creativity and allows you to think beyond any construct of safety. You are yearning not to be imprisoned by the forces of fear, but to celebrate the extension of love. Passion propels you to reach outside of that fear and to make movement as a calling of excitement in creating a permanent story of celebrating the oneness of love.

Passion is strong in individuals who are creative or participate in sports. You love your heroes to hold passion. But it is not allowed in the mainstream of everyday living. You slowly leak the passion of life, of love, and of light out of your beingness so you too can play safe and feel successful in a linear equation of being in your body. Many, who are passionate, yearn for others to join them in their passion of being so true to their souls calling. If you take that soul's calling away, they find that passion in other forms. Yes, many passionate souls who were born to be propelled in the delightful creation of passion end up self-medicating themselves because their passion is reckless and because their passion is a force that has been taken from your vocabulary of how you want to teach a soul and how you want to condition a soul. Schools are masters of taking away passion. A young soul who is asked to sit at a desk for hours upon hours negates the youthful passion of hands-on learning to get dirty in the soil and to understand the sacred relationship that grounds their body to something permanent; Mother Earth. She will be here longer than you, yes? Yet, her passion to provide you with everything is also destroyed. Souls come in with this delightful journey of saying yes, yet how often is it that the souls in the classroom who can't sit or are loud are deemed bad and they need an attitude adjustment. How often have you shouted for joy in a space that others believe you have broken that protocol of the conditioning of that space.

Joyful celebration of you in saying yes to you is the passionate movement that needs to be grounding in every individual, so they feel their purpose and their destiny. As you take away that passion a person loses his or her ability to fully ground into their true-life purpose and their true destiny. This is a great game that the ego is playing because then you only get to play with half your energy field in the world around you. The more you give up your passion for life, for breath, for sacred contracts, and sacred relationships in your sacredness of you the more you believe in the paradigm of fear and the timidness takes over. You stop feeling passion, slowly numb, and become a place holder of the structures that need you to be that place holder.

Now is a critical time in the fabric of your Earth to celebrate and bring back passion that is not in a competitive way like sports, or not in a very niche way, because even the most passionate artists feel they must hide in their space of being so connected to the forces that are beyond. Your youth are dying because you have taken their passion. You have given them leftovers of what their soul yearns for. There is a crisis on your land of these highly evolved souls who have come to uplift you in their knowledge in your society, with their depth of understanding the connection of passion. Many souls who show an early sign of passion are immediately drugged, or shooed out of the classroom and made to feel that their way of being is wrong.

I come forth as a gift within this discussion of passion to have you see these souls who are journeying from their space of passion to be self-medicated, to understand that if you are not going to listen to them in one way, they will find another way because they are your teachers. They have a message for you; they aren't doing their life wrong. They have tried to help your society, your communities, and your families to bond and to hold a deeper communion that moves with a magnetic force of saying yes, and gluing that yes to manifest a more loving, a more united, and a more celebrated space. As you are a part of the gift of celebrating with all souls, you know you are part of the anchor of souls to come to help them share and remember that they are truly the teachers, and to help them leave to soon. For all is critical to remember that we are all each other's teachers and we are the students of all these sacred relationships that unite for passion. Passion to be creative in living in love.

Mike: Can you add faith to this conversation?

Raphael: Faith hugs your passion. Faith allows you to deeply engage within your knowledge of you to be connected to something that is way beyond your mind and way beyond what you can envision. Faith is stepping out and knowing you are safe. Anytime you step out of yourself, you are invoking faith to hug the love of you in allowing your passion to expand. In passion, you expand into the highest of your vibrations. In pleasure, you stabilize safety and security. You do not expand into the full placement of you celebrating you as a united force of all that you are within your mental, emotional, physical, and spiritual fields. Faith says there are mysteries. I need to expand for my passion of loving me is saying yes to this project, and this project I know is part of my predestiny. In faith, you know you are hugged. You have faith that there is something more than just you because if you felt it was just really you, you would just please, right? Because you would need everything around you nodding for you to take a leap of faith. Passion bubbles within your cells. It is predestiny for you to say, "Love, love, love; so, I am saying yes, and this project is my passion. This project for me holds the love of me that I know I came to share with the world." Thus, in moving forth with your passion, you invoke faith.

Many say I do not know every other second. Do you know how much you say you do not know? Yet, your faith is huge. This is the glorious part of you in creation. Because you, Dear Ones, know. You know that you are here fulfilling divine destiny that is in oneness with your passion in the love of you as you love the oneness that you created in front of you in your landscape. We are your faith. We are hugging you as you step into unknowns on an emotional, physical, mental, and — even — in a more spiritual level, seeking beyond what has been conditioned. This is faith. You are all hugged with faith, for all of you — no matter who you are — have faith in something more. There is no one upon your Earth who doesn't hold faith, for everyone is creating into the unknown and that is what is wonderful within your energy fields. None of you play small. None of you genuinely believe in duality or the ego. You just have been conditioned well. In being conditioned well, you color within the lines and that is glorious, for it allows you to know the comforts of safety and security. Once you know that, you are ready to expand within your landscape for that is the creative souls that you are. Expansion and creativity are faith, and in faith, we know you are so buoyant in the expression of love. Love raises you all to new levels of commitment, comprehension, and completeness. You are all doing your joyful work in rising in your awareness on this Earth.

Passion is the faith that others are exploring their truths and becoming safer together as you expand in your qualities of love and light. Many of your ideas of conditioning are eroding, and bring in that fear of sitting at crossroads, looking at fear head-on, and deciding what decision for them evokes passion or pleasure. This is a gift of your time because all your lines are blurring. Faith is real and it is an active protection field that gives you movement into creating you with the love of all that you are.

Elizabeth: As I am moving into higher vibration, I find that I do not have to experience the extremes of polarity the way I use to experience the highs and lows. It is almost like moving into a neutrality. Will we, as we move into the fourth and fifth dimensions, be able to maintain this passion as you speak about without having to live in that extreme duality?

Raphael: Passion is the wildflowers that hold the vividness of what you seek. Duality is the weeds. All that you plant can rise above the weeds. Those flowers celebrate union in their essence of just being. Thus, the weeds have no meaning. They are but a neutral part of their landscape. Your essence of passion is a spectrum of you that allows more light and electricity as you move into other dimensions. You speak in light language. You are all stardust. Your essence has been seen by many throughout your etchings of time and your ecstasy in lighting darkness is the vibrant spectrum of light that colors your skies. You do not pay attention to the stuff of duality, for it is just a prop that has given you a way of discerning your passion in loving yourself and loving all that is around you. When you love yourself, all props of duality hold the gratitude for showing up and giving you the opportunity to know your oneness in love and light. In expressing that in the freedom of vividness that you are, your spectrum of your own light are colors beyond what you can imagine in this placement of you. As you go into different dimensions, that light and electricity move faster. The ecstasy is beyond what you can experience but what you know of you to be and why you yearn for those dimensions. You know these props have been placed for you to clear out your garbage to recognize in your core the freedom to create in all spectrums of color and all spectrums of electric motion. This holds you as the purity of light and love that is your holy creation.

Yes, the greatest gift of you is to love and work on yourself. The props of duality do not even hold an awareness. Yet there is a gratefulness of being a part of the movement into your passion of expressing what you know is heaven on Earth.

Mike: If the infinity of you is held by passion, does that mean that when we were first created in human form we decided that all our incarnations would involve the same passion?

Raphael: You always hold the same passion of oneness and in creating in that pivot of oneness. When we hold passion, it is that gift of oneness. You all are happening now, right? This idea of passion from source is part of your whole oneness. What happens is that the mind of duality wants to pick apart any of these essences that you hold from oneness. The split mind must dissect, analyze, and separate to recreate a new understanding. What is permanent is permanent, so love is permanent. Passion is permanent. As your mind wants to dissect this in duality, you then believe in your analysis of a split mind instead of the core truth in oneness.

You carry that oneness passion throughout your lifetimes. It is within you through your free choice of how you then want to manifest with that passion. Manifestation holds passion. They are interwoven together creating what you want and what you don't want. Any vibration that you are in is always holding passion. In another dimension, you would still hold the passion of oneness. It is a vibrational frequency that is different than the world of form.

Your physical form is constructed in a dense way that your passion becomes what you feel. There is a feeling you have in every lifetime as a soul that is going to be a part of your woven destiny to awaken. Once your soul remembers that passion piece, it is easier to then ground into it in other lifetimes because you have remembered that. I can ground into that passion piece of me and manifest even more. Older souls are more honed and willing to harness passion in a deliberate way of creating what they want. Young souls get their passion burned out in creating what they want. Sometimes you see where they are passionate for a month, then it goes away. They are not yet grounded into the whole idea of this stream of passion that is a part of their incarnation. The same can be said for love. You are always grounded in love. That is part of your permanence from Heaven. You are going to hold that to in every lifetime. Your free will of experiences and of saying what you don't want and what you want in that lifetime can change in how you ground into your passion, or ground into what you love. The more you remember that strength of passion as a positive quality of you, then you are going to use it in a more deliberate honed way. That is what older souls seem to do. They seem to have wisdom of when it is right for them to really take on something versus when it is not.

Elizabeth: You said to recognize when you are with someone what is their pleasure and their passion. Might this be the secret to a good relationship?

Raphael: Yes, acknowledging there was something within your passion and your partners that magnetizes you to be strong as a unit, than you could do alone. Once you can hold that sacred space and not compete with your processes of passion, you hold a magnetic force of strength that of course no one else can undo. Then, scarcity doesn't hit you either. It is why sex can be such a strong gift within a relationship because it brings that physical passion into a chemical response within your body that makes you bond even deeper. If you didn't get excited, it would be very hard to not say yes to the call of expansion. Souls in relationships get nervous if their partners expand when they don't or when the expansion is outside their realm of understanding within the way they ground themselves and even hold their family budget for instance, which can often break up a relationship when they are called to expand beyond their resources and one partner is says yes while the other doesn't. If that passion is the true calling, then you will make it through if you stick together. The more you are grounded in your passion, the more you feel that excitement. It is like Christmas and the excitement of knowing there are presents. The excitement of waking up and saying there is treasure to be had today. That is passion. It is an excited space, and it holds electricity that magnetizes what is yours to expand to. If you don't hold that excitement, it is very hard to on your own get into the expansion of you.

Mike: Does that cover how we can be passionate and not preachy?

Raphael: Preachy is the belief that you are somehow better than another. It holds a top-down philosophy and there is always an agenda when you preach to get somebody on your page. When you are in passion, you are excited to share and that excited energy is for all. There is no, I'm better; you are just busting at the seams. You want to share what makes you feel alive. In that sharing, others might see you as preachy because excited energy is not allowed in your conversations. When you are excited, you are pushy. How often is it when you see someone who is simply excited, and maybe you are tired and not ready to feel that heightened vibration? Then you tame the ideas and then they can become preachy. Somehow you have made it into a space where you are overflowing with excited passion for whatever you are moving forward to, instead you now got to get their okay somehow. That is why you are preaching. If they get excited, then you can go back to your original excitement. Many times, you cannot go back to that original excitement because you have allowed someone to dilute it from you.

When you are first excited about something and you can ground into it with Mother Earth, as she is the goddess of manifestation, you can walk with her and say, "Mother Earth, I am so excited for this new adventure and I would really like you to nourish me through it, and guide me in my manifestation." Once you ground into Mother Earth, then you find that person who is going to show excitement with you. By saying what you are excited about with your people, you are grounding it in heart to heart for they will be excited with you. Now, you are grounded and your heart is fulfilled in its expansion of passion. Once you do that you take a step into what you are passionate about and you find how it feels on you.

You take a walk towards passion, and then you feel it without it going into a conscious thought. You are not dissecting this passion at this moment. You are feeling it. Your mind is your heart. As you feel and think through your heart, you see if this is the right place for me. The more you feel that the passion is still there, you will take step after step because you will keep feeling it. Your body is drawn to it. Your third eye got the first impression, then your body feels the passion. As you step in and your passion is still vibrant, you know it is part of your destiny. When you step in, it is holding that excitement even if people around you are saying "crazy."

You are your own truth. Your body, breath, mind, emotions, and spirit have all the answers of you. You are wired for you, not for them. Knowing and feeling you with passion, moves you. When you move in passion, there is a permanence to it because you have an addiction about it. Your soul strengthens in its communication to you the more you can step into that space. Then, you acquire the confidence. Passion and grounding are pivotal so you can lead yourself in what you have chosen to be.

Elizabeth: I worry that the masses are so mesmerized today that many never allow themselves to explore their purpose or their passion. Could you talk about this and the impact on our youth?

Raphael: Your goal of passion in your 3D world is for work and to make money. Many do not get a choice of their passion to really understand what they came to be truly passionate about. Unfortunately, your schools' script a child from preschool on to understand a passion of end results. In your capitalism created environment, the top need many to do the end results for them so they can make their passion of their money, yes? Through the great advent of your internet, you have a new world upon you. This new world is one where work does not equal a result, and there are ones who hold the power of your land and hold all the keys to your prosperity. Prosperity is how you make the money for you to thrive in the gift of your destiny. That is how you feel prosperous. Abundance is the full horn of plenty of all the textures, all the space, and all the elements for you to hold passion

Chapter 8 - Passion

with to create an expression of you that ultimately should provide you with your prosperity, which right now in your environment is money. It is sad that it is the equation of society today.

With the advent of the internet, you have unlimited space to create. It is a precursor to the Age of Aquarius, and it is pivotal to bring in now to see how you as a mass consciousness felt about others expanding into this new portal of creation. You have found that it does allow you to connect more and work from home. This wonderful tool of the internet provided an explosion of expansion, and all of you are falling in fear to some degree because when you create with expansion, the game is all inside of you. You take the risk to open a certain site on the internet. You take a risk to connect with a new friend. You are responsible. Adults have more fear of this universe of creativity and expansion than your younger ones. They came for this and they will be the power of the Age of Aquarius. For them, this expansion in this new universe of thoughts is passion. They were born to participate in this. It is in them and they do not need to learn because it is an intuitive system, and in that they have all the power. Many parents are scared and you feel they are lost for hours, yet they are doing their destiny. The more they understand how to collaborate with a person in Europe while they are in their bedroom, they bring their world to oneness. You might not deem the quality of their game healthy, but for them it is not about the game. It is about an inner connectiveness that lights them both up when they share a true passion together in that game.

This movement for the youth is one way that they can hold their passion without the schools, the governments, the religious institutions, and their families taking their passion away. They are not you. They are a new energy form and they think very differently than you who are here to be the ground for them in this new expansion of them. To deny this learning and this passion is to deny the mass consciousness a way back to oneness.

Many young souls do not care about you, and that is what makes you mad. They are invested in their destiny of collaboration and creativity in thought. Their passion is to expand beyond a nuclear family, a community, and even a state or country. They expand in their mind to be fully exposed to all the creative impulses this medium can bring. That is what hurts, because they don't give a crap and you deem them entitled. They are entitled to their passion, for they are the doors that open into the Age of Aquarius.

Young souls came with a deep purpose and it won't look like the institutions you hold dear. It does not mean they are not grateful for all that you have done, but their reality is so big in the expansion of mind and spirit. Many souls hold the whole spectrum, so you will have gender fluidness, yes? You are also going to have where you no longer can claim that this is just a job for a woman or a man, but it will be a job for a soul whose destiny and passion fit that. In the process, you, Dear Ones—especially the old souls who like their ground of their prosperity—they will fight not to give into the newness of this expansion in creativity but to police the kids in their passion. That will cause you all to spin downward instead of as a collective to spin upward and to truly unite with spirit. Most young souls are spiritual and they will claim that to you. They recognize a greater oneness than many older souls, meaning older in age. Those souls who have lived and worked hard want kids who work hard.

Through the expansiveness of all the gifts you have given these children, like drugs that help you not get sick and to allow you to live longer, your dishwashers where you don't have to wash every dish by hand, cars, airplanes, computers, and cell phones; you have given these souls the foundation for them to live in a more refined mental way. That was your job and there is great celebration for you to be really in your passion to create ways to save time, so you can live longer, to save time so you can do your passion, and to save time so you and your children can create in an expansive way. These kid's passion was a part of their destiny and when you take their passion away you have clipped their destiny, and when you clip someone's destiny they self-medicate. You have also given them all the drugs to self-medicate with because you, Dear Ones, held the energy of the Age of Pisces, which — as I said — is very much the healers and love drugs. So, they are taking exactly what you put your passion into by creating more drugs to live longer. Thus, they say, you have clipped my destiny so I will use your tools that you have created to self-medicate. And then you want them in jail? They took your gifts of your passion and you think they are entitled? That is very backwards thinking. No wonder why these souls are opting out in big chunks. You cannot move forward if you clip the destiny and the passion of the youth.

On an organic level, spirit always celebrates the connection of you. Many are awakened to how they have clipped their children's destinies and are also willing to truly collaborate in this expansive movement that youth is showing up with passion. Again, the water rights are about the children. Standing Rock was the passion of those children to stop being clipped in their destiny of their heritage in the land (crying) and, again, as I cry before you about this death of motion the kids need from you, Dear Ones. They came before the elders and said we cannot allow the destruction of us anymore. Their passion to draw the line in the sand created a momentum throughout your globe. Those kid's lights have expanded forever. They are now the spokespeople to hold passion for every youth and to say, "I am worthy of my destiny."

You have brought in many old souls and these spiritually old souls are here to hold the movement of expansion with integrity, love, compassion, strength, commitment, and purpose as they acknowledge their grace as they stand forth with the potential for more. The riots against your president is mainly youth. They will not stop expressing in social media, or with boots on the ground, the destruction of their destiny. Where you are right now as a nation does not hold great expansion for you. The energy of the youth is the movement to bring America to greatness again. Stop shoeing them out of their passion. Allow them the right place next to you in solving the problems you face.

Chapter 9

Abundance

We celebrate an awareness of holding our divinity outward, for creation in your landscape is from the inside out. Once your creation is created or out in the world, the celebration of you being vulnerable to bring your creation into existence is then able to create a conversation to see how you have woven in your mastery of love, of spirit, and of oneness. There is great anxiety when you put out your truths and your knowledge. For putting you out, the vulnerability of being judged, of being shot down, and being marked as bad resonates strongly. You, Dear Ones, do not want to fall from grace for you have already felt your fall from grace, from joy, and from love. Why put yourself out for others to gossip about what you severely held and cared to put out. Creation is no small thing. It is no small gift as you put things out one way or the other, through your body language, through the way you dress, and through the way you hold or withhold the core of you. Joy is a part of celebrating your anchor in wholeness and being a creator to have an intimate conversation with us, spirit, with you the holy self and with another. With all the particles around you, what layers of intimacy are you willing to go to? What layer of nakedness are you willing to be?

For in creation, you all are naked. You began in this world in your holy temple in just the beauty of your body. In that space, you were able to present your note of you, shiny, new, and blameless of all that you knew to be and not to be. Innocent, shiny, vulnerable, and needing depth of connection in intimacy to thrive. Each creation is that innocent space of being born. In that placement, innocence is enriched with love as the space that is being hugged. Creation is scary for the duality of form makes one not know the good or the bad that might be exposed in the innocence of now. You fight to claim your innocence. What a gift to behold for your truth is that you are innocent.

In innocence, joy is. Joy is the buoyant elixir of unconditional love. Joy is a remembrance of cocreating with the source of Absolute Love. Joy is the profound connection of being together. Love is always held around you holding the vibration of joy. Joy is the oasis of true innocent connection in all that you do. Movement in joy is knowing you just being you. That you are and that is all you ever need to stay. Love is, Source is, God is, Yahweh is, Allah is, and simplicity of all is. There is no story beyond is. There is no additive beyond is. Joy is. It is a recognition that you are and that I am. That you, as a statement of you, is holy, is innocent, and in your innocence you are abundant—for only if you believe you owe a debt does scarcity take over the totality of you. The identity of scarcity, the identity of separation, the identity that the story is more than just is. Somehow you need to build your story of is to be is; for God is and so are you, which evokes the loss of joy.

Curtains fall over and dampen your beingness and your expressions. Curtains of doubt, curtains of insecurity, and curtains of not enough. You live in forgetfulness and this scares you. How can you create the big love, the big job, the big abundance if somewhere deep within your consciousness you have forgotten a pivotal truth, a pivotal identity, or a pivotal strength? Many say that I can forgive but not forget. That not forgetting energy creates karma for you to eventually release and truly forget all the stories of your creation back to I am. I am joy, I am love, I am and God is, and Love is. The depth of forgetfulness is part of the veils, curtains, or gravity that holds you down to play out duality. You have forgotten your strength as creators of love. That is the deep whisper you feel that calls you through nature, through music, and heart to heart connections that says, "Oh I am not forgotten and I have played with you before and that we know this music do we not?" We were created in this expression of notes upon notes. Look at forgetfulness and understand the grace of being able to forget your stories and to remember your truths. The fabric of your knowledge of you buttons up this wonderful temple. Through your energy centers, which are these beautiful chakras of yours helps bring an identity in strength to your holy temple to celebrate joy and be abundant of all there is.

    Love is abundant, for love is the vehicle that excites the particles and brings you to expansion of more abundance. Fear, separation, lack, and duality dampen the particles and dilute the expression of your creations. Be willing to forget your identities of duality and to remember your innocence in connections of love that are abundant and you will expand with all your buttons vibrating in the highest placement of your note. To be fully in joy with everything around you, identify and give gratitude to what is abundant right now is knowing yourselves are abundant. Your breaths are abundant. Your depth of breath is not just one breath but billions. Your heartbeat is abundant. Again, not just one beat but eons of beating. Grass and leaves are abundant and everything around you as well, for each element within your form holds the raw materials to bring it to you. Yes, there is stress in conversations around how you hold the highest regard to the raw ingredients as they come to you, but there is great abundance in being able to share all that you have within you and the landscape around you. When you connect in this abundance, you bring the resonance of joy to your heart. Your heart holds the connections of everything within your landscape. Your heart is the placement of knowing and feeling and being connected to what is around you. The more you can have the sacred conversation; this vulnerability within your heart, the more you connect, and in that connection, you are celebrating your innocence of being a holy creator and moving love to connect the depth of the experience you are here to claim. All of your experiences are abundant, for each experience gives you clarity of how you self-talk. It brings you back to saying and recognizing yourself and giving yourself the gift to forget the stories of duality and to really connect with your, "I am one, I am anchored in this wholeness, and I grow in joy as I do." This I am one in finding joy, and the depth of connection is the simple wonderment of remembering the delicious placement of simple connections. Connections that say I am good, I am abundant, and I am one with all there is around me. If you are one, there is no scarcity.

Abundance for you, as you hold your voice, is about value. It is about how you share vocally your value of you and how you claim that value, for in duality all that you do is a transaction of understanding value. Value of good and bad, value of payment, value of purpose and service. Are you adding value? What is your price? Are you priceless, or are you feeling that the price tag of the transaction did not express the abundance of what you brought? The conversation around what you deem as worthy, what you deem is needed for you to live, opens a way of celebrating the raw materials that you are all here to create from. Your day-to-day world is structured to meet your needs. You have created this to be so and maybe what you really need is not being met, for in the

Chapter 9 - Abundance

creation of your need the expectations of what you need and how you should get it might be outside of what truly you are here to make in your needs and what your needs are truly meant to be. Your body or your physical temple lays down and needs sleep. It awakens into a sitting position to celebrate and give gratitude to a moment of time and space. As you rise, you become an instrument of showing your priorities in your actions for your needs within you move you to do things. But your body just needs to be in those positions of lying down, sitting up, and standing. You create stories around that need of lying down in the best bed ever, or sitting in the right perfect chair, yes? Also standing and making a statement of you as you move and show all that you are in claiming your needs. Your bodies needs are quite simple. It needs food, it needs nourishment and the gift of Mother Earth provided you to match all your needs. The love of nourishing your body and expanding your creation is to create beautiful elaborate food for others and yourself and that is a gift of love that is priceless. That is a way to share the love story of yourself and others, but Mother Earth meets the basic need of food. Your trees are abundant in their fruit, your land is abundant, even in small spaces, to provide you with vegetables, fruit, and with all forms of nourishment. With abundance, Mother Earth says yes in her celebration with you to provide exactly what the body needs to lie down, to sit, to stand and to meet all the needs of your form. You as you are here celebrating your creation of you gets to remember your love and share your love story.

Money is just a tool of a transaction and it can never hold your true value and that is why there is much resentment and bitterness around people who have money and those who do not, for it will not ever fully express your value of your gift as a holy creator. Yet people who have money are sometimes in duality looked upon as somehow godlike for they have gleaned something that is so far outside the world of possibilities for others. The flow of money for everyone has the flow of rhythm in it because money's vibration is like stones skipping upon the water. Really there is no rhythm or reason as it skips and falls to another, except that it is your time to have that gift of a raw ingredient, a raw material of expressing you more. The law of attraction works to call in the abundance of the form of money, of the form of value in ways you hold transactions, for the more you excite your energy in love, the more expansive the surface area of you is, right? The more expansive your surface area, the more you are gifted those rocks to fall into your field. How exciting is that? For then you gleam that raw ingredients like the waves of the ocean bringing forth all that you look for on the sand as you walk, to be able to see the value, and the money. Appreciate its gift and then send it forth once again, for in your love language of sharing your abundance on every level brings in more abundance because the surface area of your vibration of your aura, of your being, is as big as the ocean to be able to bring in the value of you. Therefore, at times it is hard to give you specifics about what will bring in your abundance of financial worth. Each person, through their mind, has accepted what abundance means to them through their self-recognition, which is different for everyone.

We see all of you as billionaires. But you as you serve your needs in this form through the stories you have created again which brings the curtains of lack around you. Thus we can only bring forth and help you remember your value from that awareness. As you awaken your celebration in your joy to connect in the sources of all great places that you want to connect in, it becomes a priceless expression. Those who hold wealth recognize that you all can have it too, but in duality they also know they can

Chapter 9 - Abundance

work against your forgetfulness and even use your forgetfulness to deaden your joy and your expression of you so you forget that you really are priceless and you could demand more for everything you do as the holy creator you are. Lack and separation, makes you feel guilty to ask for needs beyond your body's awareness. You need clothing and then your shelter, but even in that if you have fallen from grace sometime in this reality, that might be denied. You feel these cloaks of having to be so good but never recognizing that your good can be on a scope of just maintaining basic needs. When you filter life with joy in the depth of singing your love language it widens your energy field and there is no one in duality who can keep you from getting those wonderful pebbles of financial abundance to fall within your field. The more you do that and celebrate with each other, the more you get the financial freedom you seek; in love, your needs can be the love story of truly connecting in all the experiences that you came to be. What you see for yourself in the dreams you hold on those vision boards that celebrate you extending to the highest possibilities of you come true.

Vision connects your divine blueprint to spirit and back to yourself. When held with your true gift of love in your purity of knowledge that you can ask and you shall receive, brings in connections that make this vision happen. These connections play through goosebumps on your body, connections of just knowing in your heart that yes, this is my truth. Connections that what you expect is a certainty and not an expectation that if you do not get it somehow you have done it wrong. Your karma that you are paying for is all about the way you have held separation with yourself in love. Each action yes, is a gift of love, or it is somehow holding a space of separation. When you know that you are connecting in love, then all that you see for yourself does come true. The more you have the knowledge of it, and you see it happen, the greater that your field expands and that to comes true. Your vision has worked with all the connections of spirit, or yourself, of Mother Earth, and the abundance of people that are upon this world. Talk about abundance. All of you celebrating all the possibilities of creation.

Connection in joy resonates your note. I share your note again, for it is your calling card of knowing your oneness in love. You are here in a holy vibrational frequency to hold that note so purely that others harmonize within your field. In harmony there is peace, and in peace you can become vulnerable. In vulnerability you celebrate the newness of coming here and saying I celebrate my holiest creation of me. I celebrate nakedness. You are all naked are you not? No matter what stories you cover yourself with, no matter what clothing you cover with, you are naked. Naked to the rawness of judgement. Naked to the heaviness of separation and you are naked to be able to shine. Joy is accepting and allowing nakedness of your soul to be the calling card of you as you hold the purity of your note and vibrate your frequency of your placement and all there is, for you all hold divinity in the now, where there is just the note of you.

Coalesce in your strength that you are the exclamation point of your love story, and that your note is the radiant force to celebrate the gift of joy in the abundance of your eternity.

Abundance is the gift of saying yes to the moment, receiving and sharing all of you. For you are a miracle in motion celebrating and connecting all movement and all creation within you, to a greater expansive awareness of your world. Because abundance is such a part of your everyday placement, you keep it in the back of your mind through the autopilot of your essence in the survival of your day to day living. You forget the glorious union and the

Chapter 9 - Abundance

sacred communion of giving and receiving. It is automatic in many ways. You do not have to tell your body to breath in and breath out. That system is automatic. Your blood circulating through the pumps of your heart, again, hold an automatic space. The sun receiving and giving is automatic. You do not have to do anything but just be and to celebrate these systems of abundance.

It is quite a leap in your mind to understand the difference of what you consider abundant and what you consider prosperity. Prosperity is an ego alignment of having to get and hold. It doesn't allow the true communion of giving and receiving in your paradox world that you are in. Many hold both these principals as equal, but they are not. When we come and speak of abundance, we are sharing with you your divineness, which is automatic in all that you do. This divine placement of you is abundant. Your gift is to bring forth that depth of abundance that is your divineness, into sacred relationships in your world of duality. This is a great mantle of responsibility for each soul because in this position of understanding your divinity, the gift of allowing the sacred flow of all of you to another is your truth in celebrating your desire for prosperity.

Prosperity is a principal that you as a mass consciousness equate to stuff. You equate it to all manmade wonderments of your lives. In this, you get lost in communicating your divineness within this manmade wonderment to proclaim your prosperity. We, as the Holy Spirit, talk about this prosperity as making a huge cancer upon your land. It does not hold divinity. But the truth of the ego is that it wants to be special and have more than others. I call this cancer because it holds in tumor places in all the different constructs through your corporations, governments, individuals, and religious placement, which seek to be known for their success, prosperity, and glowing with their self-importance of their value that has accumulated through these man-made principals and wonderments. Money is definitely a man-made wonderment and it is wonderful for you, yes? This is manmade in the process of showing how you want to bring your divinity of abundance to an arena of expression. For money is just an energy field of expression. Money allows you to choose what you want and do not want in this world of duality. Many will hold that you are more divinely awakened or divinely chosen or have a huge divine purpose if your bank account somehow super exceeds those around you.

I would like you to remember that prosperity is not about your divine abundance. It is a token responsibility to infuse the gift of giving and receiving in a profound sacred relationship as you hold the prosperity your soul came to harvest. Those who hold the divine abundance of their sacredness in the deep communion of that abundance in all their relationships will fertilize all the beings around them to celebrate their joy in creating and remembering their souls' journey into the sacred gift of giving and receiving. Your position of cultivating and grounding into the divine abundance around you is the greatest movement of your alignment with your mind, heart, and body to be the divine instrument and to cultivate your string of wealth as your soul propels you to your destiny. Gratitude then becomes the grounding piece to remember and to acknowledge and allowing it to ground in the abundance that is your divine right. Leaves are abundant. Blades of grass are abundant. Buildings built in your landscape are abundant. Cars are abundant. Acknowledge this abundance that you have all created to celebrate the remembrance of your divinity as creators of all that is before you. Hold joy with the expansion of this abundance of creativity, watch the power of passion that makes movement exciting in all that is happening.

There is an abundance of excitement in your world now. What a wonderful gift to ground yourself and to fully cultivate a communion with this abundance. In gratitude, you are grounded to accept the mantle of leadership, to bring your divinity into prosperity. That is the call that we are giving you right here and now. Step into your desire, your vortex in the Law of Attraction, to be prosperous within your divinity of abundance, for you are abundant. Your prosperity is your joy of owning your divinity. Celebrate the prosperity in communion with your soul purely open to the gift of giving and receiving. For all that you give does come back and when you give without conditions, it allows for the expansion to be divine.

I celebrate your abundance and ground into the gratitude with you to be that divine instrument in holding the amazing joy of prosperity.

Mike: In a previous message you talk about "falling from grace." I have always heard that, but maybe I didn't understand it from your perspective. Could you define falling from grace?

Raphael: Grace is the glue of your innocence and wholeness. When you hear people say, "She holds grace," that person is holding that vibration that glues their wholeness and innocence. In that grace, miracles are here before you because all that holds grace, finds all is right, for there is no fear of the moment. All is whole, and you are innocent. You fell from grace within your own perception of your divinity. Falling from grace created the ego to be your antagonist for you to question and remember who you truly are. The ego is but your creation because you fashioned this amazing story of falling from grace. When you fell from grace, you lost your glue of knowing your wholeness and innocence. You fell from that essence and texture and what did you create? Gravity. The depth of heaviness betrayed the underbelly of all your denials. It is hard for you to believe that you wanted to understand the concept of being more than God, your creator. You deny this awareness and it is what you run from, but it wasn't because you were bad. It was one moment of asking, "what if." You fell, and what does gravity do? It makes you fall from grace.

When you fall, you are no longer whole or innocent, and because this one paradigm shattered you into millions of pieces of the creation of this world, you judge anyone who has fallen from your sense of grace. You as a contingency of the son and daughter of Absolute Love hide from your truth of just being a creator who asked, "what if," and acted upon that. Any soul who acts upon a desire of "what if," and fails your sense of what is grace, becomes pebbles of humanity that get shifted to the fringes of your reality. Your fall from grace is your gift to understand your abundance. You did not fall, you were caught. When you were caught by the beautiful gift of us, the Holy Spirit, we gave you all the tools to be the divine creator in a reality that wants to prove to you that you are not whole, not abundant, or not good. And yet, as you find your gift of your divinity in each incarnation, you say and remember the abundance that you truly are, and reconnect in grace, and not in gravity. A lot of times when you are in these movements of accelerated growth of your divinity in the remembrance of this, you get very dizzy, because you are no longer being held down to the principle of form, but to the creative flow that is held in grace. Movement of your soul is the movement to have sacred union and sacred relationship with all that is around

Chapter 9 - Abundance

you and to disappear your "nots" as in you're not good, and moving back to the ease of grace that is you.

Elizabeth: It is my understanding that manifesting is happening faster and faster as we ascend. Is this true, and how is that possible?

Raphael: As you ascend, you are no longer beholding to take the elements of what you just create in form. Many who first feel the strength of gravity through cause and effect of the elements of your world learn about air, fire, water, and Earth, and learn how to manifest with those beautiful elements. It is labor intensive. It brings joy as you bring something to fruition, but it is a highly intensive expansion of energy to receive something that is sometimes very little if you feel that you must equate the energy of output with your abundance. As you ascend, your vibration allows you to manifest not just from the elements, but from the weaving of the elements to connect in a more expanded way. You find that it is a collaboration at first of many souls coming in and bringing out more abundance or prosperity. You come connecting as a group to move the elements. That is a level of manifesting from a bigger place of higher energy, because you are collaborating with another. That allows your sacred relationships to expand beyond what just your labor output could do. You all played creatively with this idea as souls for a long time. Then you created machines to step in for a person where the output of this machine could occur throughout the day and night. This allows you as a physical form to receive more prosperity. I would not say abundance, but prosperity of your human ingenuity, to be able to have more possessions that show your wealth to others around you. This is when the breakdown of sacred relationships started to occur.

Some people got to own the machine and some didn't. Why? Some would say it is because you who own a machine have more ability to receive more prosperity without the physical output. Abundance is our divinity. The ego set this up by saying that, "I am going to be creative for you in this thought form and show you who really is divine." The ego does not want you to remember your divinity at all. Many rich do not understand their divinity. It does not matter how many possessions you have. You always hold the fear of needing more to show that somehow you are chosen. You know that money buys you. Thus, these beautiful machines became a way of releasing some sacred relationships. When you lost these sacred relationships of acknowledging the gifts of your neighbors and how they, Mother Earth, and the elements celebrate you, you started to fall into forgetfulness. You began to forget that you are abundant and prosperous with sacred relationships to all. You have slowly unraveled any place that holds a sacred relationship. If you forget to be in relationships, you are an island that the ego can control through fear.

When those who are moving more into their divinity manifest, they seek the divine relationship from the highest potential of their world. There are no sacred relationships with your machines. You created the machines so you can understand them. Machines will never be in relationship with you. People want their phones to be in a sacred relationship with them because they store all their information on these phones, so why can't that phone be a projection of them. The information on your phone is a grand projection of your actions and, in that, the data companies make them feel like they know you because this is how you have acted. But they do not know your soul destinies. They do not know the gift of your inner awakening essence. Many will rely on a machine to manifest their next car for they have the data fields that you absolutely have shown how you act. But no, there is no way that information will ever feed your soul to the next point. It is you understanding your abundance, and the greater weave of uniting back in sacred relationship with the elements around you, which is not a laborious act. It is a joyful art of bringing what you love as the abundant elixir to manifest your depth to celebrate in sacred relationship your prosperity in a human body. Because you have more time on your hands and you are not labor oriented, you are able to hold the energy fields that can weave a higher energy of the elements so you no longer need to go cut down a tree to create the table. You no longer must saw the wood with handmade tools. You have given yourself opportunities to have the abundance of raw ingredients of the elements in the format that you can hold to express your creativity in manifesting. This beautiful industrial age has given many people this opportunity to manifest what they see in their minds eye or what they feel in their heart, to have it come forth without much output.

Now, you are entering the energy age and this shows you global awareness of finding materials to celebrate your desires in manifesting. Now you don't even need to go to a store. You get to go on a computer. This vibration of you to have what you want allows you this time for what? Sacred relationships to remember to reconnect. If you keep losing these sacred relationships you find that you fall into the underbelly of all that you have been denying of making a world that holds the haves and the have nots. You all feel the desperate pull of this creation of lack. The gift out of the desperation of lack is reaching out and making a union with Mother Earth, with your neighbors, and with your beautiful animals, celebrating that you do hold the gift of wholeness and innocence.

Mike: Why is creation so hard?

Raphael: Creation is not hard. Manifesting in duality is hard. Creation is your divinity just like abundance. You are creative always. Your cells are creating, your mind is creating, and your world is creating. You do not put creation into your manifestations. You forget you are a creator because manifesting means you must work. Ego loves you to work. To keep you marching to its drumbeat helps you to fall into the cloak of forgetfulness and not be the creative essence that you truly are. If you all celebrate your creativity, all the problems before you would be solved. The ego must not let you celebrate your creativity, in fact, it makes you fully aware that you are here to work and not be creative. Only a few creative souls are prosperous. They can fall from grace in the mass consciousness quite fast. You fear creativity and you put yourself to work to manifest a safe awareness of prosperity. You are true to the safety net that you all individually hold in working towards prosperity. If you allow someone to know your prosperity, they might take it away from you, or you might have to give more than you want. You might have to do something that you don't really want to do. You all cloak this idea of what you feel as your true sense of prosperity.

Souls who anchor in abundance celebrate the expansion of giving and receiving in their prosperity, because when you hold that gratitude of abundance, you hold the forgiveness of creating a place that only celebrates work and not the joy of an expression. You work hard upon this land and it is amazing to see how some of you work so hard to really get out of work. For you must be very creative to not work because work is the motion that you have chosen to show up for, to make a commitment for, and to honor the giving and receiving of money. Even the contract of giving and receiving of the people in your company that you might be going to work for is a contract of money. There is no sacred relationship that exists in this idea of work. Many, in the end, create sickness if they always have to show up for this relationship, because there is no essence of you within this dimension of being in contract that something that is just money is just a means of expression. You have made it something more and people want to give it that, but then when they do it is never enough. When you put your sacred relationship of all of you to the identity of money, you become only expression of having that money or not. You, then, are never fully anchored to your full abundance. When you bring creativity in celebrating your connection to all that your work gives you, of which money is a piece, you get to expand in the buoyancy of joy that celebrates the giving and receiving of all that is around you. That holds abundance for it holds wholeness. You begin to recognize then that is your true choice of going to work.

Elizabeth: Isn't the financial situation that we find ourselves in partially determined by the journey that we chose before we came into this life?

Raphael: Yes. That is hard for you to understand once you are in embodiment. You came for a purpose of uncovering your divinity in your abundance even if you maybe chose a lifetime of not high prosperity. Some get caught into being one of the have nots and yet some find their way out of that and rejoice in the gift of showing up in celebrating relationships wherever they are. Many of your relationships are free, yet you don't hold them as sacred because you don't feel that you are earning anything by showing up in these relationships. For example, by going for a walk on Mother Earth it is free. When you see the sacred union of that walk, the abundance of all the sights and senses that you take in and out, you start to feel a greater texture of safety within your community. That sense of safety has value for you, one that will let you expand in the way that you chose to show up in social environments. When you show up more comfortably in social environments, you get people talking to you through giving and receiving. That value is free. Do you have to pay anybody on your walk to be safe? You just got that from being able to ground into the abundance of all the sights and sounds around you. When you show up within your safety to the person in the store, they look at you and connect and ask how is your day? They celebrate you as a human being who is safe to them because you feel safe. That relationship then builds another layer of trust that makes you safe. That acknowledgement that they trust you even for that moment gives you confidence to take the step out into how you want to manifest your prosperity. All this that holds you together is free, if you chose to see the sacredness of grounding into the abundance that is around you.

Once you feel confident in your safety and in trust, you expand into asking for your divine pay in the place that you chose to celebrate your giving and receiving of work. Once you are there, your expression of you allows you to know that you can ask and that you will receive through your gratitude and grounding in abundance. The art of recognizing your reality of how you are to create these sacred relationships allow others to celebrate an expansive connection with you. Then you build your business

Chapter 9 - Abundance

through referrals. They are the grace of your sacred union with others, and you do not pay for these referrals. As you work in a new paradigm of expressing the gift of abundance in celebrating giving and receiving, it expands exponentially to all structures that you participate in. No one can stop divine relationships. The world of human duality fights hard for you to not only bring your divine relationship into the way you celebrate religion, but also your partnerships with another and in kids and friends. That isolates the power of your abundance, which is the power that ripples exponentially when you connect with all that is around you. You are living in a time that is calling forth isolation. Your expansion of prosperity is limited and thus, you are fighting each other for these pieces of stuff that truly is short sighted in your growth and in your divine abundance. In isolation, you do end up taking everything with personal fear because you then must protect what is yours. You don't have a divine relationship with your neighbor, so then he can become a terrorist in your mind. It has been a slow forgetting of how you are invested in every being in your now. You are here to help remind others to play in the divine gift of abundance, and to give and receive in sacred union for you all to prosper. The call to all is to ground in gratitude the gifts of abundance to give and receive even if your logical mind tells you not to. A smile of someone at a curb to give them money gives them union with you. It is free and it does help that soul to connect in a place that he or she matters. Don't shy away, but respond with a nod and smile, and say thank you in your heart for your creativity to do this work, for they are working very hard to receive a sacred union of you.

Mike: As you have stated that joy is in innocence, is the only way to get to joy through innocence?

Raphael: In finding how you are innocent, isn't that the riddle? Because you are told from the moment you are born that you are bad. You are created in original sin, you poor soul you. Then the riddle of joy and innocence is your great uncovering through your destiny. That is why it is hard to imagine that you are divinely whole and innocent. Because the gravity of sin is the heaviest of conditions to walk with. And you are all very heavy energetically. Those who really work in the idea of sin in your religions really want to work that even in buildings without windows because they do not want you to understand your light. Joy resonates when you start trusting your innocence. Many souls come in to have to work off some heavy cloaks of karma, so they do feel their depth of sin. But they also come in with the depth of strength to break through that karma and be free of that sin, pain, and suffering and to celebrate a union in joy, which could be your wonderful dog who gives you Absolute Love. It can be a tree that holds you when you need to rest. It can be the bubbling brook that offers you the nourishment to quest your thirst. Your journey out of sin is not your prosperity. Those who have more can be burdened with great sin. Many say, "Look at this man or woman without sin for they are so prosperous. You who have illness must have really sinned somehow. For your illness is the reason for your sin." Those are not true at all. What you have created in the choice of this life and show up for is an inner destiny that makes your creativity problem solve how you are innocent, and how in the innocence you can bring joy. You judge a journey, for it might not equate to your conditioning of a life that looks joyful.

Many on social media love to post their pictures of joyful encounters, yes? But that picture does not speak to the depth of you in sacred union with yourself and another. It shows an idea you manifested and as you do that, those who find the depth of

Chapter 9 - Abundance

connection will always solve the riddle of their innocence and joy. You can live alone and have great union with everything around you, be in total joy, and understand your innocence. You can live in a bush and have great connection with the giving and receiving of the elements and of all those you participate with. You can find in that simplicity of your creative experience that you have joy in having a breath and quenching your thirst. If your gratitude in that moment grounds you to your divine essence of abundance, you will connect in a safe way to your destiny. That pivotal piece will move you to your next creative experience. Your machines make you have experiences that you never thought were possible. Travel and conversations all over your globe. But are you in the depth of gratitude in this ability of you to connect in the abundance of the moment. This depth of connection of abundance, gives you joy.

Elizabeth: Will the shift that we all feel is coming with the global economic reset bring abundance to all and not just the US, and will it include the trees and everything else?

Raphael: Yes, that is what the collective desires. It is an organic bubbling of the elements expressing to you the divine creator how abundant you are. It is a movement that is very physical, emotional, elemental, and spiritual. That is why it is organic because it is the reinvestment of your heart, of your mind, of your soul, and of your body to know and trust that you are not playing the haves against the have nots as a collective. But the movement allows all to be prosperous. There is so much more here that is available to you in this way. As you hold your Divine truth in abundance, you allow Mother Earth to be more abundant. You all prosper. It is all for one and one for all through prosperity and abundance. That glows in the choir of all your souls to know that you have all that you need, want, and desire, and that you are complete, thus whole and innocent. It is happening. Forces around the world will try to take away that paradigm. It is the way you must digest and release the excess beliefs, and really come back to the union you all desire. Abundance is so much more than wealth; it is a union. It is the moment of knowing all is possible because you are the Divine Creator of your now.

Mike: This is going to sound selfish and personal, but I think it may apply to all. Transitioning of living in society and being in the box of what society allows, I want to use the gift that I think I came here to do. Keeping the faith and hope that by coming out of the box and trusting that you can be supported in this society; can you speak to that?

Raphael: Everything is working for your abundance and joy. We celebrate and serve the tune of your pure note as we dance in an extension of the highest and best for you. The fabric woven into this placement of now in your landscape is a path of your need to be right. Who is right and what is right? You are all rewriting the story and so what could be has changed. Rightness going into righteousness will be humanities downfall. For not one person can claim that they know all that is right with another or the world around them. Right is a need to feel safe in a world that is changing drastically. What you envision five years ago is much different than what is now and what is now will be different from what you will have five years from now. You are all touching a virtual screen that changes reality on a quantum level. You feel this because you are going into vision and communicating beyond what the form can do, and your value is no longer how long the

Chapter 9 - Abundance

form can work as in the industrial age, but it is on how you can support your environment twenty-four seven.

Every moment there is great change in your now, and this is why you have a need to be right, for being right gives you a sense of safety. Yet every system changes. How often do you have to download a new operating system to your phones? You feel twisted like a pretzel and you are dancing to so many different needs just to feel right. Then, because of separation, righteousness slowly creeps in and allows the haves and have-nots to really camp in what is right. This is a time that brings the twisting of you into the deepest understanding and value of you. What is your truth now as you celebrate your love story and your joy? The experience of your reality changes what you are doing now with your gifts of love and joy to match what your value of being here is. Jobs that once held great value no longer exist and other jobs are put in its place. Believing that anything in your world can be permanent is no longer true. Your permanence is your love story and in sharing it there is permanence and because your expression is greater, the way you connect to make that job stable becomes the chains of true interaction and stability. Everything is coming from a vision that you don't understand at times. A company has a new vision and so you might now be obsolete. You feel you have fallen short of that great vision, yet you did not fall short, for in this time the gift of your purpose is even stronger than ever. Your mediums of communication are showing you every spectrum of creation of love stories to pain stories, to lack stories, and to victimhood. All this is out there. This is good for healing and good because once something is out there, the honest integrity of you in a discussion can be put forth.

So, yes, what might seem like a lower job because a company thought of you as obsolete can be the greatest gift to celebrate a new connection of your integrity and truth in sharing your love language. Temporary agencies are everywhere now as it is a new creation. Because things are changing rapidly, companies can only know a vision for their company for three to six months. They do not know how to project outward and so they keep all of you temporary, even if you are on their payroll. You feel that and in that you have a large force of connectedness with each other to say what can we do beyond the normal ways of finding work? People all around you are questioning this world of having to participate 24/7, to participate with each breath and showing your value to get a paycheck. You can no longer separate yourself from the needs of what is part of your value to maintain your needs. This feels scary but it is a great gift to shout out with free choice, and to make a collective of all of you and strengthen the collective in a world that is permanent, because you are all celebrating your love language. There are many ideas to come forth in exchanging value so that you are no longer beholding to one way of being and knowing your value. When something resonates very strongly and it brings great joy and smiles to you and others, connect in that. Seize that moment and move into that as an expression of you. It might have to start out as just a way of sharing. But eventually what you are needing is this permanence of knowing your needs are met.

Chapter 10

Love

To hold an identity is to hold a space of separation. In that space, you find the premise of lack of love. Once you identify a moment, person, or anything all of you holds that identity as a way of separating you from the whole, you from another, you from you, and eventually you from us. Awareness of self, as you've defined yourself, is a strength for the renewal of understanding constructs of conception, of theory, and of love. For your understanding of this great paradigm of love is one that is an identity that you shift in a space of truth for you, and not your truth.

Love is patient and kind. Love allows you to shine your light to heal the places where you hold an identity of lack. Yet, as humans, you are not patient in love. You push others and yourself to be in love. You make this journey of seeking love to be a motivation of identities of self. Are you kind with yourself, if you are not in love? Everything that you decorate your body with through such things as clothing, jewelry, tattoos, etc., says to you if you have love or not. The quest for love is an esoteric idea that you have broken down into a possessive identity. Love becomes the enchantment of possessions. For enchantment of the idea, and the identity, of unconditional Absolute Love is hard for you, who are in form with the ego's strength that bubbles through you, to hold even a moment of identity with.

You are all pop cans brimming tightly and ready to explode with all your ego identifications that prove, to yourself and others, that you are loved. This tightness around yourself that integrates anything else into your constrained understanding of love makes many explode. Explosions in your paradigm are not pretty, so you hold dearly to the belief of your ego realities of love. What we do is hold you so you can slowly evoke the knowledge, of the textures, of the smells, and of the whispers of the essence of unconditional Absolute Love. Throughout your beingness in duality, you have created love stories, poems, and songs in many descriptive ways to celebrate a union of unconditional love. These paradigms of thought become the goal for your identity to match, but there is a lot of stress as an individual to match these big paradigms that you have put out as the true way to celebrate and to share unconditional love.

That is why most of you feel you have failed in love. This big failure makes you fight for survival instead of expanding you into the trust that it takes to absolutely be in love. Most humans have a hard time doing the work that you have done to understand what makes you hold you and others in a concept of love. To know love, you must fall into its essence and feel, know, see, or hear its beauty of giving you the knowledge of wholeness. How far does one trust him or herself to fall into a principal that is not understood but motivates expansion in all of you to become stronger? Love is a principle you must create a relationship with and fully explore within your own identity , and realize that there is a lot more to it.

Think about the pop can and like a baby it is new and not shaken too much. You help to hold that baby with softness. You don't rattle its interior space. You accept and allow that being that is innocent and new to become and grow without you shaking its

Chapter 10 - Love

awareness of how it should love or not. As this little being grows, you, the divine parent and source of knowledge, create behaviors for you and then for others around conditions of identities of what is lovable and what is not. The kid, who is extremely busy and cannot sit for the teacher, is labeled as unlovable. What if a kid decides that it likes nighttime and not daytime? As a baby, you allow them to sleep. But, as they progress in needing to follow your rules of living when it is light outside, it is thought of as not optimal, and you give the child direction that might not be patient and kind. You shape that soul more, and through the beautiful integrals of growing, you have learned what shakes you and shows what makes you lovable and what makes you not. This can go against every fiber of who you came in as a soul. Then you shake these contents through your emotional, mental, spiritual, and soul awareness. You shake them in stress, because you know you came to be something that your dear mom is not. You hear that that is a sin, yes? You hear that you are not honoring this beautiful soul, yet you know that you are trying to love in the way you came into love, and not the way you have been shaken energetically, emotionally, and mentally to love. Each of you are under high pressure in a human form. You can explode at any moment. Your ego world loves this because it can then prove that you are unlovable; you exploded. You have now become a terrorist or harmful to yourself and to others. The science of vibration would have said that you will explode, all because of a paradigm of how you have chosen now to celebrate love.

Your reality is so conditioned and controlled that you must explode if you have come to show a new paradigm. This explosion might not be like throwing up all over your parents. This explosion might be a journey into addiction and self-medication; it might be to defy all reality in a way that allows you to become a whole new name. This identity of you will explode. You have all done things that made others question your sanity, yes? In humanness, you just want survival, so you do not want to explode. You want to keep moving on but the more you move on and you have the awareness that you can't do the human equation of love the way it was set out for you, you will explode. For all of you have come in to show us, and the world around you, a way of celebrating Absolute Love. This is all part of your destinies to come in and celebrate Absolute Love.

Can you understand why you are in an explosive time? You have slowly been shaken in this current timeframe. It makes people feel that they are beholden to an identity others have given them, or that they have found themselves in the pages of a screen, yep, that is me and that is my identity.

Be careful when you label, because it takes you into a space that you must then be loyal to. Being loyal to a label of an identity that holds an ego story will only make you live in survival mode. Therefore, you all just survive. You have spectrums of people who are enlightened and know how to be above the survival march. You are always at war with how much you will be shaken if you don't do the ego identity. None of you want to explode, but you must. To go through understanding that egoic love is survival love to the expansive light of unconditional love, you must hold patience and you must be kind.

The world is not woven in any equation, for the ego has no equation to make you safe. As we hug and whisper to you, we help you to not be shaken. We give you the balance and the grounding to walk and talk in duality, and to hold grace under fire. We help you to be more in light, and the more light you hold, the less you are shaken by any events, identities, or by any pain and suffering. Even in love it can shake you, because once you

Chapter 10 - Love

believe that is the only way you are loved, it becomes quite a burden, yes? When you are not shaken, the ego cannot sway you and point fingers at you because you are not exploding but instead celebrating and enjoying all moments of your beingness with love.

You are under pressure, and it is hard to believe in love when this happens. We all get that. We see you white knuckling each day not to fall into the trenches of pressure. Remember that when you are under pressure, it is part of a hybrid engine that you hold within your heart in a way of motivating you to an experience to see how you hold love. Do you hold love as if you are always lacking in love, or do you hold love as if you are truly part of the divine wholeness? When you are under pressure, it is hard, so I do know what you would say, but do you know the moment I am yelling at my kid for not cleaning up their room as I asked them to, that this pressure to have others be on time with my needs to make things look so right that I prove to others and myself that I do this for love? I would say, "Yes, I see your strength and your loyalty in bringing in a commitment of staying true to your space and have others stay true to their space." This loyalty says I love you to your child, yes? In that space of saying I love you, as you pull yourself back from yelling, are you being patient and are you being kind?

But is it because you want your will to be done. You saw that room as messy and you gave a limit and it didn't happen, and you exploded; then that is lack of love. That is saying to yourself and your child, I can only love you if you can dance through my conditions. Only you can answer these questions. In that, there is no judgement. Do not be hard on yourself for whatever way you have decided that the moment was an issue. Your life is not a Hallmark card. You have memories of celebrating your ideas of love and you post them all over on your social media. This does not mean that you are living a life of love. Let's be honest if we can, because under pressure, which you all are by being born into duality, you will fight to just survive. In survival, love is conditional. It must be. You have lost the glorious connection of truly knowing wholeness. The ego can never take away your memories of Absolute Love. You are created and woven in Absolute Love. That cannot be taken away from you.

When you hold each moment in the celebration of how you must come into your remembrance of love to expand it, you will find that your memories that you do show on all your social media will ripple to everyone the remembrance of Absolute Love. This is the gloriousness of your social media right now. You can really ripple the divine principles of spirit. It helps you to get out of your bubble in your pop can so to speak. Don't be afraid to explode in joy, laughter, and celebrating your remembrance of Absolute Love. Be kind to others as they explode and be kind to yourselves, for your selfcare is the most critical piece in being grounded and balanced.

You beautiful souls who say yes to moving all the walls, and dynamic energies of fear, and came to trust in something more of the glorious space of love will disappear any boundaries that separate you from the active celebration of having joy in your life.

As we draw in the remembrance of Absolute Love, let all your cells be nourished by the simple reality of *Love Is*. To ground into love is to accept that you are fully created in love. Love is a word full of mystery, mystic, intrigue, and impulses of connecting the electric essence of your Holy Spirit. Love is always woven into all you do for love is your oneship of knowing that you are in the creation of the holy Absolute Love of your father.

Chapter 10 - Love

Passion and love create spectrums of pain and duality within your space of now. Passion ignites placements of your divine pattern to be whole and manifested in your now. Identification of self in love is the quest that brings you here repeatedly. This quest to identify you as Absolute Love is a journey of remembering you, the creator, in a space that shouts to you to remember you are the creator for you in the illusion. Once you see yourself as Absolute Love, then you magnetize the space of oneness with your holy father and mother and with source of creation.

Hearts of love connect with one another, bringing particles together to create reactions of feeling, of knowing, and of believing that you are connecting to you and peace in all there is.

Words shout, words whisper, and words hold you to us. Words are your mechanism to share what you see, what you know, what you feel, and what you hear. Words allow the expansion of you to be everywhere. Words ripple, creating currents of highs and lows. Your ability to understand the power of words and to use those words in the highest vibrational frequency allows you to tame the logical mind of duality, to gift calmness, and gives you the strength to reach beyond the physical placement and to ask; as you ask you shall receive.

The beauty of your mind's eye allows your holy creations to become a pattern for purpose and to project that pattern of purpose to the landscape around you. Much of your mind is held in connection with your soul and your spirit, creating a wonderful vibrational highway that connects you to all realities, souls, and you. Traveling in this vibrational highway requires you to take the leap of faith from your logical mind, step into your imagination, and accept that all realities are happening now. Go into this space with a bubble of love and the mysteries and answers you seek shall be known to you. If you go into this world on this highway with a bubble of fear, the distortions that cause people in your world to go crazy can happen. For in this highway of all that is now, what you seek will be magnetized consciously and unconsciously as you journey to this space. Your mind is connected to eternity yet getting there takes practice and partnership, especially with the Holy Spirit. This brings you to a place of remembering the source of laws that you hide in pain and pleasure. The source of separation is the dark mass that you must acknowledge and know to forgive in every placement of your reality. You do not look upon any space with lack but you see creations, the reactions, and the dance of love.

Connections are the greatest high of all. This high is eternal and is never lost. There is no mistaking those moments when you connect to these highs for its remembrance heals your doubt of you and makes you continue to reach to be fully in that high. Each layer, thought, and feeling of your story has been complicated in understanding the simplicity of love. You create such amazing complicated systems that excite your every moment. You are the most pivotal anchor of all expressions. You are so complicated to yourself that it is hard to understand that life in love is simple. Each moment places you in a divine decision to see, feel, hear, and know love. This placement of love can hold much discouragement for the dance of duality needs the expression of highs with pleasure and the lows with pain. If you choose to love simply to be at peace and hold calm within your hearts, you take yourself out of the game of giving and receiving pain and pleasure. You, who strive and need connection, then feel betrayed by something each lifetime that you quest for. This betrayal in love makes you slowly share stories of pain and pleasure. Notice within your day how you like and love yourself when you are in a space of love in your heart and calmness in your mind.

We want you to know that you are not betrayed by love that has created you, love that you are right now, and love that you will grow into in each holy moment you choose that love. The connection of love creates its own magnifying effect that brings true friends and true holy spaces to you. You will then know that you have never been alone. You will see the truth of family that you quest for. You will understand the abundance that is yours for in love, giving and receiving, is not a catching game but gifts that strengthen all in their unity of their connection of love.

Taking time throughout your day to register within your logical mind that this is love rewires that beautiful logical brain. Do you take time to say I am love? Do you take time to introduce yourself as love? Hi, I am love, and so are you. How wonderful to share this love? I extend this to you to do as you see people with a smile and as you smile, think to yourself, *I am love and so are you.* Celebrate you so I celebrate me in the simplicity of love, and when you look into someone's eyes as you smile and say I am love, the ones who twinkle back are your family and they will help weave this grand momentum that allows your logical mind to really see that love is participating in your now. If you can see that in your logical mind that this love that you thought betrayed you is participating with you throughout your day, you will settle deeper into your grounding of love and that grounding of love harmonizes with your beautiful Mother Earth as a gift of loving you and in loving you she shares all that she has with you. Her sources of nourishment are given unconditionally. She pours all of her to you to honor that you have come to partnership with her to build structures, to build temples, and to build beauty.

Knowing how grounded you are in love, that flow to her will help to bring forth more abundance that she is creating for you so the belief that you have no water will allow water to show up some place; for no matter is destroyed in this world of yours, it just changes form. In the gift of your love to this beautiful partner of elemental joy, it can create for you your desires to hold your physical form in the purist placement of you. The gift of sharing connections in true love unites all particles. Uniting particles creates a wholeness of you bringing you into your full power, your full power that you have felt has been scattered beyond any hope to reclaim. Imagine a world that holds your wholeness powered by your truth and Absolute Love. Harness the space that will be, for imagination is the divine blueprint of your sacred truth.

Love has no beginning or end. Love is the constant that all is from. Love's wholeness holds no barriers to you or another because love is within each placement that you seek. Love is a strength that must be yearned for. Love comes to you when you undress your identity and stand naked before yourself to recognize that yes; you, Dear Ones, are Love. The placement of you bringing this love is the greatest triumph of freedom out of pain. Your love brought us to you. Your love, from source, brought us to connect you back to your home that is eternal. We whisper delightful gifts of your love back to you to awaken you now to the vibrant being that you are, so you can flourish in our arms to walk in love always.

Hearts are profound within your holy temple, for your heart is the beat that allows you all to create magnetic understandings of your truth. Your hearts unite in music with the placement of all your notes to unfold great compositions in being the master of love that you are.

Chapter 10 - Love

Words have such power that even a trivial moment makes a dent in your reflection back to you. Nonverbal communication, through the gift of your intuition, to read between the lines of what your holy temple can absorb makes you want to connect and communicate to be a whole unit of a wonderful body of joy. Celebrate your awareness of your choice, and anchor yourself in the undressing of your identity of pain and vulnerability. Shout that you are the image of love. In this love that you are, it protects you in every breath that you take. Through communication, connection, and the curious mind that you have through your willingness to say, "what if," is the strength of your mind using your third eye. Your mind is the sand that honors the waves of the ocean. Your mind is the sand that honors the waves of the beauty of your third eye to see you, Dear Ones, in a place of strength and in a place of anchoring in love. Your vision is a truth yet you allow that vision to be engraved by your mind, and to feel the crashing of your mind upon the vision that will get you home safely. For the mind holds its division, and within that division, there is lack. The mind battles the holy vision looking for truth and safety. The divided mind will always be a mystery and, in that division, there is always your chance to have decision remorse. From a vision that is whole in your love, the mind then becomes the divine blueprint for you to build permanence and for you to build decisions that are true. When you have a vision, allow the mind to be waves that bring your divine vision to action. Watch the mind coalesce around the ideas in your vision to create the magnetic force for these truths to be in your world. The mind is power beyond comprehension yet you ask the mind to comprehend a place for duality where your brain can fight information that is your truth to behold. In the mind, your spirit is one, and imagination tickles your brain to allow the ideas a container for your holy temple, and to move into the oneness in that imagination.

We are holding you so you can integrate the depth of your truth into all cells of your reality. For in each cell, there is a microcosmic awareness of you. You are orchestrating multitudes of creations within your physical form. There is a lot that is done on an unconscious awareness for you have outsourced all your cells out to a part of your mind. Also, you are creating with every nuance of thought that is around you. These thoughts impress upon your microcosmic awareness of your cells. You childproof these thoughts that come in. You look to make them safe, yet do you make yourself safe? No, you give space to just create from not to be safe. Are you policing every cell in your body? No; you have given it to a space that you recognize is helping to orchestrate and compose you in this physical reality.

What wonderment one cell holds. What divine placement that the one cell is expressing at this moment for you. Your cell knows exactly how to be. Its joy to express the vitality of you is inherent. Your mind somehow believes that that cell does not understand its mission. And when I say your mind, I am talking about your brain holding the conscious duality of left and right hemispheres. The mind of source knows that cell's perfection. The mind of source knows your perfection. Duality in its own essence when things become divided creates the need to worry about your creations in front of you. In this worry, your mind still holds the wholeness of that cell but the programming of the right and left hemispheres through a split reality creates the scenario whether that cell is right or wrong. The heaviness of the placement of separation and being split creates disease within everything you create. Your conscious mind is always double guessing whether it is right or wrong, is it love or is it hate, and is it dark or is it light.

Chapter 10 - Love

This programming of the split mind then becomes a conscious pattern that overlays your cells. In the mind, the more you home into belief, the more you own that belief, and the more you are that belief. That belief then becomes a pattern that overlays the perfection of the cell, and that overlays the perfection of your mind connected with the mind of love. That overlaying of the cell becomes its memory that its creation starts weaving from.

Water is an incredible element on this planet. The gift of water is that it is programmable to your thoughts. What a gift holy water is, and in all sacred temples, water is holy, because it is programmable. Your cells have holy water, yet they are programmed by the weaving of your thoughts within your split mind. These programs are what your body moves through and they become part of an automatic process that then is orchestrated within your form. The gift of water is that it is programmable and we are here whispering into the water of every cell within your being that love is the truth, love is the answer of wellness, and love does conquer all. This is not cliché language or flowery wording to romance your duality thinking to accept the truth. Programming yourself back to love is the quest that you do. The story is and has always been about you, and when you accept the negative programming, you have given your rights to your story to the duality split mind that you call the ego. The ego is an energy placement that you created. You have such guilt, shame, and decision remorse of losing your full connection in loves eternal embrace of Absolute Love. Again, another mystery that the duality mind cannot behold is this Absolute Love because in Absolute Love there is no division.

You are undercover detectives of love. How amazing that even in this busy and complicated world of yours, you know that subconsciously we tickle you. You hear faint whispers, surely, but you do hear, you do know, and you do have that vision of us, and your heart yearns to be safe with us. Each one of you has been gifted a guardian angel that never leaves your space. This holy present is from source to you so you will know that no matter what, you are part of Absolute Love. You are made in that image of love. Being reprogrammed is what you are doing now.

Now in your landscape you have been gifted to yourself the elements of the planets, which are aligning to bring you out the great density of darkness and open to the communication of love. Again, you give yourself great passageways to find the joy of being the source of love that you are.

The three wise men that came to you are the gifts that life in, and through, love is laughter. Laughter is a profound way to reprogram your holy temple of water. Laugh at yourself. Laugh at the gifts of you. Your brain cannot decipher between false laughter and real laughter. Amazing, isn't it, that the love energy of the elves gives you the joy to hold love in a cell and it knows its creation to you is youth, vitality, and breaking patterns of pain that are in you. Laughter then is a way to be brave as you stare yourself down when you are holding fear for it is a reality in this world that the landscape here holds fear. You came as the son or the daughter of source to bring light to darkness and you all are bringing light to the darkness of your time. During the holidays you put lights everywhere celebrating that you can alight and sing your holy song in communion, in connection, and in conversation with another. You bring presents to others but is that present really you? I suggest that you truly bring you to this time as you share your light, laughter, and love and bring you as the holy temple of sacred oneness. This gift of bringing you as a sacred being of source also reprograms your cells. It programs you to create and know that your creation is good. It allows the dance with the left and right hemisphere of your brain to join in harmony so that your blueprint of you, and the visions that you see, can come to be. You are in complete control of bringing forth renewal, light, and love to every aspect of yourself.

We are helping you as you choose to be reprogrammed back to love, to hold that space so only love becomes the cause and effect of your world. Moments of joy, moments of oneness, and moments of being totally safe anchor you back into this holy temple that you are here to fully engage in. At first, these moments seem elusive. We know this, so we sprinkle you more with these moments because you yearn for home that is deeper than any placement of your now. We know that a holy moment in absolute remembrance of Absolute Love will heal every identity that does not match your perfection. Your gift to us is asking us to bring laughter to your life, to bring magic to your heart, and to bring vision of more to your mind. We engage with each other; you and me together. As you soften you allow us to sink in deeper, creating a heart that matches all. If you do not soften, your circular energy takes what we do into cycles of patterns, then history repeats itself. Softening to us allows the circular pattern within your dual mind to soften in and create a crevice of hope and a crevice forming a heart of something more. And we hug deeper and deeper into that space to allow all of you to be one heart and to be the gift of the heart that you truly are. Once you are that one heart, that heart becomes wings and you then are fulfilling your passion as you wrap those wings around yourself and others allowing them a great space to soften. In that softening, the elixir of forgiveness enters the hard surface of the dance of history and patterns repeating themselves. As an Earth Angel, your wings and heart are a mighty force to awaken and break the bonds of duality and pain, to break free and honor the safety of connection and not separation, and to hold another and give them the placement to take the plunge into their mastery of love. Be an Earth Angel. As we are with you, you are with us. Be in the choir of Angels and sing love in every facet of your being. Together love is assured, and you are anchored always in the home of Absolute Love.

Through the heart we recognize aspects of us participating in fields of color. Hearts resound to harmonize and blend the full energy of man, spirit, and love that is not separated but cherished in pieces connecting to the whole. There is no separation from a heart space. The true hearts connection finds no boundaries. There are no identities but one. The heart, which is your motor, encourages you to live in an identity that is your holy temple, and move in grace to honor all sacred spaces that you occupy and to reflect and project the essence of you, your love, and your wholeness to other hearts that come to play before you.

Love is an abstract understanding, for your reality holds spaces between spaces and makes love a program that must sift through boundaries to unite and to blend and see your truth of you in the truth of another. Experience within your heart gives you the full awareness to awaken into your totality of love that you are and provides the full spectrum of love to be known so that love is not abstract but a hands-on heartfelt dance that allowed you to be fully in your life, your body, and to be in every decision that you make right now whether consciously or not.

The heart is the motor saying, "Yes you are love, you are feeling, you are emotion, and you are your past and present." How divine and sacred to hear, to feel and to know you are one in you.

I connect with you right now through communication. I, Archangel Raphael, hold the strings of your needs, your wants, and your hopes, weaving them together in a tapestry of communication. I affect you as you affect my communication with you right now. I do not have one pure message. I translate for you the messages that you brought to be heard today. I become your hologram to hear what you needed to hear, to feel what you needed to feel, and to know what you needed to know. Your future is a part of this tapestry that we are weaving right now. Your past is also part of these beautiful threads that are all woven to you and me. A divine message came through each of you today. This holy placement creates communication. I honor you with great gratitude that you have felt your right placement to be here with me. In this gift, you are woven anew. Choosing to step beyond what is rational, what is scientific, and to move into a space of extending you to hear, to feel, and to know words that are my joy and my honor to sing back to you. You called upon me and I resounded with a yes to celebrate you in this time of awakening, and in this time where boundaries are erased and you are given a nod to do what you love and create your heaven on Earth with all your needs and desires. I weave this tapestry to communicate on every level with you that you are safe to journey into unknown territory and take some risks this year. Risk what has been but a dream of an adventure, or a dream of someone else; we just say yes. I hold the net of grace, and as you move, so do I because energetically, we connect. Many risks are felt and then you must see it to really believe that you can do it. The vision quest that you are on becomes a push within you to not become complacent, but to extend you in your true wholeness of what you came to share.

Vision, whether internal or external, propels your energy to move your body. A child sees a toy it wants that is just out the child's reach. That vision of that toy propels that beautiful soul to take a big leap and move the holy temple of its body from a place that it has been to a new awareness. A movement in vision for you is very related. Be considerate in what you see. Look in your mind's eye. Does what you see in your landscape connect to the visions of what you hold about you? Do you see yourself on a beach with no worries in the world? It feels so good to be on that beach but outside of yourself you are under a blanket, shivering. Those extremes make you believe that the vision of you on that beach is not for you. That vision becomes a pipedream that is easy to dissolves easily. Yet there is a place in you that, when you look at that dream, you recognize that it speaks to you about your sacred placement and at this time those sacred placements of you are becoming more real. The more you think of that holy placement, during this year especially, it will allow you to step further into it. Vision is critical in understanding that you deserve the dreams of your inside to be carried to the outside. You can project your internal vision outside of you. Your beautiful child had a toy in front of him, that he could just reach out to move it. So too, spirit places your toy right in front of you to make you move. To question if you deserve those toys sabotages your movement. Children are innocent so to speak. They say, "I see, I want, and I get." Adults are vision controlled, so you don't get to have what you see and want. This allows all the levels of ego to play out. Yet you are so creative that you can become, once again, that child and know that spirit gives you a vision to move forward into having. The equation is still simply within the vision. The movement of your mind with the self-talk is to clear away paths so then like a child's mind, your mind says I want that, and it does receive.

It is extremely hard once a program is within your mind to remove it. The gift of erasing these sabotaging thoughts you have

Chapter 10 - Love

will slowly move the conditioned and safe part of you, and release it so you can see that your heart is engaged in that step and it says "Yes, there is a home that I am ready to buy." Your rational mind says that you do not have the financing for it, and you will have to get another job. Your heart says that you love that house, and you see yourself living there. Spirit shows you that the house is fine. Let go of the bottom line; the buts, can't, won't, and seeing that spirit indeed wants me there. I feel my highest awakening there and I connect with the crown of me to the totality of spirit to help me achieve the goal of my desires and what spirit has given a nod to.

Connection is always there so, again, like love it becomes abstract. In the rational mind you must make connections part of a ritual, and in that, there is a feeling that you can trust this connection that is and always has been you. Walking and feeling one with nature, prayers, singing, cooking, cleaning, and watching people all help you connect. Your awareness of a connection, which is through the ethereal field above your physical form, is an energetic blueprint of you. Connection to spirit in the etheric field produces goose bumps so you know then that the energy around you is activated. When you feel this, there is a power that coalesces around you stating you have powers beyond, and you do. Finding ways to really hold your electricity creates movement of negativity or anything that would hinder the ability to have what you want. Connection is power beyond you in form. It is an energy that once tapped into cannot be controlled, for you know the mastery of the spiritual connection. It is your sixth sense. It gives you exponential ways of living. That is why it has been hidden so long. For humanities fear to really own this field of spirit can be overcome and creates the beauty of heaven. And yes, there are many ways black magic plays too, for this field around you is connected to your higher self, and if you dilute your holy self the ego will, and has, created what you call evil to participate in your field. Many religions worry about how to control your power. To be fully in you is to understand your freedom. Your freedom of movement, of choice, and your freedom to create.

As you look at you at this year, you will find more meaning to your freedom that before you might not have seen. To love yourself is to accept your power and celebrate the freedom it provides you, knowing you would never hurt others, and that you are here freely to share your message of love. Never sacrifice your freedom, for it is the gift of how you were created. In this freedom, the first place to look and connect is that physical place of you. Find how you feel fully in you. What is right when you are fully in you and then you make choices from that placement? In a physical awareness, it is easy to look at your parts, and to assess those parts for the good or the bad. Do they fit or not? Yet your parts are all one in the energy field and everyone reads that first, so even if you are in a crowd and shy, if you go in with the acknowledgment that you are fully in the yes of being here right now within this crowd, all who are around you will acknowledge that yes. They will see your yes and not your parts. Parts get to be stories of discussion that trip up how you connect with us and others. Reinventing loving yourself is saying "Yes, I am in my body wherever it is right now. Yes, I am here in this body and I thank you for you are giving me a holy awareness of my breaths and my movement as I celebrate my love."

The next awareness is emotionally. Be attuned to your emotional field just like you would attune to a choir, listen to the note that you are all on to celebrate together. Listen and attune to your emotions; if someone next to you arouses fear, understand how you protect your emotional field because in a world filled

Chapter 10 - Love

with many holy temples, you are always protecting your emotional field. To be totally honest and vulnerable with every emotion that filters through your field, which moves your energy to really share all your emotions, you would end up alone, for your world wants and needs everything to act in a specific tone.

Energy, this vibrational currency, pulses and adding the liquid of emotion makes it heard, felt, and moves it. And if you are all the same you are safe. How dare anyone say they are sad? When you walk the streets, you are supposed to smile and numb your awareness that you might have to sugarcoat words or emotions that might need to be said. But to go outside the small spectrum of how you are to share your emotions can cause you to feel that you are a walking ghost, because the mass conscious rules, at this time, that everyone is supposed to play nicely so as not to ruffle anybody's feathers. You are ruffling what? Their emotions, right? You are supposed to pet each other and withhold truths and then somehow take them on for yourself to weigh you down. When you take other's emotions, it weighs you down because that may not be your true knowing. How amazing your world is set up to only play a child's piano of twelve notes. If you stay here, you will get through life without any pain. Most at this moment cannot fit on this little spectrum emotionally so, if they do not there is a way that it needs to be regulated.

This is changing. There are many new methods for people to celebrate their truths in their emotions and to be able to widen a spectrum of motion. Emotion, when you are happy or sad, moves you. To deaden your emotions and visions is to deaden your movements. Yet as the creators and spirit that you are, you need to move. You must change, evolve, share, grow, delight, and play. The norms that have been restricted are being stopped all over, and some emotion is harsh, but it is shattering a mass conscious belief to keep you under a spell. For if you are truly in love with yourself and genuinely happy, that is all you resonate with and then there is no need to childproof your freedom.

Your mind is eternal, and vast. Duality placed, in your physical reality, left and right hemispheres for you to gather and to access information and to create space to make meaning out of information in a logical manner. Accessible and analytical information that has data to support or oppose becomes tools of fear. More data makes you have less freedom of what your mind's eye can really believe going forward. And this collection of data is only wonderful for a moment. For all data is a moving target just as all of you are. What you believe today can change tomorrow. What you feel is the most important placement can change. And so, the ego wants only to give you tidbits of information to keep you under its spell. Those of you that seek beyond this data of being under the "human radar" of existence feel your world could be threatened from an outside source.

Originality in love is never threatened, and this is the time to be original and give yourself that quality of really being under the true management of your mind and to examine who you are when you believe a story you're told, or when you accept what everyone else is saying. The vision of you in your mind's eye knows when you lessen your power of you. There is so much thrown into your sphere of information that it is hard for any one person to really look and say, "What do I truly want to wrap my love around in belief?" This time of reinvesting in your beliefs from a pure love energy will move these souls that keep coming in who are so ready to be part of an experience of understanding love. Many souls come in because the filters of how you present are lessening. People are fighting to maintain structures, but these structures are changing and the belief of how you go to school, how you get paid, and how you live are actively revamped.

You, as a collective, have said yes to be fully in your body at this time, and to make a stance that you do not need any childproofing to have your freedom of choice in love. Standing out and claiming freedom is true terrorism on the ego system. To be fully you is a program that the ego cannot let you have, because if one can do it, so can another. If you gather into your awareness that others are doing it, it creates exponential movement. It is just like a video going viral overnight. Energetically, you—in your full power—will create an economy to change overnight. This gift amps up the playing field so mastery is especially important. But you are already masters in knowing yourself. You have played different stages of awareness by taking on different parts to see if you really like that placement of you or not. But you are already masters because you would not have come at this time to be part of this true freedom that being one in spirit is. Spiritually, your connection can come from any place because it is everywhere. Where isn't your energy located? If all of this is about you and is created with you, from you, and to you—it is all still here. You extend an invitation to participate with yourself. How fun right? Are you afraid of yourself? If not, then this awareness of connection becomes a coming out party of knowing the full spectrum of you.

All of you now participate in fighting for freedom. This call to connect fully in mind, spirit, emotional, and physical ways was an easy yes for you because freedom is worth participating in. Alignment of love within freedom exponentially generates the power to create beyond you and to be here saying yes to all of you. Acts of yes make freedom stronger. I say yes. I own my love of yes and in that, I celebrate your yes for we are not in competition or separate. But we are strong enough to move reality for ourselves and others, and to feel their highest yes of love. You will feel as you start saying yes that you love to smile and see others smile with you, or you love to sing in the shower and feel your full power. Yes, you love to go on a road trip and see unknown places and know that you are safe, for you are connected beyond to such love. Yes, you are ready to do your own business because you believe in yourself. You are ready. Say yes to drinking more water, knowing that your body hums easier with your emotions. You say yes to clothes that bring more of you outward. You say yes to rolling on the grass and giggling with the great arms of Mother Earth. In saying yes, you fully take on that power of knowing that you can hold the love of that field. Responsibility of saying yes to what you love is not heavy, but it is joy of cultivating other yesses. Shouldn't being happy make everything else lighter? When you are fully aware, that is what saying yes is.

This is a great year to look at those three physical fields around you: your emotional field, your mental field, and your spiritual field. Find out how you are already saying yes and, in that place, step out, step over, and side step a doubt that might make you say no. Kind of say, "Whoa, I am ready to say yes to the delight of sharing my love."

You all hold the space to come here and journey on a sacred path, which is at times difficult. Love, that many cannot remember, is incredibly veiled in your world and beyond any words that I could put forth. Love through the connectors of grace of tolerance, compassion, and saying, "Yes, this is me and I am here to raise my hand and connect deeper than ever before."

You all are on this journey in this lifetime to complete your heart essence in love. Love is the healer. You all hold this great healing capacity of love. You raised your hands many times to say, "I will be on this planet, or another planet, to share my love story."

Yes, there are many detours of humanity. The smoke and mirrors presented to you are always amazing, aren't they? Creation in duality can and will change in a moment, and that is hard because you journey with many truths of eternity that are absolute. Yet the human fabric, the human design, is not absolute. You wish it was and you would like others to participate with you in absolutes, with continuity and consistency. Yet they are different each time they enter your awareness. Love acknowledges that a journey has many ways to show up and become accountable. Your expression allows the freedom for others to know that they come from love too. All is love and you hold that acknowledgement deep within you, and that awareness will create flow and synergy and essences of joy within places of chaos, for love knows how to forgive. In creation as things come before you, by using forgiveness, it can be a truth in recognition that you are one, you are more together, or that you are all on the same team. Your team unites to sing your holiest songs. Many have and will share in darkness to learn some self-forgiveness and to forgive that creation is the eternal experience of knowing that you are a messenger of love.

In your world, duality creates great havoc amongst you, and this havoc is easy to become a part of. Do not feel bad that you become entangled with places that seem wrong or feel unjust. This is a priceless experience, when you are there, for all of humanity to crack through that shell of imprisonment and to remember that you are vulnerable and you are all scared, for everything is temporary and you do much just to take your breath. If you see how you are surviving, acknowledge that you're playing and that you are participating in something grand. In that self-acceptance a new awareness will happen. It might not feel like it at first because the heaviness of this dual form requires much to let light in, but it will happen and you have already been a masterful space of love.

Many of you have already journeyed in spiritual placements within humanity throughout time while sharing wisdom, connection, and love. You are here again this time in your existence, and it is the time for many to shed various skins, to feel light more than ever before, hold love deeper, and truly connect in journey with each other.

Right now, you are all feeling the salad bowl effect. Humanity feels like it is a giant salad bowl, let's say, and it is spun, cleaned, and energized. Chaos, in that spinning, feels like it is ruling many points of your placements, your structures, and of you.

When you feel a spinning motion know that you are being cleansed deeply of all guilt that you hold in conscious or subconscious mind. For guilt does not serve you. Guilt is a fuel that sabotages. We are holding the sides of this bowl, acknowledging the harsh realities of your daily awareness. In that spinning, you will see more earthquakes for the Earth is spinning too. We are spinning to create greater vibrational energy to lift you into awareness beyond just form. You will see more earthquakes and more wars for all of humanity is in the salad bowl attacking and feeling the force within and feeling the war of that force within their will be done.

It is not that we are taking your free will, but we invite others to give and take, to share, celebrate, and enjoy in love and peace. This celebration of connection will happen. You are here, holding that depth of structure, weaving it like a beautiful, sacred web paralleling the grace of all heartstrings, strumming humanities harp of glorious notes to create anew. The spinning salad bowl will eventually relax, which will take many years. For some, though, this will take a few hours or days because we are hugging you as you spin and you will be able to root back into this placement of holy beings who weave your destiny of grace with your Mother Earth, with yourself, and with the other beautiful planets and souls that are there to "Yes," the holiest hum of love.

We eternally thank you for helping to convert the fight, the pain, and the fear into the story, the holy memory that is and has already been the oneness of love, for as above, so below. And we thank you in raising your hand and acknowledging us in your journey to be a part of the humanity choir, singing beyond what you know today to eternally hold the highest essence that you truly are. We thank you eternally for you are one in us.

I have come to help paint in greater hues of life that you are participating in with your holy form. Your colors share your rainbow of awareness's and of love that create your purpose in your placement. The joy of all of you before us is recognizing that your total purpose together is the renewal of commitment in holding love for yourself and for each other. You have united with all that you are to celebrate love as a way of holding your space of you to others in their space of love. The dance of lights that you are is like the *Aurora Borealis*, celebrating that your light among all participates in an awareness that many can rejoice in to join in the dance of life in love. But to take the highest road, so to speak, in a place where the darkness roots is to trust in something greater than what your mind can comprehend. Many are called to be liberated in the freedom of just being love yet how you share your love can and will be perceived in a spectrum of do's and don'ts.

This conditioning of do's and don'ts creates a straitjacket of energy, which squishes your heart from fully engaging with another.

Celebrating, again, the gift of your heart is to release the straitjacket, right? The straitjacket provides on some level protection and definition for how you are here sharing your heart's space of being vulnerable. But eventually you must leave all constraints that inhibit your celebration in who you are and to totally trust that it will be received. Once you trust that you are guided; you are one, that you are the focus of love, then what you share, you will not be in fear. What you share will be wisdom to all around you for as you share love wisdom filters into spaces in your world for your world is more space than solid, yet for your definition, you like solid.

Vastness scares you so you create these energetic placements of a solid to help you like a toddler learning to walk. A toddler touches, creating the definition of what it means to be upright, independent, and trust their body and steps. What you have placed in solid is like that toddler touching and saying, "I am trying to walk in my own space and in me." Like that toddler, he leaves the furniture and walks in the space that to him is vast. As he walks he might fall and in falling the gift of renewal and standing and trying again is the trust that he was naturally born with, and the ability to stand upright and walk. In walking we feel alone as a toddler because it might begin by holding the furniture, then a parent holds his hands, and later the space is his to explore. For you this is true also.

Your straitjackets of definition and the way you create solid beliefs and refuse to budge is again your need to let go of the furniture slowly and find your way in the vast space that you are. You are not alone as you let go of some belief structures for we, all spirits of light, hold your hands and tread with you, helping you trust that you are safe on a journey in a world that has a lot of uncertainties to your rational mind. Trust that in the, "I don't know," the inspiration of your holiness will seek you to light the way. The eternal connection of your love is your heartstring that lights your way to your delightful home. As you journey, you build the trust that you are here now to relate love and love remembrance to others around you and, in that connection, you will find you can trust what you see, what you feel, what you hear, and what you know. Once you trust everything it becomes easier because you created you to summon the courage to find out all of you and the strength to know yourself intimately. Knowing you gives others permission to know themselves.

Like the toddler who walks and discovers his journey in the big landscape of a living room, you find yours in the big landscape of your community, of your family, and of the world. Once your foundation of trust is solid, and this does take time, when you let go of the straitjacket of definition that has been handed down, you will encounter crisis' or opportunities to find your true place of how you can build trust in this new idea that you are always one with the source that knows all

As you trust your placement you trust that you are here to be exactly who you decided to be, and you are a gift in the remembrance of love. As you trust more, the light that shines around you, which is like the light of a firefly in a jar, will gradually encompass throughout all the spaces of your physical form to your aura form and through the space to touch another. That light will then shine as your purpose of giving light to yourself and to others. Trusting that you are perfect love, and glowing to everything around you, creates opportunities to release your energetic straitjacket.

Yet it takes energy to break the bonds of what you constructed here into the freedom to fully expose you. Showing yourself is the great 'if' in enlightenment, awareness, and journey that you are here to do. The exposure is not to make you weak but give you strength that you trust the whole fabric of oneness, as it hugs you and others, and together that love holds the space in love to connect heaven, and the creations of you here. For heaven is love, all spaces are love, the joy of being hugged, and the expression of creating is the greatest motion that heaven is, that love is, and that oneness is. You will celebrate within you for your cells, your emotions, your mind, and—of course—your spirit will respond through that celebration, that sharing, and the love that you are. The willingness to imagine and participate in the creation of love reminds all that it is the place that connects you. Not fear, but love.

Mike: We talk about love all the time, but what is the spiritual realm's definition of love?

Raphael: Just to be. For you are Absolute Love. Words cannot define love. Love for you has definitions, but it is a force just to be. You fight being and the ego has made you want the grass to be greener. It is a personal exploration into your truth that you must undergo, and it will take you all your lifetimes to undergo this grand principle. It is a journey worth taking, and you do because you keep coming back. When it is complete, you are whole.

Elizabeth: Since love is all there is, how did the patriarchy take over and make love a weak or feminine thing?

Chapter 10 - Love

Raphael: Anyone that must win in survival will make love a weak or feminine thing. All great civilizations, whether matriarchal or patriarchal, have known that one way to usurp all your power of a human essence is to make one feel less than another and treat them with lack of love. They have to somehow prove that they are not enough, that they are a failure, and they are condemning you to make you wrong. Survival is the game in ego land and that survival quest can only work if you see the haves and the have-nots. Survival needs a winner and then an absolute ruler, yes? Then it gives you a place within the system, and that is why I ask you to question identity and your attachment to it.

Ideas of how one is loved and not loved has more of a stranglehold throughout time. As a child you might question something, whereas a young adult, if you have lived in a system that makes you feel like you are less than, you would not question it; you would just accept your role.

Civilizations become afraid when you start exploding with love. If your explosions are in love, and you start connecting with others who also believe the way you do, you can overturn that patriarchal system. That great system must have many soldiers who march to the orders that make you instantly feel you are wrong for having a new paradigm. Many civilizations that are small need each other to survive, yes? They celebrate their communities win in love. As the civilization gets bigger, it is easier to plant the seeds of why you are bad and I am good. You get creative on how you plant and control these seeds. Your whole system of laws control the seeds of telling someone that they are a felon because they broke the laws society decided to put into place and that makes them unlovable. Many raise their hands within the marching orders of that society to judge those souls as forever bad.

Once they believe this, through the Law of Attraction, they will continue to get that. You don't want to be them, so you create reasons to blame others to keep people in this conditioned space. The more you stay in a conditioned space of what society prescribes to as a way of them saying, "I love you and want to keep you safe," the more you will follow. It is like being a stay-at-home mom and making you feel like you will never be able to move from that. But they say that you must love them because society is keeping you safe. Maybe that beautiful housewife feels safe and loved and maybe she doesn't. The patriarchal world doesn't care because its paradigm of what is love usurps her truth and her remembrance of Absolute Love. In patriarchal societies, it is the overall belief in the system that makes it run effectively and you are slowly not believing in this system. That is when you start to have the fall of society. There is a tipping point where the ego can keep everyone together in the belief that this way of celebrating communal living is good. It builds up but then there comes a tipping point when you have too many people exploding and from the insides of that system with all the explosions, people lose faith in the bigger paradigm of that patriarchal society. At first you feel safe, so you are not going to do anything, but slowly people don't feel safe and the comfort zone has pressure, and that is what is happening in your world right now. No comfort zone is safe. You are all under pressure. The patriarchal society can no longer keep the people it needs to follow the marching orders to the patriarchal song of liberation in their sense of love.

You explode and start to question your identities of what truly love is. What wallpaper do you want to put on your skin to show yourself and others how you want to truly shine in the way you know that you came here to. You all wear dressings to share what you do and that creates a space of how you identify with the

Chapter 10 - Love

greater world around you. Once you are in a tipping point, which you are, the people at the top must up their game of controlled love, so everything you will hear is, "I am doing this for you." We need to stay together for each other. We need not to let anyone else in because we need to first take care of our county." The more you build walls, the more you hold the absence of love. The more you build love, the more fear and pressure enters your world, because society is saying you are wrong, which creates much more pressure in feeling fear.

Like shaking a can of pop, you are facing fear and you have been shaken through the whole experience. Do you think that you would not explode? Anyone would. How would you explode? Would you resist and say this is not who I came here to be in this transaction? Would you explode in that face of fear, and say, "I am calling you out in the name of love that I am, and I am saying no; I deserve this and much more from any system that I am asked to plug into?" Do you think that is your death if you do that? Or do you leave the can, walk away, and decide to ignore that fear is really in control? Your choice is part of your destiny. None of these choices are wrong but it does break you, and it breaks the system that you just walked into. In that choice, you decide where you trust and where you trust to fall and really be. That is your choice, but we are there with you. We are your soldiers of love. No matter what you do, we are proud that you can look at fear. That moment of looking at fear has disappeared it and will break it. By looking at fear and breaking it, it allows love to shine. As you are tipping, look at fear. Celebrate that you can stand in fear and acknowledge that you are loved. Your success of you is not equated to all the possessions that you have just bought or the transaction of value, but you, as a being, chose to look at fear and have a decision of your own trust.

Mike: It seems to me that love is the "prime directive" like in Star Trek. Does Absolute Love, Source, or God manage or direct all species whether on this planet or not with the prime directive?

Raphael: It does not direct. Ego directs. Love just is. Love is being. You are not directed with love. The ego gives you marching orders in all the "would have, should have, or could have." The prime directive is not coming from Absolute Love at all. You know there is a better way to celebrate and make that your prime directive. You have chosen that (laughing). I laugh because once you believe that Absolute Love can give you any directive, you start seeing that gift of you in a split mind of duality. Your directive comes from you because you love the entirety of yourself, and you want that wholeness to be part of a conscious awareness. You accept each time that love is it and you are going to go in and do that. You do find it and you each show love in such creative ways that your journey is for certain, and you will succeed in your vibrant passion to be in love.

Elizabeth: You mentioned once that now in our landscape we have been gifted the elements of the planets, which are aligning to bring you out of the great density of darkness and open to the communication of love. Would you elaborate on that?

Raphael: The ego must explore, right? The ego believes the grass is greener and wants more. The ego will bring into your paradigm of awareness the new lands that it is exploring. Within that, you see that you are going to have beautiful instruments of science to go to Jupiter's moons and Mars. As you are going deeper into your awareness on your conscious mind of space and planets, the ego wants you to say, "There is more and if you behave, I will give you more." Of course, those who follow the rules might get to board spaceships and have more, right? What great things to tempt you to stay true to the ego game? As you know and have been studying, you are more than just Earth. You have multitudes of solar systems that help hold the different energies around Earth and within the great galaxies that you call space.

Those you call E.T.s, offer all beings a way to celebrate a greater expression of how to live without a world of heaviness in duality. Each great system of beings, like the Pleiadean's, has their own way of celebrating and expanding love and fear. It is not that they do not hold that system, they just work with it differently. Some beings are more in tune to love and hold that strength, and others hold the paradigm of fear in their space. You call them the greys. As you are expanding in the expression of love, you will receive input from these other sources, which are the intelligences that are beyond what you know at this moment to help you trust and expand more. The ones who work in fear will be exposed more as you trust in fear more. There is a collaborating effort that the universal energies bring forth in the alignment of your planet, but also in the alignment of other solar systems. It isn't just about you. You are fun, and you bring interesting ideas to your reality. Participating with you in the world of becoming more in alignment with absolute truth is like catching snowflakes on your tongue. All of you are such individuals and souls celebrating your moments of being that we just celebrate with you as we catch you to hold you in the vibration of the being that you are. As the alignment happens, you are going to have more resources for you on a conscious intellectual level to see the strength of how connected you are to all the elements that participate in your now. What happens in another solar system ripples to you as you ripple to those beautiful sources of beings? Your light is its own constellation, and you are seeing within your own light system as well as the lighted system of Earth, and as you are ready to trust these great beings on a conscious level, then they will share with you. Especially, the ones that come to expand your awareness of love.

Your fears make the greys greater because it diminishes your light, and you can be brought into their system. Many in power have been brought into their system. It takes other worlds to hold you captive because all you beings have brought in the truth of your divinity in love. It takes more than just your presidents to keep you under the cloak of fear. There are other forces at work. I do not discuss them much, as you probably know, because I don't want your mind to dwell on that. Humans have a way of dwelling in fear more than in love because that is how you have been conditioned. I am helping to undo that conditioning. It can be a way that you can understand the nuances of fear but not buy in.

Mike: Will we as a planet ever be able to come together in love?

Raphael: You will always have this pressure of fear. How you are held and shaken by it is what your planet is asking. Earth has its duality and in that duality there is strength of experience, which we cannot belittle. What we ask is that you balance and redirect what you believe is fear, which is lack of love, into the light of love on a conscious level. This is to show patience and kindness. Trust that you can go to your neighbor and they will open their door with joy and not think you are soliciting, that you only want their attention for a transaction or to grumble about the neighbor next door whose kids play drums all night and no one can sleep. More gather around a source of pain and fear than they do to celebrate in love and joy. That is what will dissipate as you awaken and trust love more. The ego is created by you. You, as a collective, must disappear the ego. That doesn't just happen because of a friendly force from space comes to you. You might want to tear down the gift that you are giving society. It will take time to remove the conditions and it is a collaborative effort to disappear the ego, which is what? Fear. It is going to take a conscious concerted effort, but you have reinforcements to hold that truth, and to help it slowly dissolve the shadow, pain, and hurt of duality. It can be in the blink of the eye or snap of your finger if you believe. What you believe goes back to that identity that you will use in a transaction of survival. If you believe in love, the transaction of survival is a hug fest.

Love is and will always be love, but you have made it a condition of crazy. You all love, but you can be crazy in your expressions of love. Love's purest essence is to take you out of the conditioned land and be part of your divine essence, fully holding the wholeness that love is, for you are one in love. To quest or to make any rules around how you celebrate love is to undermine the full vibrant creative space that love's truth holds. As you are participating in your journey of love, you find your creative texture of how you celebrate your one on one with others that enter your personal space. How you celebrate your exchanges with society in your world, your community, and with yourself becomes more vibrant and collaborative in sharing an expanded awareness of you in how you trust yourself with others as they are celebrating their expression of love. You are all loved, and that I know is a wrapper that is hard to fully understand. As you hold space in meditation around this premise of being loved, allow that to soak through all of you into your cells so you can rewrite your program of fear or lack of love, allowing that cellular memory to remove all your pain and boo-boos of not knowing your divine essence of love. Each time you do this beautiful meditation of just seeing love, or seeing someone you love hugging you, and feel it move through your energetic space and into your cells and the memory of those cells, you will feel your body slowly letting go of the fear and pressure that is so inherent. As you let go, you soften to allow the memories of all the ways that love has shown up for you. Then you can show up for another. Because truly, love is patient and love is kind.

Chapter 11

Forgiveness

Creation unfolds when you are ready. You, as a holy creator, are always moving, expanding, and connecting; allowing your vibration to meet and greet all realities that spirit holds. Creation in your world can look very messy. The movement of particles to be whole takes a lot of will on your part. You must actively engage and hone, as a creator, your will be done. Understanding your will in the creation of illusion, or your ego self, is very important. Also, understanding the creation of your true self, which is the Divine spark that you are, is a destiny that you came to know. Your world has made the duality of everything fluctuate your truest and highest vibration of what you want to manifest.

Understanding your duality, your wing of the ego self, and the other wing of your higher self—which is your Holy self and the self that you came to expand in this work of art, even though you might not consider your world a work of art—is important. For us, you are incredible creators weaving in your mastery of light and love, and your mastery of your human condition.

Forgiveness is that pivot point that attaches your wings of duality or your ego self and higher self to your heart. As you forgive, you bring in Divine motion to your destiny and to fulfill it in the most lighted and loving way that you are here to do. At this point in your mass conscious destiny, you are asked to heal duality on a vast level, to see people through the lens of spirit, and to release the egoic judgement. You must not judge in the world of duality. When you guilt yourself into thinking that you are bad for your judgement, you have created a vibrational texture that doesn't allow you to soar with the love and light that you are.

Know that in duality, certain things are. Judgement is. You perceive through your own lens a point of awareness to know within your heart that you are not a bad person, and you are not unspiritual if you judge. Give yourself judgement as if you are taking a temperature, or mark, of how you relate within yourself; as you judge outward, you judge inward and bring that inner voice, which is your self-talk and programming—both consciously and subconsciously—into your heart. Love yourself, for then your judgement becomes discernment. In discernment, you find your destiny points of your true self that help you to forgive your egoic self, to help you fly above the conditioning of your world of form. Please look at the space as a beautiful way of weaving in the sacred dance of how you fly with the wings of your will and of your God's will be done. That will—which is spirits will, which is us—shows that we just love you and so our will is not for you to stop something. Our will is for you to shine in all the ways you chose before you got here. If you see that you are stuck in your will be done and you are creating from an ego aspect, we will shine light into those ways that your ego aspect creation is taking you off your path of destiny. It is a correction that forgiveness holds to know that your will and God's will are the same. You are here as an instrument to fulfill a purpose that is individually yours.

Your personal communication with Source is acknowledging your will be done and God's or Sources will be done. In creation, you show who you are. The solar plexus of self-will shows your vortex of what really matters to you now. What you see before you is a creation of the vortex of your solar plexus. The Law of Attraction holds space in that vortex energy. You can hone in your will, and Sources will, to celebrate the gift of love in everything you create. Love is the language that connects you eternally. All love holds the sweet nectar of everything you have been and will be. Love is all that you have and will ever become within a body and within an expansive expression in spirit. You are love, and love provides the fluidity of motion to help you forgive and heal.

Forgiveness is for the greater good as well as for you, the creator of what your eyes see before you and what your body has memorized. Your body holds all your incarnations. There are many pivotal pieces within your DNA that as science evolves, you will be able to have snapshots of your past. Also, within your DNA, you have the DNA of your ancestors. You are all related. There is not even two degrees of separation within your DNA. When you die, your cells go to Mother Earth. Your physical form is made up of materials from the Earth, and it is a beautiful gift of her elements. Within your physical death, your cells, which are ashes to ashes and dust to dust, become part of her landscape that then becomes part of the food chain. Your vegetables hold elements of all that you are and all that you will be, and everyone else around you. In doing so, you are all part of this beautiful cycle that allows you all never to lose connection with the total sum of you. As you gravitate to that recognition and as you ground into Mother Earth and realize that we are not separate, you realize that we are all the same.

What makes us separate is the visual places that you perceive in judgement. Having a visual expression makes you define and identify good and bad, love and hate, and happy and sad. What a culture believes is the right way and what others perceive is the wrong way is a visual experience and those who say they are not visual perceivers cannot see at this time but are still receiving a visual experience. All your eyes receive light impulses of everything around you. Your body is receiving those light impulses, and those who may not physically see are seeing the expression of their landscape through their heightened senses of hearing, tasting, touching, and knowing. As you hold this visual experience, give yourself the permission to fall in trust with the elements before you. Do you trust this creation of you? If you do, you are in your destiny and gratitude ripples forth. If you do not trust what is before you, you can hold the space where you do not trust. That awareness within your body, within your emotional field, and within your mental field will provide you with your own unique awareness of how you accept the illusion of the egoic self and how comfortable you want to be in that story.

This is all your wings to fly with. You have built motion to weave and leverage the place of duality to fully heal trust with all that you created and to expand that trust with love.

Forgiveness holds a vibration of voice that when you say the word out loud to forgive, it sends energy to release the knot of contention you have in your heart and whatever event you cannot heal or forgive. Forgiveness is the first step to unfolding and claiming your earth angel wings. The wings of yourself and the wings of accepting your egoic story, and how true they are for you, is the perfect tool to slowly bring in the highest vibration of joy. Joy is the vibration that spirit holds of true flight or flying in any dimension of expression.

Words hold power as you impart them to another and to yourself. Looking yourself in the mirror and saying, "I love you and I forgive you," gives your body the gift to release post-traumatic stress, suffering, and pain. You all hug these elements of pain closely and they are energetic bruises within your Holy Temple. Bruises that can fester bring you down to your least common denominator of fear and pain. Bruises, when held with love and forgiveness, become a portal within your system to channel the creative problem solving that you came with spirit to heal. You all hold these portals of healing within your body because you all have been on a serious path of forgiveness. These portals that your bruises change into, some call the wounded healer. You are more capable of holding empathy, compassion, trust, and true joy in your physical form with others around you. You are held down through pain and you don't want to forget pain, because dang, that really hurts. That is part of the conditioning. It is very hard to childproof everything in your reality so that you don't get a boo-boo. In fact, you came to get some boo-boos because there is grace in learning who your true self is in that moment of that journey. None of you are here to sacrifice your whole life for pain. That story is not yours. Your story always comes in to go to bruises that have festered in the past lives, and it requires your DNA to bring enlightenment to that portal so that it can become a gathering spot for others to hold their truth in uncovering the spectrum of pain and turn it into love.

Your vision in forgiveness between what your mind's eye sees and your physical eyes see are two different things. This is where you get confused. In your mind's eye, you all hold that portal to spirit. In your imagination, your vividness of love always trumps your vision of pain. In your mind's eye, you know, feel, hear, and see the texture of love and spirit around you. The dissident energy vibration of data that you take in with your eyes make you believe differently in the illusion. Your eyes see the pain and your social media loves to share your pain story. You connect more through the energy age in pain and that is why you feel an implosion of chaos and disruption. Pain is a portal that allows your illusion to dance without connecting in the heart. Illusions are always around you and they are not wrong. You can choose any illusion that you want but in that illusion, as it connects to your heart, you hold the compassion and empathy to join with the souls of humanity for love and light. When your wing of the ego becomes disconnected from your heart, you operate visually and consciously in that illusion place. That false ego then holds the portal for all that you have deemed evil in the past and you will deem evil in the future to come through. It must disconnect from your heart that holds unconditional love. If you have disconnected, you dance to a different master. Your will be done is in alignment with this ego wave, for it does wave. Recognizing that you are there in this portal gives you the clarity for the light of remembrance to choose differently and to be rerouted to your heart. Rerouting is all forgiveness.

You do not need to ever know what you are fully forgiving. So much of what you forgive is the unconscious collective guilt that you have greatly created as a way of trying to have some type of definition to explain how bodies must be. If a person is not doing the definition of what is right, you throw guilt at them because that is one of the greatest energies of the self-illusionary worlds. Forgiveness of guilt helps you to know you are innocent and your world loves to let you know you are guilty. You are guilty of even looking cross eyed at somebody. You are guilty. Once you sit in that space and hold it with your heart, you will find that a lot of the things you feel guilty for are not your truth. As you release that guilt by simply saying, "Forgive, forgive,

Chapter 11 - Forgiveness

forgive," the rippling effect of the word forgive said three times heals the collective unconscious guilt.

Fear and hate are really grounded because it is the least common denominator you all play with. It is the lowest vibration, so of course it is very grounding. Once you are there, there is a comfort because you collectively acknowledge your pain stories more than your love stories. You have a way of really being buddied up with your pain. When you are in that heaviness, who wants to forgive? It is very hard. Then it is the space of just having gratitude for your breath, for your body, and for the place that you are at. In that gratitude, you open for us to lift you out of the heaviness of pain and guilt. As we are lifting you within your great gift of gratitude, the lighter you become, the more you see that illusionary space was just a dream. Dreams are easy to forgive or to be able to bow to and say that there is a lot of knowledge in any dream you have. There is great purpose in analyzing your true dreams if you can remember them. It is the same when you disconnect and become part of the egoic illusion of self. You are in a dream. When you resurface and hold an awakened place, it is easier to see the symbols of your journey. Those symbols can then be easier to forgive, than the placement of your active movement in that dream.

As you do hold that space of forgiveness, those symbols give you the key to be emboldened and enriched in your true self, which is the self of your highest light and love that you came in to be. Forgiveness is a weave around all your principals of faith, of hope, and of gratitude. As you weave forgiveness just by choosing hope, you have forgiven. When you choose to smile instead of frown, you have forgiven. When you have chosen to connect with a stranger, you have forgiven. When you have chosen to give yourself a gift, you have forgiven. Your priorities change in your authentic self as you choose the highest vibration and then your mind's eye will celebrate what your physical eyes see, for dissident energy will harmonize into a perfect picture of your true reality.

Your mind is vast, and in the vastness, your holiness is permanent, because your mind holds your eternity. You close your eyes, and you can feel and see eternity. It can be scary to some, but it is there. Your mind is that gracious divine instrument that connects you into your Holy Temple in allowing you to physically, emotionally, and mentally live a whole experience of a world that you created with your eyes in duality. Your mind is fully forgiven. It is innocent. The duality of the split mind is the ego impression. It is like a box that got put into the vastness of your mind. It holds you like the genie in the bottle, and that who you are can only come and be expressed if somebody gives you that permission. As you forgive, the box of duality disappears. Your mind within this beautiful Holy Temple of yours becomes whole. In that wholeness, your flight then becomes one of oneness. You no longer see duality; you are in unity. That beautiful aspect brings a vibrational force to the wings of you, to uplift you in a permanent space of just being in your authentic self.

We hold the paradigm of you as the greatest force of remembering love. You are all here celebrating a journey that feels so heavy and chaotic into the bubbles of joy, which allows you to fully find your voice and be the portal of love and light.

We seek and, in seeking, we look for answers to many questions. Many times, those answers are through creativity of your whole mind with spirit. In your creativity you connect with spirit to find a way that makes you sing with joy in completing the task you raised your hand to do. All of you have come here to this place to seek more. In seeking, you are questioning a little "what

Chapter 11 - Forgiveness

if" or a bigger "what if." Your bigger what if, for example of becoming a nurse, makes you start looking for answers that pave your journey to that desired outcome. Other times, a what if is just asking the question; is there a better way? What does love have to do with any of this that is before me? What if I am not who I think I am, or who I was told I am?

In forgiveness, the what ifs are what you are slowly breaking down to understand that you came from a true place always of curiosity, and in curiosity, there is no sin. For all great ifs have achieved for you in your environment, the luxury that you do really hold onto. Acknowledging that you are a seeker gives you the acceptance again to question the quieter what if in your mind. In your mind, you hold your most personal antenna for communication with spirit, however you define that. What if I am not a good mom? What if I don't love my partner as deeply as I should? What if I were to leave a job that brings me great wealth to seek an unknown what if? A lot of times, these what ifs play the see-saw of duality that makes you hold a lot of anxiety within your form and, when you become anxious, you run through the survival patterns of behavior and not the truest holy love pattern of your soul. When you chose your scarcity thoughts and you work all your what ifs from that vantage point, the outcomes usually lead you into many dead-end places. For in scarcity, you will always find that your answer is just another way of creating your story into victimhood instead of the story being the promise of more and that you really have come to be empowered with.

Forgiveness is holding those teeter-totters of your mind as in I like myself, I don't like myself, I like my marriage, I don't like my marriage, I like my job, I don't like my job. In those spaces of duality, you find your truth as you hold them for some of you are in a job that no longer suits you and it is time to no longer be the victim of that setting, but to bow graciously out of that scenario and into another what if that has been calling you for a while. Sometimes what you don't like about a situation, once you can under-stand it and why it is happening, is that you can give yourself that opportunity to fall into a space of acceptance to level the teeter-totter of your mind while fulfilling that destiny within that space. All your destinies have come because you chose to be true to your what if that you incarnated to do.

Sometimes we get put off our true patterns of our heart because the equations of the macro and microeconomics keep you thinking that you must stay in a job for benefits and that those benefits are so important that you are willing to give up your life force to be there. Know that it is scary to say goodbye to something your economy has structured for you to believe it is important, and it no longer is. The incredible story of looking at your heart and being true to your destiny is that you receive a lot of grace when you say yes to the bullet point that you came down to do. The more you know it is your destiny, the more you can forgive everyone else around you who might be opting you out of that destiny. Your destiny points are very specific to you and they make your body feel different when your mind holds a destiny that you came to fully say yes to. All of you have felt the switch within your body. Some people call it a gut level instinct. Some people feel it in their heart. Others will feel a knowingness of that destiny and it gives them more energy to do it, where every other idea was just so humdrum.

A destiny point is cleared by forgiveness and then holding gratitude for your journey as you are now ready to say yes to your what if that you came to express. You will all hold some type of guilt within your body, emotional field, and within your mental field. Guilt is different for everyone. Sometimes you feel sabotaged because of guilt or the belief that you have done something wrong and you deserve punishment. There might be a belief that you are liked or not liked and deserve to have a time out, because someone told you that you are too much for them. Recognize that as a collective, this guilt is what you all come in to forgive. When you say, "I forgive," at the simplest level, it means that you are forgiving the collective guilt. When you say, "I am grateful" for this wonderful moment I am having, you are also on the flip side of that gratitude, showing forgiveness. You are forgiving your belief that you aren't worthy of having this precious moment. How often do you believe that you are not worthy of the joy that is in front of you at this moment? Within each gratitude space, forgiveness is hell. A lot of the time, people say that it is harder to forgive than to be grateful, but in gratitude, you have forgiven. That is the gift of seeing your journey as your choice of a great adventure, uncovering your what if and finding a way to know that no matter what your choice is, the gratitude that you hold gives you the knowledge that you are not going to keep coming up against doors that are locked and closed but doors that have an opening just for you.

Your what if is the biggest story, legacy, and momentum of you. This beautiful gift of expressing your what if allows the landscape in front of you to have its joy be part of yours by saying yes to seeking the answers that you are really looking for.

You are in a great time of global economics, yet the microeconomics should be very exciting for souls who are seeking and looking for what ifs. Because the chaotic essence that is the frontier you look upon as you make your daily decisions about your life and long-term decisions, it makes certain that you understand your microeconomics of your own personal life. On an organic level, people are connecting deeper than ever. It is hard to be reassured of this because the louder voice and all your social platforms want you to be aware of the macroeconomics of emotions, repression of ideas, and even the mental and moral reasons of why things are happening. These connections on a macro level are not truly connecting to be the truth speakers of what is happening going forward. What is happening at the community level is that it is trying to connect so you as an individual can make yourself feel part of the grand what if that you are wanting to celebrate. Namaste

Mike: Can you talk about forgiveness and past lives?

Raphael: Your past lives are part of the reason you say, "Yes, I want to come back." Why be here? It is tough. You are squashed. There is so much constriction in everything you do in this place of 3D. You come back because you want to fulfill your journey of wholeness in love in not only the personal stories but the collective. When you do review your life, you see the places of bruising that are still festering and you say with the wholeness of love that you are, "I shall return, to be one with that bruise, bring angel kisses to it and have it disappeared from my energetic awareness and the totality of all that we are." Pain is not a true vibration of you as a spirit. You do not want to leave things undone. That is why you enter back and reconnect in that portal of bruising. You might find it in DNA that you have never been a part of and to just go into that pain story that you are ready to heal with your destiny that you are choosing to be at. Every lifetime has portals of your egoic self and your holy self.

When you choose to come into that pain, you also bring all that portal of good with you. It is like the beautiful claps of your hands to be one with all that you were in all your good, to bow to this bruise

Chapter 11 - Forgiveness

of pain and say we got you and we are going to love you till you disappear. That is why the fabric of just holding your hands together as one by your heart is a place of grounding your acceptance of your duality and then the forgiveness of that space that duality holds. Past lives, again, offer you an understanding that you might have never gotten unless you allow that lifetime to become part of your now. When you do past lives, it is good to be with somebody who can help you through the story for there is a lot that you can remember. If you do it alone, you might overstimulate your awareness of you at this moment. But, giving yourself that opportunity to look at your bruises and to kiss the pain away gives you more of an enriched place to claim your divine placement.

Elizabeth: I have forgiven all beings in this lifetime but how can I be sure that I have forgiven all the past lives? Also, since we know that all lives are occurring simultaneously, can we forgive our future lives?

Raphael: Yes, for it is all now in the expansiveness of your mind. In your mind and not the box of your split mind, all has already been forgiven. Thus, you are already whole and innocent. You in a physical form do not feel that. In your physical form, your body tells you that you are not forgiven. You look in the mirror and look at your body, and you typically do not like what you see. How then do you feel forgiven? Your body is the best thermometer of knowing your strength of your divine destiny in this gift of forgiveness. You have all brought in a forgiveness puzzle to work on. It can be from a past life, future life, DNA, or just be the knowledge of the destiny that you are going to go through this lifetime. Forgiveness puzzles are part of a soul contract. You said yes to solving this puzzle and, many times, what bothers you the most is your full forgiveness puzzle. It is something that you just can't let go of, and it can be something simple. Like how someone smacks their lips as they eat. But it can also be something with a person who keeps coming back and forth in your life and you know in this incarnation at this moment that this person has you do a dance that just does not fit your true understanding of your authentic self, but you keep dancing to their music. You will hate yourself for that because you have this great collective knowledge of what is abuse. You work the story and you really need it, ponder it, and try to comprehend abuse. Abuse really is not what your split mind wants you to hold onto. You have been every character of the book in your incarnations. You have been the victim, perpetrator, and the hero. You will continue until you acknowledge the triangle of drama within the egoic self doesn't have a long-lasting effect. It depletes you when you live in the world of drama. But this dance you have with this person is just so magnetic and no matter how much you work on your authentic self, you still see this person, or someone that is acting like them, until you find your understanding of this puzzle.

Once you understand the story, you get the forgiveness all at once. The story no longer holds the magnetic attraction that it did. You have all come in with a great forgiveness puzzle and in that it is an initiation within yourself to trust you, to choose love, and not hold on to pain, fear, anger, and hatred in all those places that at the end of the day make you feel bad. Your truth is the celebration of joy. It is one of your greatest gifts that you will give and when you do your forgiveness puzzle and you understand it, your alignment in you has expanded a hundred-fold in light and that is a vibrational reaction to all that you just let go of in that moment. That is always exciting to see as you uncover that placement.

Mike: Once you recognize the puzzle and you embrace the forgiveness path, why is it then still so hard to solve each puzzle that comes along?

Raphael: Because that puzzle reacts on your physical form, your emotional and mental fields, and your trust with spirit. Your body can mentally understand it, but emotionally you are still reacting. Emotional fields have a different vibration than a mental field. Your physical field has a different vibrational field than your emotional, mental, and spiritual fields. What you are holding as you forgive is a crescendo throughout your life. It is a practice that requires a daily conscious movement in, for as the crescendo goes, so does your energy field crescendo. As you forgive in your mental field and your mind gets it, the journey is confrontational and is in the lowest vibration—which, again, is your physical field. To reexperience any abuse in your field feels like it happened in the moment where the first abuse happened, or the first pain, or the first idea of shame happened.

That vibration is known in your body and your body is the most vulnerable place within the world of form for you to hold onto and reside in. As you are healing the mental field, then the emotional field is the mid vibration, and in that it takes time to really allow yourself to sink in to the emotional experience of pain, to forgive it, and to be okay within yourself for that vibration of forgiveness. Then it will hit you in a physical way and many times in your body when you are forgiving something, it will be doing a detox process to help you release those memories within the cells. Even in forgiveness, your body is not yours. Yet, as you clean out that story on a physical level you won't be so anxious, or you won't have memories of all the details around you would of, should of, could of. You will hold the space that you really have come to learn, which is this gift of what is being alive for you. Many give up when they hit the emotional placement of forgiveness because to feel any amount of discordant energy in your emotions is like plucking a string that is not in tune. There is a resonance of disharmony and why be in disharmony when you can choose not to. You have chosen this space, but you could always choose not to. Eventually you will come back to heal that place. Some lessons you will bring into one lifetime with the emotional field and you will say, "No, I don't think so." That is okay. We celebrate you with that. You do not need to do it all. We are here to help you. As we hold space with you in your heart and become part of your wonderful GPU (God Positioning Unit) of your heart, you will find that you can go into your physical form and release. If you are dancing with another, they start to release, too. They are less on edge around you because you know when you are with somebody who you have a forgiveness lesson with, you are kind of edgy in all ways instead of being able to lean in and trust. The gift of forgiveness is that you know when your forgiveness is complete, you can lean in, mentally, emotionally, and with a physicality and be like, "Oh, I can trust me with you and if I can trust me with you at this moment, I know that you can trust me too." Their trust becomes their way to fully seeing you, and not the story.

Elizabeth: How can we best resolve the anger and the conflict in our world?

Raphael: You are in the most expansive time that has ever been. You have been through many expansive times in this place you have called home. This time, you have many souls who say yes to enlightenment. The process looks messier than before.

Chapter 11 - Forgiveness

Understanding duality is the first gift to ground into this expansion of love and light. You as a collective have said yes, especially thirty years ago with your harmonic conversion to bring in harmony. As you said yes, you were reminded of all the garbage that your human egoic placement has brought you. Part of the energy again, of hate, is a collective knowingness that it is time to forgive your collective guilt for being in bodies. The war on your body must stop. In stopping the war on your own physical body, you help stop the disconnection of people playing in the illusion and not being connected to the heart. Through your last generations you have been trying to connect with the mind, which is beautiful, but you have taken it into an intellectual space. Knowledge is critical. In an intellectual mind, data points of knowledge provide you with a roadmap to exist in harmony with your fellow beings. Intellectually, you stop engaging in your heart. For everything then is an idea and not an experience. As you know if you have been a parent, a manager, a friend, or a lover that what you have agreed on in theory changes when you put it in action. It is what makes you feel that you are always wrong, or damned if you do or damned if you don't. Mentally, you do get it within your mind.

Then, you come to the box with the split mind and all those theories need to be woven in an ideological presence, like religion, that on one hand is to make you all feel safe. But on the other hand, it can really make you resonate in guilt and fear. You are imploding all places that show a disconnect of your mind and of your heart at this moment. That really is the great divide. No matter how much you want to believe in a principal, the movement of your body changes that principal. You all have a specific way that you create within the theories that you believe and, thus, you are in a very chaotic point right now because you are very disassociated as a collective with your mind and your heart. You need to reconnect as a group and therefore you all came in because you knew that it is the greatest time of enlightenment. What is enlightenment but the connection of the mind and your physical form of the heart? Because you have said yes to this great momentum, you must go deep in the trenches to all the bruises of the guilt of your collective. All the pain of your Civil War is upon you at this moment, for that story in your history never fully was integrated and healed. There are a lot of bruises that fester. Your Revolutionary War still is not healed. Nazi Germany is not healed. The destruction of Tibet is not healed. Tiananmen Square is not healed. Russia is not healed. How many bruises did you enlightened souls take on? The pain of uncovering these bruises are brutal to the egoic story. It fuels that story to make you believe that war is the only way to achieve nirvana, a new beginning, or enlightenment. People really love this story because it is disconnected from your heart, soul, and spirit.

The story is the wheel that turns in humanity to make you the pinnacle and then the valley. Know that what is happening now is the beginning of setting vibrational energy to have the harmony that you all said yes to. It is scary because it is not what you thought would be in form. Yet the vividness of anchoring in yourself and grounding in to be here fully, and to be an advocate of love, is the greatest gift that you can have. It is happening organically all over this globe. Love is the resounding answer to people who are saying I need to reconnect. No more shows that keep me hypnotized in the illusion of ego but saying yes to being one to all that is around me. Mother Earth allows you to step up for her and to acclaim global warming because you are all warming up. Light is warmer than darkness. You create warmth around you as you say yes to love, and your passion will be the energy that moves you with Mother Earth into a place that resonates the highest harmony. Warming is a way of saying that you are here to be warm with your advocacies to become that heater of light and love that warms somebody that is feeling so dark.

This time allows you to look at the symbols around you and to find out what piece of the bruise you are here to work on. If the Nazi flag is your stimulus of pain, then you are here to heal that. If the Klu Klux Klan is your stimulus of pain, then you are here to heal that. Look at these symbols around you and acknowledge them as a gift that allows you to sink into that bruise and heal with forgiveness that memory that created it, so you can be strong in your advocacy. Now is the time to raise your hand and stay connected to your heart and honor this wing of duality, but you leverage all this chaos with your quest of love to see and hold forgiveness in this place so you can be clear in your path not to be afraid and get pulled in. This time is amazing. It is like all the hot spices, like cayenne, and when you take a bite it opens you up. This time is hot and spicy, and in that openness it is for you to have that clarity of your connection in how you are to say yes going forward with that.

Chapter 12

Life Purpose

It is a joy finding the love of duality and balancing into your now and finding you, for you are the central core that facilitates all your opportunities. You came with factory spiritual presets that offer you the guidance to fulfill your destiny. As I, Archangel Raphael, connect with all of you, one thing is certain; you will do your destiny. You are all on the right path for your destiny. Some of you are in your destiny and others are still dancing around that lovely pivot point of saying yes to the true joy of you, which is your destiny.

Life Purpose is the creation of you that you came to ripple forth with. Your Life Purpose is, and always has been, your choice in spirit as you come into form. How you want to dance, create, play, and be in your life is the answer of purpose and how you want to purposely be in this beautiful form that we call your Holy Temple. Each Chakra holds energy that allows you to find a greater expansive connection with yourself and all that is around you.

Life Purpose comes in when you tune in to each of your Chakra's, and you ask, "Am I here to be the ground for others, and am I here in the root Chaka to hold and find a profound sacred union with the Earth that is below me and within all the spaces that beautiful Mother Earth provides?" If you resonate there, your purpose which is very sacred, gives you the opportunity to be the witness for others. Allow that space as witness to be the conversation of love and joy.

Many come in as creator energies. You are now at a profound time of holding many souls whose Life Purpose is creation energy. That is why many of your institutions are imploding because you can no longer think in boxes. You are creators. You see stuff, you know stuff, and you bring stuff forth as creators into this world of form to be out of the previous boxes that have been and will now be changed. Are you one who can be an advocate for your creativity? Can you honor that sacred union and say yes to the brilliance and the risk that creators are? For there is great risk when you plan to be a creator. Because, within that field, you have put yourself into a placement of being outside any box. Again, many souls at this point are creators and in creation there is chaos. Your world is in chaos, which is very scary and risky. But know, that through the soul's purpose of being a creator, change is for the highest and best.

The next Life Purpose space are those that want to come in and understand their self-identities, and to understand the Solar Plexus of connecting with self and being able to bring that self to center stage. Many of you still live in a dream of what you want to become and have not yet stepped into the stage of being who you are. Claiming who you are in the life path of this important Chakra allows humanity to rise with integrity and trust. For those that can be clean and clear in themselves, it offers that placement of rightness to others. Not in religious rightness, not in political rightness, not in due diligent rightness but in the clarity of yourself, and the clarity of saying you are a Holy Temple, and you hold the true sanctuary for others to come and not feel judged, but to know that they too can build their own sanctuary of their truth.

Chapter 12 - Life Purpose

You have been living through the Age of Pisces which is a very heart Chakra placement. During this age of being in Pisces, you swam into understanding what is love. Really, what does love have to do with your human texture, your human commitments, and your sacred commitment with yourself and others? The heart Chakra has expanded because you holy souls did come in at this time to expand that energy of claiming oneness that you and I are the same and that we all vibrate in the perfection of home. This energy of expansion does get diluted and, so it comes to be very hard work for those souls who have chosen their Life Purpose in the heart Chaka. The heart energy is the most vibrant force to celebrate a sacred union with everything around you. This time has been critical as you have all shown your true commitment to facilitate the beautiful heart that glues you to the remembrance of Absolute Love that is your home.

Before you could go into the Age of Aquarius, you needed to know the light and dark expansion of a heart centered commitment. When you expand into any vibration, you go through the whole spectrum of the darkness and the light. Many are afraid to encounter the darkness as you expand, yet it is a powerful place to flow with all the things that you fear. In that space, we are here. The spectrum of the Holy Spirit is here to help you to continue to expand and know that whatever you touch with love, it holds that memory eternally. Those that have worked in the heart Chakra are extremely tired. Know that we are here to hold space with you as you continue to watch the world around you expand in the question of what is love, and what does love really have to do with any of this? Yet, you are the gift of love and that you sharing you creates the remembrance of love and holds space of oneness.

The throat Chakra is increasingly important because, in the Age of Aquarius, you are more and more balls of energy that celebrate a connection of communion with each other. You no longer need to sit next to each other to communicate. Your devices of energy have given you a global voice, and that is why you are learning right now to discern what is safe and real. The voice of truth is the voice that will be organic at first, and then it will build into a crescendo of yes for all. If you are here to work on the throat Chakra, make a note to yourself that you to will take time to build your practice into the crescendo that you are looking for.

Many come as visionaries but loose this, so many do not stay in the space of imagination. Those souls, who have come and committed to their Life Purpose from the deepest vision of themselves and others, are quickly told that their visions are dreams that can never become reality. Destroying someone's vision is the biggest body pain that you can experience and I know you all, as a collective, have experienced the pain of visions or dreams being taken away from you. Those souls committed to this lifetime must use every ounce of their energy to claim that, so this is why they are here. It is a calling to do what you do when you are here to be a part of the Life Purpose of your vision center, or your third eye. There are great teachers, authors, and communicators of all types of theories in this life path. Sitting in your visions and claiming that you are fully here to be that dream will provide you the strength to hold that space, and say yes, to make the destiny that you came for a certainty.

You are all connected to the crown, so this is a oneness path to nod to all around you and to know that your destiny was to connect with spirit. Whatever that personal place of spirit is, for spirit is everything and everywhere, and all ground is sacred with spirit. All buildings, people, and all your Holy Temples are sacred with spirit, and it is why we say you are your Holy Temple. You all brought in a personal way to show how you are connected.

Chapter 12 - Life Purpose

This personal connection cannot be taken from you. It can be dimmed by other voices and other structures that tell you how you must celebrate a sacred connection, but no one can ever take it away from you. There is no way you will be disinherited from your true holiness or from the Heaven that you all came here to create. In that, our pledge to you is if you do feel that you have been disowned, displaced, dislocated, or you have just been disked we are there with you. You are what makes fear disappear. We whisper and celebrate your movement in this space of you, but you in your commitment to your sacred placement makes fear disappear.

What I ask you to do is to go in, hold each Chakra, and look for a response to see if that is your life's journey or not. You all live in this beautiful energy flow that is constantly renewing your Chakras and to expand into a whole unified energy field. As you are learning you and figuring out where you need to be inward, ask each Chakra; "Are you my destiny?" You might feel a yes, or you might feel a no. You might hear a yes or no. As you work through the Chakras, you will find that in doing this, there are two or three Chakras that answer yes. As you get more yesses in playing in the center stage that you all come here to play, the individual Chakra will blink or that yes will be strong. Give yourself permission to feel those Chakras and to fulfill that promise you gave to yourself because you gave yourself all the answers you are seeking. It might not be you who can answer for you. You might not be able to go inward, but the person next to you might say a word to you and you realize they are going to advocate for something, and you feel that you need to be part of this something. That advocacy work is your Solar Plex and your voice woven of course with love. As you find where a feeling is hugged into you, it will help you hold the energy in your body to be strong in that yes. You might not be saying yes outward, but you are saying yes inward. All it takes is to say yes for us to help you into this sacred union of you.

You are all doing your purpose. Purpose is not to work. Purpose is finding that place that when you are just being, you have great joy in doing. Your world works on work, and in that process a lot of people confuse Life Purpose with their career sets, and if they are not doing their Life Purpose, then they must change their job. That is because your ego system has created you to think you are workers and not creators. When you hold that you have created the vastness of your life, you start to claim that your life is the purpose of creation. When you are creating the creation flows into form, and when that form is celebrated by everything around you it starts to be this wonderful system of movement, then that can—and might—become your job, your worth, or something you claim to see some payment for.

You are all coming into a time because it is part of the Age of Aquarius to find the energy of you that makes you love the creation of your day because that is where you receive nourishment and pay from. The new paradigm that many are wrestling with is this idea of having to love what you do or to be in love. Yet, this expansion of love has brought in good and bad. You will still question what is love. Know that as you are working and going into the Chakra that holds your destiny, the love is there. It is like a child who wants to be a doctor and, as he grows, he takes classes and he recognizes that to help and be a healer is what his heart says he loves. But that boy cannot handle blood. The belief that his soul's destiny is lost can make him stand in a belief of unworthiness. Yet, he might be the most pivotal healer as a shaman that the world needs. Your journey of how you identify work changes when you start to hold the destiny of you within the vortex of connection that you came to do. You will always be what your destiny is supposed to be. It might not be how you had envisioned because you got stuck on the identity of words instead of the identity of creation. If you feel that you are pushed up against a wall around something you know is your destiny, I ask that you contemplate looking at three hundred and sixty degrees that I call around sound of that identity. You are all teachers, healers, advocates, and creators. How you can show up with the totality of you and take that center stage and be the light and love, is your gift that you allowed yourselves to stay connected and have creation uncover the right identity of the word, or of the placement for you to be.

You are mighty, you are loved, and you are all one. Your placement here is no accident but part of a holy design cocreated with the Holy Spirit to bring love of all to the anchor of creation with all elements within the human form which we hold as your holy temple of awareness. You come in your physicality, your holy temple to work out, to work with, and to work through opportunities of deeply understanding your power in creation, your power in love and your power as the oneness of God. Each time you come in, you are here in the holiest purpose to remember, yes, that you are a holy child of Absolute Love, that you cannot deny yourself what you are, and you cannot deny yourself love. For when you deny yourself love, the pain you inflict upon yourself and others becomes your karmic pattern to heal and yes you do come back to heal that karmic pattern for you did create that karmic pattern of pain. Only you can heal that karmic pattern and you seek to do it as often as you can for you know that when you heal all karmic patterns of pain you are complete. The complete awareness of Absolute Love that you are will shine to all and in that holy moment all will be forgotten, and all illusions will shatter in your placement of how pure you are in love which will resound eternally.

To ground is a way of holding gratitude in your now. Grounding provides a purpose to feel, to see, to know and to be. Grounding from your root allows a structural alignment of all energy fields within your being to coalesce and strengthen to the Divine moment that is now. Anchoring, grounding and being settled are constructs that make you a spiritual being and to be at peace with the physical endurance test that you have challenged yourself to within this incarnation.

I come into you through a process of anchoring. Anchoring within each cell, each space, and each vibrational frequency that all your energies together hold. I am anchored in all of you as I bring in a remembrance that you are not your body, you are not this moment; you are eternal.

In creativity, we share a magnetic pulse to move the denseness of all particles in this world of duality. The pulse of your heart magnetizes the flow of all of you to pump up and make a body hold action. Our creativity of space, and our creativity of each other, is a magnetic pulse that accentuates your courage and strength to bring in a new stroke like with a paint brush of you to celebrate claiming a space that is just nothing if you are not here.

With identity, this is what causes all your pain, for you identify in spaces with words to make you somehow powerful. Identity is a construct of fully encapsulating your Divine destiny that you chose to be seeded and to sprout into the holiest essence of love. You do not play small in identity ever. For once you choose an identity, you have chosen to bring forth a statement of you. Be wise when you chose an identity because identities are cracks of your heart that can splinter and slice your love that you share in your wholeness that you are here to be.

Most run from their heart space, for going into the heart you magnetize the currents of the universe. You pull into you all that you are when you are fully in your heart. Your heart hears all. Your heart frequency can attune to any vibrant placement of your choice. Your heart is the most fluid, and unlimited source of your power as the creator of your universe.

Your voice and throat are the bridge between the mind and the heart. They are the tollbooth that you pay at as you share your heart and your mind. Most species in this universe have moved away from using their throats and words in communicating. Words are linear structures that make you hold identities with time and space within the constructs of a duality placement. Words when spoken are payments of interaction. This payment is about an expression of voicing your perception of your now. The voice for you has much power, so I come with words out of my voice so you can hear a vibrational eloquence of a language that is here to show expressions of love and to unite each other in the wonderment of dancing in your light. Yet, words become punishment in the harshness of reality through perception in a duality place. Birds sing with joyous freedom sharing their love. Your voice as a species is the most critical awareness in this energy age. Your voice when spoken holds the truth of your mind and your heart. This power will be your redemption. All should participate in taking this payment of your core identity and celebrating it in love to unite those that have become lost.

Your mind sees beyond form. Your third eye acknowledges that you are more than your placement of your physical form. In your mind you are always eternal. So, as you daydream, you know that all is possible. You do not lack in your mind. You do not have any boundaries. For in the mind, as ideas come and go, they share feelings throughout, they excite, they depress, and they give hope, and understanding. The mind is touched in spirit. This is where we slowly kiss you in your physical form to become one with you in this beautiful embodiment. Do not fight any vision in your mind. Give it credence and forgiveness for you are fully in the power of now.

Through the crown in connecting with us you have the realization of full body oneness with each other. How can you do something with purpose if you do not feel a full body connection for yourself and with another. I share this grand placement of knowing that you all fight to fully be in the creation of your body. Most people hold very detrimental body images. If you have any angst around your sacred temple, you will never fully embody this beautiful vehicle to fully connect to the totality of your Divine purpose. This body is a part of an identity that you created to find what truly makes you be fully exposed to God. For when the underbelly of darkness is brought to light, how you hold your physical form, and how you hold that magnetic pulse with yourself and others, shares the depth of oneness you have, and the joy of being love.

Part of the structure that you have created is to come to lives with a *Life Purpose*. That will erase the patterns of karmic pain forever. Your journey of love is so deep that you jump at every opportunity to heal the source of pain that you caused with the great *what if*. What you create, Dear Ones, you will heal for it is already completely done. You are now one in eternity with your holy source of Absolute Love. What you do in human form, or other forms, when you replay the games of illusion is to help erase those memories of pain. So only the truth of love stands before you and is your full vibration wherever you exist.

Chapter 12 - Life Purpose

Your life purpose for you is to have the greatest impact on breaking karmic patterns of pain in whatever holy temple you chose. Breaking karmic patterns of pain is through the gift of forgiveness. To look at everything and to know that all is forgiven is the grand eraser of pain which allows love to glue the pieces of a shattered illusion into a mosaic of love's divine placement. Your life purpose can be the momentum of knowing that when you share your heart with another, you accept in that moment their holy placement before you. Forgiving all that has gone on before and all that will be allows your hearts to beat as one in kinship of embracing the vulnerability of humanness, and the vulnerability of your form in anchoring trust with another in the most vulnerable place which is your body.

Life purposes take on different meanings when you decide what placement of the illusion you are ready to shatter karmic pain in, and bring in the mosaic of love to the awareness of you and all that are around you. Those souls that are here to really know the gifts of Earth bring in the patterns of taking and shattering karmic placements of pain with the Earth and all Earth elements, bringing security to the foundation of loving and sharing with the holy aspect of Mother Earth. This life purpose ties directly to the Root Chakra which is red. Souls that resonate here bring forth to hold a vibrational pattern of love of all the environmental aspects like the trees, the animals, and the ocean. The renewing of love with your holy placement on your holy planet is the most sacred gift to give in your life purpose and in your life right now.

Other soul's life purpose will come to celebrate passion. This life purpose ties directly to the Sacral Chakra, which is orange. These souls will bring the passion of understanding creation, of having a thought and using the elements of love, using the elements of earth, wind, fire, and water creating from a thought something to behold, something to share without any concept of ownership for all of you are one. What one has, one shares. What one has, one already owns for thus you share it more. Passion to remember oneness in all that is created within your world is a holy gift to take away the belief of lack and to celebrate the gifts of passion in all you do.

Some soul's life purpose holds the knowledge of what it is to understand the claiming of an identity and bringing forth that identity to all places they journey. This life purpose ties directly to the Solar Plexus Chaka, which is yellow. The identity is not letters beyond your name; the identity is not certificates on a wall. The identity is the identity of the greatest gifts of the holiness that you are which are the gifts of honesty, the gifts of truth, and the gifts of openness. These are the identities to choose and play with. These are the identities that shatter karmic patterns of pain. Celebrating holiness in the identity of your form clearly states the anchor that you are in the love of your divine creation.

Some soul's life purpose is to renew and heal heart to heart, and to bring peace everlasting to all around. This life purpose ties directly to the Heart Chakra which is green. These souls work in the heart. These heart people bring a divine service in knowing that others heal any illusion that you are separate for you are composed of the same amount of water that others hold, you have the same heartbeat, and you are so much more alike than you want to believe. For if you believed that you are truly one with another you would stop all the wars and renew the depth of kinship that is sincerely yours.

Some soul's life purpose is for communication to have holy understanding and to bring that holy understanding to others for in words; the power of you creates ripples that extend eternally.

This life purpose ties directly to the Throat Chakra which is light blue. Words are so powerful within your space that creation is within each bubble of the words spoken. Ask and you shall receive is a sacred law for all. Communication for souls who journey here is to release the pain upward and to bring love back as they bring forth the wisdom and the remembrance of the power of communication.

Souls, whose life purpose is to see the big picture and to hold that big picture, resonate in a vibration of great vision. This life purpose ties directly to the Third Eye Chakra which is dark blue. This vision that they hold in their life purpose is to thread all realities to sing as one in the great choir of all particles joining their highest vibration in the life purpose they have chosen. Holding vision for others takes great patience and souls who have this life purpose hold the knowingness that what is in the highest and best will happen for all karmic pain as it releases and brings all to the highest vision. So yes, these people who come with knowing that there is more and they are adamant in this placement that you are more than what you ever know and help coach you in that grand life purpose vision.

Some soul's life purpose is to remember and connect the oneness that you are which brings depth of healing in karmic pain into the belief that you separated from source. This life purpose ties directly to the Crown Chakra, which is purple. These souls connect with the divine space for they know already that they are one. They know they are willing to take your hand and tread your pathway so you too can hold that totality of being one with the creator of you.

As you incarnate with your life purpose you come with a depth of knowing what is right for you. You know your divine placement in each lifetime. This is not a secret. This knowingness gets hidden as you play out the game of duality and then you believe that you have been forsaken and in that you did not come to celebrate a life's purpose. You came to be a pawn of the games of separation. This is not true. We whisper to you that this is not true, and you are not a pawn to be placed and sacrificed and be gone. You are mighty always. Your power is so much more than duality. By sharing a divine connection and creating a holy connection with yourself and with us, when you forge that divine connection, we help you to remember you are just playing a game of duality and your holy purpose which is your life purpose in your holy temple is what you came to do. As you do your holy purpose the joy of you will be celebrated on every level in every cell and this joy will ripple so others too can catch the wave of celebration to stop playing duality and remember their life purpose in healing karmic patterns of pain and showing the delight in the holy placement of the vivid mosaic of life that is heaven on Earth. So, I say forge your connection to us however it looks. Your prayer of knowing there is more to this story than what is before you will enable us to shine your life purpose throughout every cell in your holy temple and you will have the power before you to find ease and grace in every activity you embrace. Come with us and dance towards the light of oneness that is yours.

In grounding you find peace to share you. In passion you find energy to propel your will to connect and magnetize others will in the joy of sharing the grace of love. Identity is but what you claim to be for your identity in eternity will be the son, the daughter of Absolute Love. Identities that you will seek hold purpose to share a greater understanding of your feelings, of your mind, of your body and of your senses. Identity is not stable for your form is not stable. All that you create is not stable so recognize and put security into what is stable. Your gifts of spirit as the creation of Absolute Love are part of the platform of stirring you to rise, to nourish and to give unconditionally. The heart within your form is the grand control panel of all fluids that come within its reach creating a dance of systematic rhythm nourishing strength to each cell within your body holding a beat for you to remember your rhythm of this life that you are now in. Listen to your heartbeat and you will find your rhythm of passage, of strength and of courage creating the dance of you in your now.

Your voice allows you, Dear Ones, to speak what you know, what you are learning and to embrace your senses that allows your identity to feel more solid in the space that you have created. Your voice has power for the words that you share hold the ripples of energy between you and another and that energy creates the other one's senses to feel an intimate response of you to them so they too can use their voice to share their thoughts, their dreams, and their senses back to you. Your voice is your portal of awareness to extend you to the elements that are placed within your now.

What is true vision? What is the reality behind vision? For what you see with your eyes is just a reflection of something before you. That reflection is interpreted through many layers of identification that you have given it and then that vision becomes a tool to feel graceful in the elements of your now. Vision of truth is connecting to the greater vision of spirit and filtering spirits reflection in the identification of attributes of spirit. Vision is a portal to release duality and to know the truth of your sacred union in source. Vision magnetizes the fluidity of spirit with the solid particles of your now.

Connection of source has never been denied from you. You are holy connected to your father who is Absolute Love. Connection is scary for in all connections you perceive vulnerability and in this vulnerability the sense of loss is so overpowering to you that you veil the connection of you to source creating many games, many strategies, and many modalities to connect. Yet connection feels like a transaction of conditions instead of a truth of your beingness. All your fears are built on the vulnerability of connections and all your identities dance in this fear of losing connections. Duality says you have all or nothing in connections and thus you believe you are not connected to love.

Know my gift to you is to help you feel your divine connection in every particle of your now. Each particle is held in the hum of love's vibration. This vibrational hum is the remembrance of you, of the oneness of you and the divine expression that was your creator which is the pure source of love. Watch and feel how you weave connections throughout your now. Experience your now as you feel, see, and hear connections without fear in the knowledge of being hugged in the hum of love.

As you seek a clear placement of your connection that magnetizes what you give to be truly what you receive you will be the creator of your world. Many hold the statement of, "Do unto others as you would do unto you," to be a way of holding connections. Yet what you do unto yourself can be so hard for you know how to be your greatest critic. You know how to sabotage you. You know how to sacrifice your love for yourself. Thus, if you can do that unto you and if you can call yourself the hardest names of your world and if you can look upon yourself and judge you, Dear Ones, you will do that to another. For what you do unto you eventually is the way you connect to others around you and to us. For how you hold the spaces within your temple, that vibration, that energetic flow will ripple unto others. I, here today, want to gift you, the creator, of you the saying, *do unto yourself as*

Chapter 12 - Life Purpose

you then would do to another. If you can love yourself greatly, you can love another greatly. If you can love yourself unconditionally, Dear Ones, you then can love all that there is around you unconditionally. If you can be honest with you, you can be honest with another. Anxiety is the core of you not loving you and others will one day find how unlovable you are. Acceptance is hard in your world for yourself, for you know all the trials and tribulations and the secrets you do not want to share.

Knowing all there is about you, it is hard then to say anyone else could love you. Hiding you then becomes the true creation of your reality. When you hide you from yourself the connections of all that you created are lost. Hiding you shuts down the energy field within your heart, and within your mind to celebrate your life. Your life is the greatest gift that you can share. Your life is the greatest experience to connect with. Your life has meaning for it is allowing you to create with all the particles that surround you and to make what is before you the true reflection of what is inside of you. You are a time capsule of all awareness's. Finding the love of you to uncover the time capsule of you allows you to hold peace in all creations that have come before and will always come after in the great current of creation. Having peace allows you to fully accept you in all that you believe you have done. Hold the greatest gift of forgiveness releasing all elements of duality and being able to connect in your divine placement and know that you have always been Absolute Love.

Mike: You say we come to deeply understand our power in creation, our power in love and oneness with God. Can you expand on that?

Raphael: Everyone, each culture and each world will divine, design, and describe creation in ways that it honors its holy sacred ritual. Creation is not one thing; it is all. In creation, one is the wholeness of that creation and one is the divine instrument and conduit of that creation. When you are fully surrendering to a process allowing something bigger than your conscious mind to carry you into an unknown, that is creation. That is why it is very sacred. To go into spaces of unknown, one must hold faith in something. Following patterns is not creation. You have proven this with your Industrial Revolution, that machines follow patterns. They allow you as the conduit, the sacred instruments to create as you fabricate from the blueprints, to a construct, to become something solid in your field. Creation must behold a connection to something more. When you are problem solving outside of your conditioning, you are creating. When you are loving outside of a conditioning, you are creating.

Creation knows that it is a uniting reunion of the known and the unknown, bringing a weave to a newness that never was. Creation becomes mundane when you only use your physical sources and when you only use logical conditioning. Mundane is a practice to allow you to fully engage your landscape in safety with all your physical senses. You celebrate creators that go beyond the mundane, for that means that all of you are connected to something outside this paradigm of living. That brings you the memories of your Holy Creator as the child of God. You want to have that so desperately. When you can surrender to the texture of what is before you, it always boggles your mind. It is hard for you in duality to really celebrate a moment because it comes and goes. It is a wink or a snap. So, you who want to hold permanence in an illusion receive much disappointment in oneself, if you don't hold creation, love, and oneness throughout your day, month, and year. Yet, the moment is how it all began and how it does disappear. The moment you say yes and that you are a divine instrument, it holds your legacy of oneness. Don't doubt your power, and don't doubt that you have many, many moments celebrating yourself as that Divine conduit, creation, love, and oneness.

Elizabeth: If I am understanding correctly, what you call Life Purpose is predicated on healing Karmic patterns. But you also say that we can break Karmic patterns of pain through forgiveness. I was wondering if this must always be in the conscious state or can it also happen in the subconscious state such as the dream state or hypnosis?

Raphael: The reality of duality is that you identify greatly in your trauma and pain before it goes counter to everything you came to celebrate. You all incarnate back to say that I could love better, I could connect deeper, I could ripple love to many, so they too know their love and when you come, you hold pockets full of memories within your energetic field of pain that is very karmic for you and that you have been through before or the DNA within you has created those pockets of pain. Yet you are very vibrant in celebrating the newness of love, the newness of awakening from inside the womb to a greater expression of your physical body. As you go forth and grow, you celebrate an intuitive magnetic field that you have put into the patterning of your energy field to connect with your predestiny points to heal. In healing, it is a comprehension of a fullness of how that pocket of pain became part of the story of your family or of your soul journey in understanding love. The awareness of pain has power, and some souls enjoy power, so they like pain.

You brought in these incidents, so give yourself an opportunity to have an aha, or a comprehension of the fullness of how that pain became an identity, so that you can then erase that identity forever. We celebrate the disappearance of pain for that is not who you are. You are not a being who should toil in heavy despair. As you use all spaces to spring forth the awareness of that pain to then have the aha of it, it gives that energy field movement to dissipate and go to light. All magnetic resonance patterning holds the keys of healing. You are magnetic in your body through your heart. When you touch another within that magnetic field of your heart, you have given them the keys to understand that pain. When you sleep, your heart has the freedom to beat the magnetic vibrancy beyond keeping your body moving as you do during the day. That vibrational frequency moves into all the unconscious magnetic remembrances of pain, which then you can hold through dream hypnosis to heal. EFT (Emotional Freedom Technique), or tapping, allows that magnetic pulse of your hand which is the outpouring of your heart to touch yourself in a dance and to release the cellular tension of pain. Every movement in your day as you come across another form gives you a playground, gives you the canvas and gives you the surface to heal the pain.

When you walk in a crowd you can get fearful because your magnetic energy might touch another who holds that pain story like you on an unconscious level, and it might come into your forefront. You aren't psychically attached, but your pain stories match magnetically, and when two magnets are clinging together, their strength as one makes that pain acute and a crisis. In that crises point, you have creation. You have the ability as a Divine instrument to walk into that unknown of why that pain is and to bring in that comprehension of who, what, where, when and why, and celebrate the full release. The gift of being in your body is the gift as a creator to change all pain stories into love. Thus, we celebrate you to use this resource; your body, to be the holy temple of your reunion of knowing love.

Mike: You mentioned that your mind is connected to eternity yet getting there takes practice and partnership with the Holy Spirit. What kind of practice?

Raphael: First, be a dreamer. How often do you not dream? How often does your logic mind shut off a dream that could be yours? You don't know if a dream is truly yours to have for you have not ventured as a creator into that dream, because you are afraid of failing, and you feel the depth of sorrow in pain for each of your failures from the beginning of now to the ending of now. Failure is a huge energy field that waterlogs you to not be a dreamer and thus not fully empower you as a creator, for again, creation is into the unknown. Your mind is the universe of dreams for what you can imagine within your mind's eye, it can be. You know this to be true. How often you imagine I want a new purse and then it shows up. This creation energy is very scary for creation got you to the now. Will it get you out of the now? You childproof, you diminish your idea of yourself as a creator because you hold each failure within yourself. This is the karmic placement as you grow in your soul energy of you as God. You can create without the resonance and the vibrational frequency of failure. Many will dream and have a bucket list and never cross them off for to be a dreamer and just to dream, gives them a high of releasing identities that others have put onto them. Yet their magnetic expression with others to not hurt them might never give them the privilege to make that dream a reality. Your life purpose is a dream. It is a seed of knowledge that you must uncover to fully participate in the creation of that purpose. Some who come with less filters of failure will do their purpose sooner. Others who come with the recognition that their soul is ready to release patterns of failure will slowly uncover their purpose. Some die before their purpose ever becomes a vibrant piece of their energy field but that soul still knew that it was being led to a truth that they could hold eternally of themselves.

Dream big, and in dreaming big, create big. Creating big does not mean that you are creating the Taj Mahal in your downtown area. It is saying that I am walking with all my light into an unknown, and I am willing to surrender all my identities that hold failure, and say yes to a knowledge that I know is true. Let me bring that knowledge fully into my holy temple so that I can be that Divine instrument of that purpose. Your mind has all the dreams you have ever dreamt. Do you know that some get scared to be in their mind? They close their eyes, for they feel the darkness creeping in for the unknown is only dark if you do not share your light.

Elizabeth: You mention that there are seven Life Purposes. I am wondering do we come in with just one of these or do we move through several of them throughout our lifetime?

Raphael: It is dependent upon what you predestined for yourself. Some souls come for just a single life purpose that is so strong that for them to even think beyond that purpose would be a betrayal to every cell within their holy temple. Many souls do come to incarnate into two to three life purposes and you can see this as you age from your teens to your twenties, and then your thirties to your fifties, and then your sixties and beyond.

Chapter 12 - Life Purpose

Energetically, you do feel that resonant patterning within your body for you know when your body is letting go of something you had to do and then magnetizing into a whole new purpose of being. It is what you have chosen to create the love story in your Holy Temple. Many express change as painful, yet if you surrender into the process of recognizing that you have finished a cycle of one reason to be, you will then have a whole new cycle of a reason to be.

One must trust oneself in being able to fully engage in their purpose. Purpose means that you have raised your hand and have accepted all responsibility into that purpose. Your world in duality makes you question your decision making process. How often do you decide and then change it? To really say yes to a purpose, one must trust that feeling of a holy purpose dedicated to every breath you take. In doing so, it does become your identity. This world right now fears you who choose an identity, because for you to have that power and to trust yourself so strongly, you have upset the conscious conditioning that prevails on every level of energy fields in your landscape.

You are being advertised to consciously, subconsciously, subliminally, and overtly everywhere you go, and you are told not to trust, and that you do not know what is good for you. You must give all your powers away somewhere. Have you ever thought where you are giving your power of choice and trust to? In that mass conscious motor which right now is capitalism, and profits, which are a creation of the ego to keep you away from your purpose. What a good job that ego did for you, yes? It is so good that it keeps you away from this holy purpose that you came in to be. If you break out of the ego conditioning, you are scarred with pain, because it is painful to not connect in a whole mass conscious belief. You do not recognize your freedom when you stop connecting until you trust yourself and trust that your purpose is to bring light to the darkness that the ego is conditioning you with and that you can heal all the pain stories back to love.

Mike: From your discussion you mention seven Life Purposes, and it obvious that they tie directly to the Chakra system. Can you discuss that further?

Raphael: The world of identities and categories do not express you as a creator or the dream that you came to dream. The simplicity of working off the gifts of your Chakra Systems within Purpose allows you to truly motivate the physical body that you hate, to be the Divine instrument of your love story. That is truly the purpose of speaking in love with your physical form as you act in a world that celebrates action. Purpose only means that your Divine destiny is bigger than saying you came to be mom and have kids. Most souls want to bring an essence to flourish and to nourish themselves and others. You are all cream of the crop. You all float to the highest momentum that you can be as you clear your energetic field of pain, failure, and fear. To go into greater complications of purpose makes one believe that they can't even have a simple dream. How many times have you heard "I just want" love or something else, and then you get what you just want? You don't just want, Dear Ones, there is no justice in a life of predestiny, for you are predestined to go through what you have set forth. For do you have free choice if it is predestined? I say yes you can choose to trust in love, I say yes you can choose to believe beyond your physical senses, I say yes you can let go and have no identity but to know that your purpose has been seeded in every cell of your body waiting to be expressed when you are ready to say I trust that I won't fail this purpose. So yes, your Chakras anchor your Divine purpose that you have come to be, and you who have had kids know that some from an early age resonate with a purpose, and some do not. Because that purpose for them is to be their full creation of their predestiny. You have different purposes but you stay in the core of your Chakra System because it allows again your physical body to be seen, to be exposed and to be safe in that exposure, to be loved as it should be loved and to be released all the ways you punish yourself, all the ways you punish another and all the ways you believe you must suffer. Your purpose is for a love story. In doing your purpose, you will walk through pain to trust and to fill the sacred commitment to trust that you are a Divine instrument of love. We are celebrating love to help all remember their eternalness in Heaven.

It is overly simplistic. As you celebrate your connection, remember that your body holds all the resources you need to be abundant in your purpose. Many feel that if they do their purpose or predestiny, that it will have a negative financial placement, which is not a truth. Love is the way you grow any garden of abundance. It might not feel that it is immediate in your world of time and space, because you all have not trusted in your power to be rich. That richness is for those who somehow have made it and again the identity of making it is only a feeling the ego puts on your Divineness as a creator. Fulfilling your purpose is always financially abundant. Your karma with how you use money, which is different than how you do your purpose, can see the balance of your checkbook hold the highs and the lows of just life.

Elizabeth: So, you are saying that loving yourself is the first step in completing your life purpose and I am wondering why the third dimension Earth goes totally in the opposite direction?

Raphael: If you do not love yourself, you do not harness your full potential. The ego cannot have you be in your full potential, in your full power and in your full connection of your Divine Source. You are nuclear when you are in your full potential. You can create everything in front of you and then some. The ego cannot have you know your truth and in the third dimension the heaviest placement of conditioning is on your form. Do you place as much conditioning on a tree as you do your body? No, your body becomes your clay of identifying your pain and sorrow. Your body becomes the clay of how you identify your love and in how you express it to others. So, loving thyself and your body takes many incarnations. Many cannot just come in and love their body for no Holy Temple is the same as another. One size does not fit all, yet you are forced to be in one size in duality. You are supposed to behave in one size, you are supposed to wear clothes that fit in one size and you are forced to believe that one size is the identity of wholeness, identity of human. Huuuu (sung) is the vibration of the energy field.

Man is the physical vehicle, so you are more spirit than man or a body. Babies know this well, and it takes them a long time to really feel power in how they walk and how they talk, and how they nourish themselves. Young adults are very awkward for their body is betraying them as it is taking them into the next step of man. As you age, your body betrays you once again as it is saying goodbye to your story. In this it is very hard to love so the esoteric belief of loving yourself is a dream way beyond the capacity of a conscious mind. Even if you are consciously aware, you are still holding forgiveness in the art of loving your body or another body. Therefore, on some level, you are okay with the death of a body or the mass destruction of bodies because you never fully loved the body. There is a way you can become numb to the body and that is scary for you as the totality of the oneness. Therefore, loving yourself takes many lifetimes. You have brilliant souls who decide to leave sooner than not. It looks like suicide to you, but their soul said nope, I am ready to go. This body is not taking me to the next place I need to be. In a throwaway world you create throwaway bodies. In your identity with packaging, you will package all your ingredients of living like food. This is a fascinating aspect of the ego mind. You package your body and you become a billboard of identities and so loving your body and yourself is that holiest placement of being able to say I love myself for I am one in God. I love my body for it is my whole vehicle of expressing my story. When you can say, "made in heaven," and that this vehicle of your body is made with the light and love of eternal oneness in heaven, you move mountains through this vehicle, and it becomes a way to interact in others landscapes so they too can celebrate the beingness of being in a body.

Right now, the need of humanity is to remember to catch one another, that they are physical like you and that their pain is your pain as a collective. Their death is your death as a collective. Their sorrow is yours for you take on the mass collective as humans. Then you celebrate the love to again bring renewal of a dream of utopia which is a dream you all dream. The purpose of loving yourself is the only landscape of really uniting with us to trust that it really is just you and God.

*I do not like to wrap up or wrap down for we are eternal
and every time you put in a conclusion,
that means I have gone.
I will never go.*

*For you and I are eternal and thus it is a renewal of a
togetherness that sparks passion to rise to the
highest zenith of love that is your home.*

Namaste.

Archangel Raphael

Acknowledgments

Since joining Trisha, Michael, and Archangel Raphael there have been many years of recording, transcribing, and editing. There have also been many avenues of getting Archangel Raphael's messages out through voice, written, and video channels of communication. But without a dedicated audience, with their gracious acceptance of channeled messages, they would just be words on a page that have never gone anywhere. I would like to thank all the audiences over the years who understood that an Archangel's messages had an impact on themselves and their worlds that they live in. Whether you have or are reading these messages, attended one of the in-person group or one-on-one sessions, you are the ones who drive new knowledge into a space by combining your light with Archangel Raphael. He has always said that this material will come to a person who is ready to receive at the perfect time. So, thank you to everyone who has accepted the timing of this book. You are appreciated by all of us.

Of course, a book cannot be created without those who believe in the project and their roles in its production. These include Sharon Lund of Sacred Life Publishing who took this author on with a previous book that needed a lot of work. It was through her gentle encouragement and nature that created an environment of learning for myself and made me think I could take on more projects. Thank you, Sharon, you are true light in my life.

Editing any book is a challenge, I am sure. But editing this book of channeled information from an Archangel had to be an assignment unlike any other. I would like to thank Kaitlin Palm of Palm

Editorial for taking on such a daunting assignment and attempting to teach me in the process. It was quite a journey and I thank you for making it a better read for everyone.

I would like to thank Bill Van Nimwegen for taking my ideas for a book design as dreamy as they were and creating a design that, when I saw it, I knew was perfect.

For her input into this book and for her dedicated contribution to the questions and her love of all things spiritual, I would like to thank Elizabeth Roberts. Her love for Archangel Raphael is profound and I can say that she is thought of very highly by him.

Of course, you cannot have a channeled book without a channel. Trisha Michael, known by Archangel Raphael as My Lady, took on a role in this world somewhat reluctantly but proceeded with encouragement and the gentle touch of the angelic realm until the understanding and process became second nature. Both Archangel Raphael and I admire Trisha and want to thank her for taking on both of us in a time that needs these messages more than ever.

For those of you touched by these messages, know that you have an Archangel in your corner. As he has said many times, all you must do is ask for his input. He is always there waiting to work with you in finding your true self. As he taught us long ago, "Love is Enough."

About the Author

Mike Russell

This book by Mike Russell is the fourth in a series of spiritually based books that include *A Journey of Discovery through Intuition with Help from the Angels, My Compass, Our Story: A Journey through Death and Life,* and *What's in the Water? Our Soul's Reflection on Spirit and Self.*

Mike has spent his adult life working in the financial services industry and came into writing after the death of his first wife and found that he was opening up to the world of spirituality. His path took on a whole new meaning when with the help of his best friend and future wife Trisha Michael, they developed a spontaneous and ongoing relationship with an Archangel by the name of Raphael. Mike found this relationship to be one of opening doors that he only hoped existed. Their relationship developed slowly at first but over the years all three of them became more comfortable working with each other and know that the beautiful relationship that was created was out of love involving the past, present, and future. He knows from what he has learned that there is a lot more to life than what we see with our eyes. As Raphael told Mike at one point, "You have unfinished business here and have been assigned a project beyond your current understanding." His response was to accept the challenge as it felt like he had a purpose in life and could give back in a way that he never imagined.

Mike will continue on this path of "Knowledge Seeker" as he is known by Archangel Raphael because he is committed to sharing knowledge with all who want to listen.

About the Channel

Trisha Michael

Trisha Michael is the owner of T. Michael Healing Arts in Oregon. The magic of the work keeps her expanding with the gifts that she shares in her practice. The channeling of Archangel Raphael's messages has offered her incredible insight to the complexity of life. Her relationship with Archangel Raphael has grown with the knowledge that goes beyond duality and makes each day a puzzle piece in the development of self. She continues to share his messages and insight as a channel of his love.

www.ingramcontent.com/pod-product-compliance
Lightning Source LLC
Chambersburg PA
CBHW071807080526
44589CB00012B/718